...lish

Bryan Pfaffenberger

MIS:
PRESS

A Subsidiary of
Henry Holt and Co., Inc.

First Edition

Printed in the United States of America.

10 9 8 7 6 5 4 3 2 1

Pfaffenberger, Bryan
    PCs in plain English / Bryan Pfaffenberger.
       p. cm.
    ISBN 1-55828-384-6
    1. Microcomputers.
QA76.5.P3989 1995
004.16 20   95-18599
                                             CIP

Trademarks

Editor-in-Chief: Paul Farrell
Managing Editor: Cary Sullivan
Editor: Debra Williams Cauley
Copy Edit Manager: Shari Chappell
Production Editor: Joseph McPartland
Copy Editor: Elissa Keeler
Technical Editor: Troy Jones

Dedication

For Suzanne, always

Acknowledgments

I'd like to thank everyone who helped with this book's research and preparation, especially David Wall, who drafted several of the chapters that follow. Troy Jones and Bob Miller checked everything that follows for technical accuracy, and Elissa Keeler performed her usual fine editing job. Debra Williams Cauley was very patient with my tardiness in finishing this book, a much bigger project than any of us had anticipated. (Never underestimate the computer industry's ability to keep making things more complicated!) As usual, Debra took a personal interest in the manuscript and put in long hours during the final stages of this book's production. Thanks, too, to Joe McPartland, the production editor, for managing an heroic deadline.

Table of Contents

Introduction

Shopping for a computer, or thinking about upgrading? You're in for some jargon. Hands down, nobody beats computer people when it comes to inventing new, incomprehensible terms. For example, here's the copy for a typical computer advertisement:

PENTIUM POWERHOUSE XL-120 $2499

Genuine Intel Pentium-120	14" 1024 x 768 non-interlaced SVGA color monitor with .28mm dot pitch
ZIF socket	
16MB RAM	FCC Certified Class B
256K write-back cache	SCSI-2 controller
Small-footprint mini-tower case with 250 watt power supply and two cooling fans	101-key extended keyboard
	Microsoft-compatible mouse
540MB local bus IDE hard drive with 256K buffer	3 PCI and 4 ISA expansion slots
4X CD-ROM drive	28,800 bps V.34 modem with send/receive fax
3.5" 1.44MB floppy disk drive	350MB internal tape backup unit
64-bit PCI local bus SVGA color graphics card with 2MB VRAM	Soundblaster-compatible sound card
	Self-powered stereo speakers

If it's all (or mostly) Greek to you, welcome to the club. But there's hope—this book.

The one overriding aim of *PCs in Plain English* is to help you make sense out of the terms you need to know in order to select or upgrade a computer system intelligently.

- This book isn't a buyer's guide. It doesn't try to survey and rate the currently available systems.

- This book isn't really a computer dictionary, either. For one thing, it's topically organized, and it doesn't make an effort to cover anything besides PC hardware.

So, just what is this book? *PCs in Plain English* defines all the terms you're likely to encounter when you're buying or upgrading a PC. It's topically organized, so you can flip to the right chapter and look up the term alphabetically. Not sure what "V.34" means? Flip to the modems chapter. (If you're not sure where to look up the term, just check the index in the back of this book.)

Why is This Book Needed?

Standard computer dictionaries must cover all the areas of computing, including not just hardware but also software, networking, programming languages, and more. For this reason, they just can't go into enough detail to really help you when you're buying or upgrading your computer system.

I found this out for myself when the time came to upgrade my modem. Standard computer dictionaries define the terms "modem," "auto-answer modem," "internal modem," and "external modem." But you're on your own when it comes to the stuff that really counts. Do I need a Class 2 fax modem, or is Class 1 OK? Should I get a modem with MNP5 compression, or is V.34 bis the best choice? I can get a great deal on this V.Fast Class modem, but somebody said I should get a V.34 modem instead.

The same goes for many other aspects of computer hardware. What's the best kind of cache memory, write-through or write back? (You'll need to know, because most computer systems offer one or the other—and experts think that the write-back cache is a better design.) Should you equip your video adapter with VRAM or DRAM? Are you better off with a PCI bus, or will local bus suffice?

All these terms, and many more, are defined in this book. It's an indispensable guide to finding your way through the world of PC hardware.

How This Book is Organized

You can use this book to help guide you through the jungle of PC hardware terminology. Here's a quick overview of what's covered, and where you should start:

Chapter 1 (System Components) This chapter defines the basic components of a personal computer system. If you don't know a modem from a molehill, start here.

Chapter 2 (Cases and Power Supplies) Look here for terms pertaining to the computer's case and power supply. Also covered are surge suppressors and uninterruptible power supplies.

Chapter 3 (Motherboards) This chapter provides an introduction to basic motherboard terminology. Three of the motherboard's components—the microprocessor, memory, and expansion bus—are covered in detail in subsequent chapters.

Chapter 4 (Microprocessors) Look here for terms pertaining to the computer's "brain," the microprocessor, such as the Intel 486 and Pentium. You'll find a wealth of information on the currently-available microprocessors, including the PowerPC, and the latest high-performance design features.

Chapter 5 (Memory) This chapter covers terminology related to the computer's internal memory, also called random-access memory (RAM).

Chapter 6 (Expansion Busses) In this chapter, you'll find terms related to the slots in which you can install expansion cards, as well as the standards that underlie the slots' electronic design. Look here for definitions of terms such as ISA, EISA, VESA local bus, and PCI bus.

Chapter 7 (Ports) Here's a quick rundown of the ports you'll hear about when you're shopping for a system or upgrading, such as serial ports, parallel ports, PCMCIA cards, EPP/ECP ports, and more.

Chapter 8 (Basic Input/Output System [BIOS]) Your computer comes with built-in programs that help it to start, and assist you in choosing basic system settings. This chapter surveys terms that you may run into when you're considering how well this software is designed.

Chapter 9 (Input Devices) Keyboards and mice are covered here, certainly, but there are plenty of other input devices these days, including trackballs and stick pointers. And don't forget scanners, which are responsible for a fast-growing lexicon of terminology all their own.

Chapter 10 (Display Adapters) Here's where to look when you're trying to figure out video adapter features. Is a 32-bit video adapter OK, or do you need a 64-bit adapter? Or a 128-bit adapter? What about DRAM and VRAM? Also covered: video formats of all kinds and full-motion video cards.

Chapter 11 (Monitors) If you haven't the foggiest idea what terms such as "dot-pitch," "non-interlaced," and Energy Star–compliant mean, check out this chapter.

Chapter 12 (Disk Drives) This chapter covers all the terms you'll encounter when you're shopping for hard and floppy disk drives.

Chapter 13 (CD-ROM Drives) New kinds of components bring new terms, and CD-ROM drives are no exception. Look here to find out whether a 4X drive is what you need, whether it matters that a given drive is Kodak Photo CD-compliant, and what the data transfer rate really means.

Chapter 14 (Sound Cards and speakers) No more tinny speaker, but no more simple terms, either. What's so cool about a 16-bit sound card? Is it worth the money to get a sound card that's capable of wave-table synthesis? Find out here.

Chapter 15 (Modems and Fax Modems) Look to this chapter when you run into any funny-looking modem terminology, including all those "V-dot" numbers (such as V.32bis or V.34) and all kinds of data compression schemes.

Chapter 16 (Printers) This chapter defines the terms you'll run into when you're shopping for a printer, with full coverage of the hot new color printers.

Don't forget the index! If you can't figure out where to look up a term, you'll find a complete, alphabetized list of all the terms in the book, complete with page references.

Hunting for an acronym, such as E-IDE, SCSI, ATAPI, or MPC-2? Check out the Acronym Finder at the beginning of this book.

About This Book's Icons

Look for the following icons while you're reading this book:

 This icon flags the basic terms you really ought to know if you're shopping for a new system or planning to upgrade.

 This icon flags a definition that contains a valuable shopping tip. Get the most for your money!

 Here's some practical advice. This may be a dictionary of sorts, but that doesn't mean I can't share some tricks, suggestions, and cautions with you.

Don't Forget...

You can use this book in three ways:

- **If you know which chapter to consult, just flip to the chapter and look up the term.** Hunting down a printer-related term? Check Chapter 16.

- **If you don't know which chapter to consult, flip to the index and look up the term there.** Not sure whether a ZIF package is a motherboard feature, a port, or something weird that's found on a sound card? Look up "ZIF package" in the index. You'll find the correct page reference there.

- **If you're trying to find out what an acronym means, check out the Acronym Finder.** You'll be directed to the definition.

Note that when appropriate, some terms appear in more than one chapter. For example, the memory-related terms VRAM and DRAM appear in the Display Adapters chapter as well as the Memory chapter, because these two terms define types of memory, and video adapters have their own memory circuits.

Have fun, and let me know if this book did the trick for you (write to me care of the publisher, or email me at bp@virginia.edu). Did you run into any terms that you couldn't find in this book? Let me know. In the meantime, my efforts in writing this book will be handsomely repaid if you're able to make your way through the jargon jungle!

Acronym Finder

If you're trying to find the meaning of an acronym (such as DRAM or RISC) look here first. You'll find cross-references to the entry that defines them. The many commonly-used acronyms (such as CPU, CGA, ROM) are also cross-referenced amidst the entries.

ALU	arithmetic-logic unit (ALU), 49.
AMD	Advanced Micro Devices (AMD), 46.
ASCII	American Standard Code for Information Interchange (ASCII), 273.
ASPI	Advanced SCSI Programming Interface (ASPI), 202.
ATA	AT Attachment. *See* Integrated Drive Electronics (IDE), 224-225.
ATAPI	Advanced Technology Attachment Packet Interface, 250-251.
BBS	bulletin board system (BBS), 281.
BIOS	Basic Input/Output System (BIOS), 2, 24-25, 134.
bps	bits per second, 281.
CAV	constant angular velocity (CAV), 208.
CCD	charge-coupled device (CCD), 143-144.
CCITT	Comite Consultif International de Telegraphique et Telephonique (CCITT), 285.
CD-DA	Compact Disc-Digital Audio (CD-DA), 252.
CD-I	Compact Disc Interactive (CD-I), 253.
CD-R	Compact Disc-Recordable, 252.
CD-ROM	Compact Disk-Read Only Memory (CD-ROM), 252-253.
CD-ROM/SD	CD-ROM Super Density, 255.
CGA	Color Graphics Adapter (CGA), 159.
CISC	Complex Instruction Set Computer (CISC), 53.
CLV	constant linear velocity (CLV), 208-209.
CMOS	complimentary metal-oxide semiconductor (CMOS), 53, 136.
CMYK	cyan-magenta-yellow-black (CMYK), 354-355.
cpi	characters per inch (cpi), 354.

POST   power-on self-test (POST), 138.

POTS   Plain Old Telephone Service (POTS), 329.

ppm   pages per minute (ppm), 376.

PPP   Point-to-Point Protocol (PPP), 330.

PRML   Partial-Response Maximum Likelihood (PRML)
            read-channel technology, 231.

QIC   quarter-inch cartridge (QIC), 233.

RAID   redundant array of inexpensive disks (RAID), 237.

RAM   random-access memory (RAM), 37, 94. 110.

RAMDAC   Random Access Memory Digital-to-Analog Con-
            verter (RAMDAC), 165

RIP   raster image processor (RIP), 383.

RISC   Reduced Instruction Set Computer (RISC), 95-97.

ROM   read-only memory (ROM), 111, 138, 384.

SASI   Shugart Associates Standard Interface (SASI), 240.

SCSI   Small Computer System Interface (SCSI), 241, 259

SIMM   single in-line memory module (SIMM), 39, 112.

SIPP   single in-line pinned package (SIPP), 40, 112.

SLIP   Serial Line Internet Protocol (SLIP), 334.

SPEC   Standard Performance Evaluation Corporation
            (SPEC), 100.

SRAM   static random access memory (SRAM), 40.

TA   terminal adapter (TA), 337.

TCM   trellis-code modulation (TCM), 338.

TCP/IP   Transmission Control Protocol/Internet Protocol
            (TCP/IP), 336.

TFT   thin film transistor (TFT). *See* active matrix, 171.

UART   Universal Asynchronous Receiver/Transmitter
            (UART), 131, 339-340.

UPS   uninterruptible power supply (UPS), 19.

VESA   VESA local bus, 121-122.

VGA   Video Graphics Array (VGA), 166.

VRAM   Video Random Access Memory, 168.

XGA   Extended Graphics Array (XGA), 162.

ZIF   zero insertion force (ZIF) package, 42, 104.

System Components

In this chapter, you'll find definitions of the basic components of a personal computer system. If you're new to personal computing, look here for beginner's-level definitions
of basic terms. The subsequent chapters delve into each of
these components in more detail.

auxiliary speakers

A pair of speakers, generally self-powered and shielded to prevent interference with the computer system, that reproduce the stereo sound generated by the system's **sound card**.

basic input/output system (BIOS)

A set of programs, encoded on special circuits that permanently retain information, that enable your computer to begin operating when you switch on the power, and remain in operation to govern basic operations of the computer system. When buying or upgrading a system, BIOS-related terms come into play when you consider the user-controllable options in the computer's setup program, which allows you to specify the basic system configuration. Terms that you're likely to encounter when you use the setup program are defined in Chapter 8.

case

The cabinet, usually constructed with a metal chassis and metal lid, that contains the computer's **motherboard** and the computer's power supply. When you buy or upgrade your system, you'll want to consider which type of case you prefer (desktop or tower), as well as how much power you'll need. Types of cases and power supplies are explored in Chapter 2, where you'll also find definitions of terms related to power conditioning equipment, such as surge suppressors and uninterruptible power supplies.

CD-ROM drive

A disk drive that can read the information stored on CD-ROM disks, which look exactly like audio compact disks, but they contain computer-readable data. A major drawback of

CD-ROM drives at present is their slow speed and their inability to record information (write) as well as play it back (read), but a new generation of writable CD-ROM drives will make this technology increasingly available to PC users. You'll want to find a CD-ROM drive that transfers data at a fast rate and complies with current CD-ROM and multimedia standards. For an explanation of terms related to CD-ROM technology, performance, and standards, see Chapter 13.

Figure 1.1 Different computer case types

Figure 1.2 A typical external CD-ROM drive

display adapter

An **expansion board** that generates the video signal displayed on the monitor. No matter what kind of system you are using, the display adapter's speed and sharpness are crucial to the overall system's performance. Display adapters are covered in Chapter 10.

expansion board

An auxiliary circuit board that is designed to be pressed into one of your computer's **expansion slots**. For more information on expansion boards, see Chapter 6. Synonymous with expansion card.

expansion bus

An electronic "highway" of high-speed lines, wired in parallel, that permits your computer's **microprocessor** to communicate with the **peripherals**, such as a **modem**. Constructed on circuit boards designed to fit into the expansion bus's receptacles, called slots, peripherals add functionality to your system. When you buy or upgrade a computer, you must pay careful attention to the standard by which the expansion bus was designed (such as ISA or PCI). Expansion bus standards, and other terms related to the expansion bus, are defined in Chapter 6.

expansion card

See **expansion board**.

expansion slot

In the motherboard, a receptacle that is designed to accomodate an **expansion board**. See Chapter 3 for more information.

floppy disk

A low-capacity **storage** medium that consists of a flexible (hence "floppy") plastic disk coated with magnetic material and enclosed within a plastic cover. Today's standard is a 3.5-inch disk that is completely enclosed in a hard plastic case, and isn't "floppy" anymore, but the term has stuck. Floppy disks are covereed in Chapter 12.

floppy disk drive

A small-capacity **storage device** that is designed to work with **floppy disks**. Although floppy disk drives are not very useful for storage purposes—their capacity is too small—they are indispensable for getting new programs into the computer. Floppy disks also provide a convenient way for one computer user to share information (in the form of computer files) with other computer users. Floppy disks, and the disk drives that use them, come in 5 1/4-inch and 3 1/2-inch sizes, but 5 1/4-inch disks and drives are on the way out, so make sure your system is equipped with a 3 1/2-inch drive. Floppy disk drives differ in their capacities; some are extra high-density drives that can accommodate as much as 2.8 **megabytes** of information. For more information on floppy disk drives, see Chapter 12.

hard disk

A large-capacity **storage device** that is designed to store all of your computer programs, as well as all of the information you create with your computer. Unlike your computer's memory, which loses information when you switch off the power, the hard disk stores this information so that it is available the next time you use your computer. The storage capacity of hard disks is measured in megabytes (MB); one megabyte roughly equals one million letters or numbers. Because today's programs are so large, most users find that they need at least 500MB of hard disk storage space. When you buy or upgrade your system, you'll need to pay attention to the hard disk's size, measured in megabytes; the interface (such as IDE, or SCSI-2) that connects the drive to the rest of the computer, the size of the temporary storage area (called cache), and the disk's performance characteristics (such as access time). These and other hard disk-related terms are defined Chapter 12.

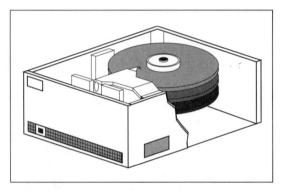

Figure 1.3 *Cut away view of a hard disk*

keyboard

A bank of electromechanical buttons, generally arranged in the form of a standard typewriter keyboard (with a few additional keys), each of which is designed to send a certain, coded signal to the computer when you depress the button. Terms related to keyboards are defined in Chapter 9.

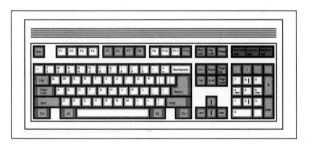

Figure 1.4 *A 101 key keyboard*

megabyte (MB)

A basic unit of measurement for both **memory** and **storage**, equal to approximately one million characters (letters or numbers).

memory

A bank of high-speed semiconductors that are designed to hold information so that it is readily available to the computer's processing circuitry. When you run a program on your computer, the computer transfers the program from the hard disk, where it is permanently stored, to your computer's memory, where it can operate much faster. Memory is also called random access memory (RAM). Memory is measured in megabytes (MB); one megabyte stores roughly one million letters or numbers. Storage devices are needed because memory does not retain information when the power is switched off. When you buy or upgrade a computer, pay attention to the amount of memory, its speed, and other memory-related performance characteristics, such as memory caches (temporary storage areas for frequently-accessed information). For definitions of memory-related terms, see Chapter 4.

Many people confuse memory (RAM) with **storage** (floppy disks, hard disks, and tape backup devices), probably because the capacities of both are measured in megabytes (MB). As a rule of thumb, most users need only 8 to 16MB of memory, while they will probably wish to have at least 500MB of hard disk storage. Memory holds the programs you are using at one time (usually no more than four or five), while your hard disk holds all of your programs and all of the information you create with your computer.

microprocessor

A tiny flake of silicon, containing as many as 5.5 million transistors (switching devices), that provides the processing capabilities for hundreds of millions of computers worldwide. Under the direction of a computer program, a microprocessor performs processing operations, such as sorting a list of items in alphabetical order or calculating the square root of a lengthy number.

More than any other aspect of a personal computer system, the microprocessor governs the system's overall performance capabilities. Microprocessors are fully explored in Chapter 4.

Figure 1.5 *The Intel 486 microprocessor*

modem

A **peripheral** that permits your computer to communicate with other computers via the telephone system, which can't handle computer signals without modification. The term "modem" is an abbreviation of MOdulator/DEModulator. To send signals, a modem modulates (changes) them so that they can be sent over the telephone line; it also demodulates incoming signals. Modem terms are covered in Chapter 15.

monitor

A TV-like display device (sometimes incorrectly called a display) that receives its picture from the computer. With most computers, a required accessory is a **display adapter**, which fits inside the **system unit's** expansion slots (see Chapter 2,

"System Unit"). The monitor and the video adapter must be designed to work together. Some monitors are monochrome and display only two colors, such as black and white or black and green, but most computer users prefer color monitors. The better monitors display the computer's picture with a high degree of sharpness, called resolution (see Chapter 11).

Figure 1.6 *A common computer monitor*

| motherboard |

Also called main board. The motherboard is a large circuit board that contains most of the computer's memory and processing circuitry, as well as the expansion bus into which expansion cards are placed. The motherboard and its components are discussed in Chapter 3.

| mouse |

An electromechanical or electro-optical device that allows the user to move a pointer on-screen. By pointing at something on the screen and clicking one of the mouse buttons, the user can select options from menus, initiate processing operations, highlight text for editing, and even make free-hand drawings on-screen. Mice are covered in Chapter 9.

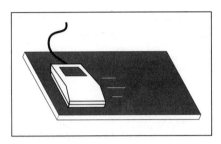

Figure 1.7 *A typical mouse and mouse pad*

on-board speaker

A small, tinny-sounding speaker that is capable of reproducing beeps and honks, but not much else. Bypassing
the on-board speaker by adding a **sound card** is a good
way to improve your computer system.

peripheral

Any device that is not essential for the computer operation,
and adds functionality, such as a **printer, modem,** or scanner.

port

An electronic channel through which the computer can
communicate with hardware accessories, such as **printers**
and **modems**. Ports are accessible by a connector mounted
on the rear of the computer's case. The two most common
types of ports are called serial ports and parallel ports.
These and other aspects of ports are explored in Chapter 7.

printer

An indispensable part of a personal computer system, the component that prints out the information you have created or
accessed with the computer's help. Printers vary in their
speed, output quality, and underlying technology. You'll

find a full explanation of printer-related terms, including the latest color printing technology, in Chapter 16.

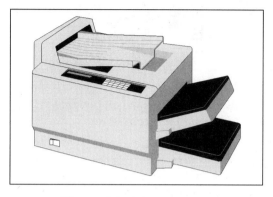

Figure 1.8 *A laser printer*

| sound card |

Also called a sound board. An **expansion board**, designed to fit into one of the computer's expansion slots (see Chapter 14), that transforms sound files into audio sounds playable on the system's **auxiliary speakers**. Without a sound card, you can hear only those sounds generated by the computer's **on-board speaker**, which is generally a small, tinny speaker that reproduces monaural sound only. A good sound card can play stereo sounds with quality approaching that of a compact disk player.

| storage |

Collectively, all the disk drives and tape backup units that provide permanent, high-capacity storage for computer programs and data files. **Memory** is designed for temporary storage of programs and data so that they are directly available to the **microprocessor**; but memory is much smaller than storage, and memory loses its contents when the power is switched off. Storage devices offer much more capacity than memory and they do require power to retain data.

storage device

Any device that provides storage capacity, such as a **CD-ROM drive**, a **floppy disk drive**, a **hard disk**, or a **tape backup unit**.

system unit

The case that houses the main components of the computer, including the **motherboard** and power supply.

tape backup unit

A tape recording and playback device that lets you back up the data on your hard disk, providing a high level of protection against hard disk failure. Tape backup units work with tape backup cartridges. You can also use tape backup units to archive important but little-used files, so that they do not take up space on your hard disk.

video adapter

An expansion board, designed to fit into one of the computer's expansion slots (see Chapter 2), that generates the output displayed by the **monitor**. When you purchase or upgrade your system, you will need to pay attention to the adapter's video standard (such as SuperVGA), its ability to present detailed on-screen information (called resolution), the amount and type of memory that is supplied with the adapter, and the adapter's graphics processing speed. Terms related to all of these video adapter characteristics are defined in Chapter 10. Also called display adapter and video card.

Cases and Power Supplies

This chapter surveys the terms you'll encounter when you're considering case and power supply options. Major considerations include the amount of space you'll need for system expansion and the case's ability to cope with the heat generated by the computer's internal components. In addition, you should consider how important it is to you that you might lose work due to brownouts or power outages; you may wish to consider an **uninterruptable power supply (UPS)**.

AT-size case

A horizontally-oriented case that mimics the size and internal motherboard and disk drive mounting specifications of IBM's Personal Computer AT, first released in 1984. The case consists of an internal chassis and a lid, attached by mounting screws. Although the AT-size case is popular and most system components and accessories continue to conform to its mounting specifications, the case has a very large **footprint**. *Compare* **mini-AT-size case, mini-tower case.**

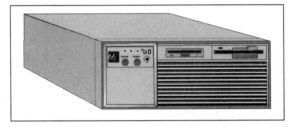

Figure 2.1 An AT-size case

convection cooling

A method of cooling the computer's internal components by encouraging cool air to enter the computer at the case's bottom and providing outlets for hot air at the top. All computer cases use convection cooling, but most systems require fans as well.

No matter what kind of case you're using, make sure that nothing obstructs the ventilation holes or grilles of either the intake vents or the outlet vents. Blocking these vents could shorten your computer's life.

drive bay

A metal chassis that is designed to accommodate a mass storage device such as a hard or floppy disk drive or a tape backup unit. Holes are provided so that drive can be affixed to the bay with screws. *See also* **full-height drive bay**, **half-height drive bay.**

---

footprint

The amount of space that a computer's case takes up on your desk. The footprint of the original IBM Personal Computer measured 21 inches wide by 17 inches in depth—a hefty chunk of desk space, by any definition.

---

full-height drive bay

A **drive bay,** 3.38 inches in height, that is designed to accommodate the first generation of IBM PC floppy disk drives. *Compare* **half-height drive bay.**

---

half-height drive bay

A **drive bay,** 1.625 inches in height, that is designed to accommodate half-height drives, which are now standard.

---

line interactive UPS

An **uninterruptible power supply (UPS)** that constantly monitors the current from the wall outlet, ready to step in instantaneously if the power sags or fails. Line-interactive UPS units provide protection for brownouts as well as blackouts. *Compare* **standby UPS.**

---

metal-oxide varistor (MOV)

An electronic device that does not conduct electricity until the current reaches a certain point, at which it suddenly conducts the current. MOVs are used in **surge suppressors** to handle overvoltages. In a typical MOV-based surge suppressor, the MOV starts conducting when the current surpasses 350 volts, and shunts the current to a neutral line.

mini-AT-size case

 A horizontally oriented case that retains the mounting specifications of the original **AT-size case**, but offers a smaller **footprint**.

Be aware that mini-AT-size cases may be short on expansion slots (see Chapter 3). That may not be of concern to you if you're happy with the way your computer is equipped right now. If you think you'd like to add more expansion boards (such as a network interface card, a sound board, and a video board), make sure the motherboard includes enough available expansion slots for your needs.

mini-tower case

A vertically oriented **tower case** that is approximately 30% shorter than standard tower cases, allowing the case to fit within specially-constructed cavities in modern office furniture. Mini-tower cases offer few disadvantages, except that they can accommodate fewer mass storage devices that a larger case.

Figure 2.2 A mini-tower case

MOV

See **metal-oxide varistor (MOV).**

overvoltage

An anomaly in the delivery of electrical current character-
ized by **surges** or spikes in excess of 130 volts.

power supply

A device that transforms the alternating current (AC) available from wall outlets to the low-voltage direct current (DC)
that the computer requires. The power supply must deliver DC voltage at the level for which the computer and its components were designed. *See also* **switchable power supply**.

Power supplies are rated by the amount of power they can
make available to the computer. This amount is measured
in watts. Most PC power supplies deliver 200 to 250 watts,
which is sufficient for most systems.

Does this mean your PC burns up as much electricity as a
couple of 100-watt light bulbs? Unfortunately, it consumes
more than 200 watts, thanks to the inefficiencies of AC to DC
conversion.

Is your computer too noisy? The fault may lie in the
inexpensive fan used in the power supply that came
with your computer's case. Consider replacing the power
supply with one that offers a super-quiet fan.

standby UPS

An **uninterruptible power supply (UPS)** that does nothing
until it detects a power outage, when it switches into action
to supply backup current to the computer. The least expensive type of UPS, standby units have one drawback: They generally cannot assist in the event of a brownout (a sag in the
current), which may cause as many as 85% of power-relat-
ed computer glitches. *See* **line interactive UPS**.

surge

An **overvoltage** that lasts longer than one millionth of a second.

surge suppressor

A power-conditioning device that is designed to suppress **overvoltages** in the AC line current delivered to your computer. Overvoltage conditions include **transients** (also called spikes), which are short-lived overvoltages lasting one-millionth of a second or less, and **surges**, which that last longer than one-millionth of a second).

Look for a surge suppressor that states that it has passed the Underwriter's Laboratory UL1449 standard.

switchable power supply

A power supply that lets the user select between U.S. current (115 volts AC at 60 cycles per second) and European current (230 volts AC, 50 cycles per second).

Don't use an inexpensive "travel converter" to power your computer overseas. Most of these travel converters use an inexpensive voltage-reducing trick that works for light bulbs and motors, but not for electronic devices. Using a travel converter with a computer can destroy the computer's circuitry.

tower case

A vertically oriented case, 21 to 24 inches in height, that is designed to stand upright on the floor, thus saving desk space. Tower cases offer considerably more internal room than desktop cases (such as the **AT-size case** or the **mini-AT-size case**), so they generally have more **drive bays** and can accommodate larger motherboards. The vertical orientation does not adversely affect most components, though hard disk drives must be mounted horizontally within the tower case to work properly. *Compare* **mini-tower case.**

A significant disadvantage of vertical cases is that because heat rises, hot components will heat the items positioned directly above them, causing degradation and eventual failure unless the system is adequately cooled. If you're thinking of buying a system with a tower case, look for one equipped with two cooling fans.

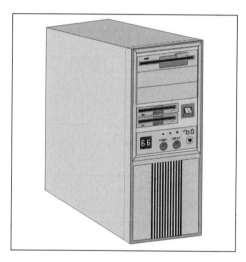

Figure 2.3 *A tower case*

| transient |

An **overvoltage** that lasts one-millionth of a second or less.

| uninterruptible power supply (UPS) |

A battery-equipped unit that guarantees continued power to your computer in the event of a power failure. A UPS cannot power your computer for more than a few minutes, but this should be sufficient to save your work and shut down the computer correctly, to ensure that data isn't lost. The least expensive unit is the **standby UPS**, which springs into action only when a power outage occurs. More expensive **line interactive UPS** units can deal with brownouts, and are well worth the additional cost.

Be sure that the UPS you're buying has enough power for your system. As a rule of thumb, a 400 volt-ampere (VA) UPS should be sufficient for an entry-level system (a 486 with a 14-inch monitor). With a larger monitor and more peripherals, you may need as much as 600 VA.

Motherboards

This chapter surveys the terms you're likely to encounter when shopping for a new computer or upgrading your system's motherboard. Key **motherboard** components are covered in more detail in Chapter 4 (Microprocessors), Chapter 5 (Memory), and Chapter 6 (Expansion Busses). For example, this chapter briefly introduces the **microprocessor** abbreviations you'll encounter while shopping for motherboards (such as **486DX4-100**) but Chapter 4 discusses specific microprocessors in more detail. Use this chapter as a quick guide for deciphering motherboard advertisements, or the references to motherboard features of a PC you're thinking about buying.

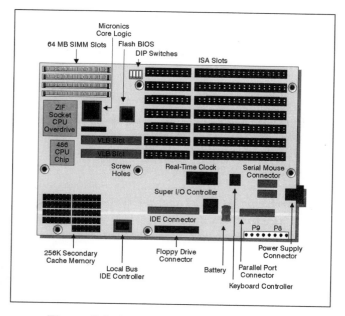

Figure 3.1 *A generic motherboard layout*

16550A serial port

A high-speed serial port that is indispensible for use with high-speed modems. For more information, see Chapter 7.

30-pin SIMM slot

A receptacle for the obsolete 30-pin **single in-line memory module (SIMM)**. It might be worth buying a motherboard with these slots if you have lots of unused 30-pin SIMMS, but the newer 72-pin design is the current standard. See **72-pin SIMM slot**.

486DX-33

A version of the Intel 486DX microprocessor that is designed to run at a system clock speed of 33MHz. The 486DX microprocessor includes a math coprocessor, giving it better number-crunching performance than the 486SX. However, the system's relatively slow clock speed will frustrate Microsoft Windows users. For more information on the 486DX microprocessor, see Chapter 4.

486DX2-50

A clock-doubled version of the Intel 486DX **microprocessor** that is designed to run at a clock speed of 50MHz. (The microprocessor runs at twice the 25HMz-speed of the computer's data bus.) 486DX2-50 processors are made by Cyrix as well as Intel, but neither is a bargain—for just a few dollars more, you can get a 486DX2-66 system, which is considerably faster because the entire motherboard runs at 33MHz (instead of 25MHz). For more information on the 486DX2 microprocessor and clock doubling, see Chapter 4.

486DX2-66

A clock-doubled version of the Intel 486DX **microprocessor** that is designed to run at a clock speed of 66MHz. (The microprocessor runs at twice the 33HMz-speed of the computer's data bus.) Considered an entry-level microprocessor at this writing, the 486DX2-66 has sufficient processing horsepower to run Microsoft Windows at an acceptable speed, but it's not the best choice for multimedia systems. 486DX2-66 microprocessors are made by Cyrix and Advanced Micro Devices (AMD) as well as Intel; Cyrix- and AMD-powered systems may be cheaper and offer a comparable level of performance. For more information on the 486DX2 microprocessor and clock doubling, see Chapter 4.

486DX2-80

A clock-doubled version of the Advanced Micro Devices (AMD) 486 DX **microprocessor** that is designed to run at a clock speed of 80 MHz. Less expensive than the Intel 486DX2-66 (at this writing), the AMD chip offers improved performance and is gaining in market acceptance.

486DX4-100

A clock-tripled version of the Intel 486DX **microprocessor** that is designed to run at a clock speed of 100 MHz. In a well-designed system, this microprocessor is capable of rivalling the performance of low-end **Pentium**-based systems. Advanced Micro Devices also makes a 486DX4-100 microprocessor, which is currently selling for less than the Intel chip. This chip is an entry-level processor in many multimedia systems. For more information on the Intel 486DX4 microprocessor, see Chapter 4.

486DX4-75

A clock-tripled version of the Intel 486DX **microprocessor** that is designed to run at a clock speed of 75 MHz. This chip offers impressive performance, but it is designed for use with 25MHz motherboards. For a few dollars more, you should be able to get a **486DX4-100**, which runs with a snappier 33MHz motherboard. For more information on the Intel 486DX4 microprocessor, see Chapter 4.

486SX-33

A version of the Intel 486SX **microprocessor** that is designed to run at a system clock speed of 33MHz. Because the 486SX chip lacks a math coprocessor, this processor is not recommended for use with spreadsheets or other math-intensive applications. This is a minimal entry-level system, and its slow speed may frustrate Microsoft Windows users. For more information on the 486SX microprocessor, see Chapter 4.

486SX2-50

A clock-doubled version of the Intel 486 that is designed to run at a system clock speed of 50MHz. Slightly speedier than the 486SX-33, this chip is still a poor choice for spreadsheet or Windows users.

72-pin SIMM slot

A receptacle for a 72-pin **single in-line memory module (SIMM),** used for memory chips that can be easily installed by snapping it into place. 72-pin SIMMs are replacing the obsolete 30-pin design, which you should avoid.

Basic Input/Output System (BIOS)

 A set of programs that govern the computer's basic functions, including the start-up routine and the handling of keyboard input. A computer's BIOS is encoded on a read-only memory (ROM) chip located on the motherboard. A very desirable feature is **flash BIOS**, which can be upgraded easily. For more information on BIOS, see Chapter 8.

BIOS

See **Basic Input/Output System (BIOS).**

---

cache

In the context of motherboards, this term generally refers to the **secondary cache**—one of the two kinds of cache memory (the other is called primary cache).

---

cache memory

A unit of ultra-fast memory that sortes recently accessed data and frequently used program instructions so that these are more readily available to the microprocessor. If the data or instructions need to be accesssed again, they can be retrieved from the cache much more rapidly than from the computer's **RAM** memory. A cache memory that is built into the microprocessor's circuitry is called a **primary cache**, while a cache memory that is physically separate from the processor is called a **secondary cache**. Cache memories are usually made from **static random-access memory (SRAM)** chips.

> Don't even think about buying a computer that doesn't have a cache memory of at least 256KB. A computer that lacks cache memory is up to 30% slower than a comparable machine that has cache memory.

---

chip set

Commonly used term (sometimes spelled "chipset") for the integrated circuits that supplement a **microprocessor's** functions. A chip set must be developed to work with a given brand and model of microprocessor.

CPU fan

A fan designed to mount on top of the **microprocessor** and to dissipate the heat generated by this crucial component. The fan is powered by a spare floppy disk cable. This desirable feature in a motherboard is inexpensive and can be added to any motherboard that lacks it.

Figure 3.2 *A CPU fan*

direct memory access (DMA) controller

An electronic circuit, usually provided as part of the motherboard's **chip set**, that allows the computer to move data from disk drives or other peripherals to the memory, without taxing the processing capabilities of the **microprocessor**. The use of a DMA controller greatly improves overall system performance when data must be moved, the DMA controller handles the job, thus freeing the microprocessor to return to other processing duties. Most of today's PCs use a DMA controller that provides eight DMA request lines, numbered 0 through 7.

direct-map cache

A method of allocating the storage space in a **cache memory**, in which each storage unit in the cache is linked to several storage locations (called blocks) in the main memory. This design is economical because it does not require additional, complex processing circuitry. However, for reasons discussed in Chapter 5, it results in frequent cache misses, in which the data required by the CPU is not found in the cache and must be retrieved from the main memory. *Compare* **full-associative cache, set-associative cache**.

DMA channel

A signal line, one of seven in the standard IBM PC AT architecture, that allows the **direct memory access (DMA) controller** to maintain communication with peripheral devices and floppy disk drives.

DMA conflict

An electronic short circuit, generally resulting in a system crash, that occurs when two peripheral devices have been configured to use the same **DMA channel**. On most PCs, channels 1, 3, 5, 6, and 7 are available to be assigned to new peripheral cards.

DMA controller

See **direct memory access (DMA) controller**.

dual in-line package (DIP)

A type of semiconductor package, made of hard plastic with two parallel rows of pins running down each side. The pins are designed to fit into matching receptacles, but it is very difficult for an inexperienced person to insert DIP-packaged chips without breaking or bending the pins. *Compare* **single in-line memory module (SIMM)**.

dynamic random access memory (DRAM)

A type of memory chip that require the processor to continually refresh the data they contain; without the constant refreshing, DRAM loses its contents. DRAM chips are much less expensive than **static random access memory (SRAM)** chips, which do not require the continual refreshing operations. Because of their economy, DRAM chips are used for **random-access memory (RAM)**; as much as 16MB of RAM may be required to obtain acceptable performance with Microsoft Windows.

E-IDE

See **Enhanced IDE**.

Enhanced IDE

A high-speed (and very desirable) hard disk interface that is increasingly built into high-quality motherboards. For more information on Enhanced IDE, see Chapter 12.

Enhanced Parallel Port (EPP)

An advanced connector for peripherals such as printers that allows the computer to engage in two-way communication with the peripheral device. Jointly developed by Intel, Xircom, Zenith, and other companies, the EPP standard may be succeeded by the more capable **Extended Capabilities Port (ECP)**, jointly developed by Microsoft and Hewlett-Packard. While the market and technology settle out, many motherboards support both of these standards. For more information on ports and EPP, see Chapter 7.

EPP

See **Enhanced Parallel Port**.

EPP/ECP port

A parallel port that supports both the **Enhanced Parallel Port (EPP)** and **Extended Capabilities Port (ECP)** specifications, as well as the standard (Centronics) parallel printer interface. EPP/ECP-capable printer ports are supported by Windows 95. By using a special, high-speed cable, Windows users will be able to use the EPP/ECP port to create connections that operate as fast as Ethernet network connections.

expansion board

A circuit board that is designed to fit into one of the motherboard's **expansion slots**.

expansion slot

A receptacle that is designed to accommodate an **expansion board**.

Extended Capabilities Port (ECP)

An advanced connector for peripherals such as printers that allows the computer to engage in two-way communication with the peripheral device. Jointly developed by Microsoft and Hewlett-Packard, the ECP standard seems likely to dislodge the competing **Enhanced Parallel Port (EPP)** design. Many motherboards support both of these standards. For more information on ports and ECP, see Chapter 7.

external cache

See **secondary cache**.

FDD

An acronym for floppy disk drive, infrequently used except in tightly-formatted motherboard advertisements. See Chapter 12, Disk Drives.

flash BIOS

A programmable read-only-memory (PROM) chip that stores the computer's **Basic Input/Output System (BIOS)**. For the user, this has a very important advantage over a nonprogrammable BIOS—if the computer's manufacturer discovers that the BIOS contains a bug, you can obtain a disk containing the corrected version of the BIOS software and easily perform the upgrade yourself. Unless convenient computer service is available locally, don't even think about buying a computer unless it has flash BIOS.

four-way set-associative cache

A **set-associative cache** design that represents the optimal balance between cost and complexity. Four-way set-associative caches surpass the performance of **two-way set-associative caches**, and significantly surpass the performance of **direct-map caches**.

full-associative cache

A method of allocating the storage space in a **cache memory** in which each storage unit in the cache can be associated with any storage location in the main memory. For reasons discussed in Chapter 5, this design solves the principal drawback of **direct-map cache** designs. Because frequently accessed data can be kept in the cache, no matter where this data is stored in the main memory. However, performance is poor because the cache controller must search the entire

cache to find the desired data. *Compare* **direct-map cache,
set-associative cache.**

Green PC

A personal computer that conforms to the Environmental Protection Agency (EPA) Energy Star guidelines, which specify that the computer should consume less than 30 watts of power when it is idle. To conform to the Energy Star guidelines, the motherboard must be designed to initiate "sleep modes," and shut down energy-consuming peripherals such as displays and hard disk drives when the system has been idle for a specified interval.

HDD

An acronym for hard disk drive, infrequently used except in tightly-formatted motherboard advertisements. See Chapter 12, Disk Drives.

Industry Standard Architecture (ISA)

A 16-bit expansion bus standard (see Chapter 6) developed for IBM's 1984 Personal Computer AT, and since published as an international standard. The 16-bit ISA expansion bus is too slow to keep up with today's microprocessors. However, it's nice to have a couple of **ISA slots** in a motherboard so that you can use older expansion cards. For more information on the ISA bus, see Chapter 6.

interrupt controller

An electronic circuit, usually part of the motherboard's **chip set**, that provides hardware interrupt signal lines. Hardware interrupt lines allow peripheral devices to gain access to the **microprocessor** when needed. All IBM PC-compatible computers use the standard interrupt architecture introduced in 1984 with IBM's PC AT, which provides 15 interrupt request circuits (IRQ0 to IRQ15). Because most of these interrupt circuits are pre-assigned to standard peripherals such as the keyboard, serial and parallel ports, floppy and hard disk controllers, the real-time clock, and other devices, few are available for peripherals.

IRQ conflict

An electronic "short circuit" caused when two peripheral devices try to use the same IRQ line. An IRQ line is a signal circuit that enables peripheral devices to get the **microprocessor's** attention. If a sound card and CD-ROM drive's controller are both attempting to use IRQ5, an IRQ conflict results and a serious system crash is all but inevitable. When you install a new peripheral device, you must take special care to ensure that the device is configured to access an unoccupied IRQ—but too often, that's a matter of trial-and-error guesswork. The forthcoming **Plug and Play** standard will eliminate this guesswork (and the crashes that result from erroneous guesses) by automatically configuring each peripheral's IRQ. *See* **interrupt controller**.

ISA slot

A receptacle designed to accept adapters conforming to the **industry-standard architecture (ISA)** standard, an expansion bus standard that was developed by IBM for its IBM PC AT, released in 1984. The ISA architecture is too slow to keep up with today's fast microprocessors. For use with a 486, you should choose between motherboards with **VESA local bus slots** and **PCI slots**. For use with the Pentium, choose a motherboard with PCI slots. For more information on these and other expansion bus designs, see Chapter 6.

L2 cache memory

See **secondary cache.**

LBA

See **logical block addressing (LBA).**

logical block addressing (LBA)

A method of organizing the storage space on a hard disk drive that permits an **Enhanced IDE** hard disk to offer up to 8.4 GB of storage, significantly more than the former 528 MB limit. For more information on Enhanced IDE drives, see Chapter 12.

maximum RAM

The maximum amount of random-access memory (RAM) that can be directly affixed to the motherboard. Don't settle for a motherboard that can handle only 8 MB of memory; plenty are available that can accept 128 MB or more.

microprocessor

A processing unit that is crafted on a single integrated circuit of fabulous complexity (current technology has pushed the number of transistors on such integrated circuits well into the millions). More than any one single factor, a given computer's performance depends on the characteristics and brand of its microprocessor. Microprocessors are also called processors, CPUs, chips, or just parts. For more information on microprocessors, see Chapter 4.

motherboard

 Also called main board. A large circuit board that contains most of the computer's memory and processing circuitry, as well as the expansion bus into which expansion cards are placed. A motherboard's characteristics are determined by the microprocessor with which it is designed to work (see **486SX-33**, **486SX2-50**, **486DX-33**, **486DX2-50**, **486DX2-66**, **486DX2-80**, **486 DX4-75**, **486DX4-100**, and the various **Pentiums**), the **Basic Input/Output System (BIOS)**, the **secondary cache**, the expansion bus (**ISA**, **VESA local bus**, **PCI**, or a combination of these), and the amount of **random access memory (RAM)** that can be directly mounted on the board.

Multiword DMA Mode 1

A method of transferring information from an **Enhanced IDE** hard disk drive to the computer that is roughly three to four times faster than the standard IDE transfer rate of 3.3 MB per second.

n-way set associative cache

See **set-associative cache.**

P100

Common abbreviation for the Pentium microprocessor that is designed to run at 100 MHz. For more information on the Pentium microprocessor, see Chapter 4.

P120

Common abbreviation for the Pentium microprocessor that is designed to run at a blistering 120 MHz. For more information on the Pentium microprocessor, see Chapter 4.

P24T socket

A receptacle on a Intel 486 motherboard that is designed to accept the P24T (Pentium OverDrive) upgrade processor. P24T brings the performance of Intel's **Pentium** microprocessors to such systems. For more information on the P24T processor, see Pentium OverDrive in Chapter 4.

P60

Common abbreviation for the Pentium **microprocessor** that is designed to run at 60 MHz. Avoid this chip, as it uses an older Pentium design that consumes significantly more power and generates more heat than the **P75**, **P90**, **P100**, and **P120** designs. Heat degenerates electronic components and may shorten the processor's life. For more information on the Pentium microprocessor, see Chapter 4.

P66

Common abbreviation of the Pentium **microprocessor** that is designed to run at 66 MHz. Avoid this chip, as it uses an older Pentium design that consumes significantly more power, and generates more heat, than the **P75**, **P90**, **P100**, and **P120** designs. Heat degenerates electronic components and may shorten the processor's life. For more information on the Pentium microprocessor, see Chapter 4.

P75

Common abbreviation for the **Pentium microprocessor** that is designed to run at 75 MHz. For more information on the Pentium microprocessor, see Chapter 4.

P90

Common abbreviation for the Pentium **microprocessor** that is designed to run at 90 MHz. For more information on the Pentium microprocessor, see Chapter 4.

PCI slot

A 32-bit receptacle designed to accept adapters conforming to the **Peripheral Component Interconnect (PCI)** standard, an expansion bus standard developed by Intel Corporation. The PCI bus architecture is designed to perform optimally with Intel's advanced microprocessors and is strongly recommended over its chief competitors, **VESA local bus** and **ISA bus**. For more information on these and other expansion bus designs, see Chapter 6.

Pentium

An Intel **microprocessor** that is designed to run at clock speeds running from 60 MHz to 120 MHz. In PC hardware and motherboard advertisements, Pentium microprocessors are mentioned in abbreviated form (a "P" followed by the processor's clock speed, as in P66). See **P60**, **P66**, **P75**, **P90**, **P100**, **P120**. For more information on the Pentium microprocessor, see Chapter 4.

Pentium-ready

Able to be upgraded to Pentium-level performance by inserting a Pentium OverDrive processor in the motherboard's **P24T socket**.

Peripheral Component Interconnect (PCI)

A high-speed, 32-bit expansion bus standard (see Chapter 6) developed by Intel Corporation, and generally considered to be the best expansion bus for today's fast microprocessors. For more information on the PCI bus, see Chapter 6.

planar board

Synonymous with **motherboard.**

Plug and Play

A Microsoft-backed standard that will enable users to add expansion cards (see Chapter 6) without installation and configuration hassles. To support Plug and Play fully, a computer needs a Plug and Play-compatible BIOS (see **Basic Input/Output System**), Windows 95, and Plug and Play-compatible expansion cards.

primary cache

Synonymous with internal cache. A unit of **cache memory** that is built into the microprocessor itself, in contrast to **secondary cache** (also called L2 cache), which is provided on the motherboard.

RAM

See **random access memory (RAM).**

random access memory (RAM)

The computer's main internal memory, where program instructions and data are temporarily stored so that they

random access memory	SIMM

are directly and speedily available to the microprocessor. RAM is supplied in **single in-line memory modules (SIMMs)**, containing 1MB or 4MB for each SIMM. For more information on RAM, see Chapter 5.

---

secondary cache

A **cache memory** that is positioned outside the **microprocessor** and designed to improve overall system performance. Don't even think about buying a motherboard that lacks L2 cache memory. A 128K L2 cache might be sufficient for most 486 systems, but you'll need a 256K L2 cache for 486DX4 and Pentium systems. Cache design is also important; the cheapest design is the **direct-map cache**, but **set-associative cache** designs are superior (the best is the **four-way set-associative cache**). In addition, look for a **write-back cache** rather than a **write-through cache**. For more information on cache memory, see Chapter 5.

---

set-associative cache

A compromise between a **direct-map cache** and a **full-associative cache** design, in which the **cache memory** is divided into two, four, or eight direct-mapped blocks, called sets. Set-associative cache designs are superior to direct-map caches; **four-way set-associative caches** represent an optimal balance between performance and cost. For more information on how set-associative caches work, see Chapter 5.

SIMM

See **single in-line memory module (SIMM).**

single in-line memory module (SIMM)

single in-line memory module (SIMM)

A hard plastic package that contains from 1MB to 16 MB of **dynamic random access memory (DRAM)** chips and is designed for easy user installation.

In the late 1970s and early- to mid-1980s, DRAM chips were packaged in **dual in-line packages (DIP)**, with twin rows of pins that would bend in all directions when the hapless user tried to press them in their sockets. By the late 1980s, memory and **motherboard** designers provided a user-friendly alternative. Early SIMMs had 30 contact pads (generally, but erroneously, called "pins"); more common today is the 72-pad SIMM, which provides designers with more configuration options.

Wondering how fast your SIMMs are? DRAMs are often marked with their speed after they are tested. Look for a suffix after the part number: a SIMM marked 398739-7 is very likely a 70 ns DRAM.

The cheapest motherboards come with slots for 30-pin SIMMs, but this technology is obsolete. Make sure your motherboard uses 72-pin SIMMs.

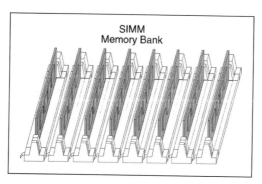

Figure 3.3 A SIMM memory board

single in-line pinned packages (SIPPs)

A hard plastic package that contains from 1MB to 16 MB of **dynamic random access memory (DRAM)** chips, and— unlike **single in-line memory modules (SIMMs)**—is affixed to the motherboard by means of pins.

SIPP

See **single in-line pinned package (SIPP).**

static random access memory (SRAM)

A type of memory chip that does not require the processor to continually refresh the data, as dynamic random access memory (DRAM) chips do. SRAM chips are substantially faster than DRAM chips, but they're also more expensive. For this reason, they are most often used in **cache memory**, which is much smaller in capacity than **random-access memory (RAM)**.

system board

IBM's synonym for **motherboard**.

two-way set-associative cache

A **cache memory** design that offers the benefits of a **set-associative cache** at a reasonable cost, and is therefore superior to the **direct map cache**. However, performance is inferior to the more costly **four-way set-associative cache** design.

VESA local bus slot

A receptacle for adapter cards based on the 32-bit VESA local bus standard. This expansion bus standard was developed to deal with poor video performance of 486-

based PCs equipped with **ISA** expansion busses, and solved the processing bottleneck for 486-based machines. However, the VESA local bus 1.0 standard does not work well with Pentium **microprocessors**. The new standard, 2.0, solves this technical problem, but it is unlikely to compete effectively with Intel's **PCI** bus architecture. For more information on the VESA standard, expansion busses, and local bus architectures in general, see Chapter 6.

If you're thinking about buying a 486 motherboard, you can save some money by buying a board that offers only VESA local bus slots instead of PCI slots, but watch out—you may be sacrificing your ability to upgrade to new peripherals. PCI is expected to dominate the expansion bus market in the coming years.

| write-back cache |

A **cache memory** design in which the cache records memory writes as well as reads, freeing cache operations from dependence on the slower circuitry of the computer's **random-access memory (RAM)**. *Compare* **write-through cache, n-way set associative cache**.

> For **secondary caches**, write-back cache designs typically score higher on benchmark tests than write-through caches.

| write-through cache |

A **cache memory** design in which memory reads are cached, but not memory writes, which must be stored in **random access memory (RAM)**. This design is inefficient because RAM is much slower than cache memory. *Compare* **write-through cache, n-way set associative cache**.

zero insertion force (ZIF) package

A receptacle for integrated circuits that does not require the user to push the device into a socket. Instead, you open the socket with a lever and insert the circuit. When the socket is closed, the contacts engage. *Compare* **dual in-line package (DIP)**.

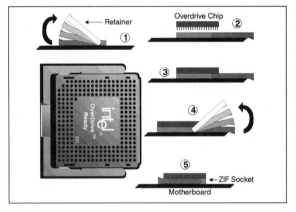

Figure 3.4 Zif socket and retainer

ZIF

See **zero-insertion force (ZIF) package**.

Microprocessors

This chapter sums up the terminology you're likely to encounter when you're considering the single most important aspect of a computer system: the **microprocessor**. More than any other system component, the microprocessor's capabilities put limits on the rest of the computer's performance. Selecting the right microprocessor is a much more important decision than selecting the right brand of computer. This chapter provides in-depth definitions of the microprocessors currently available, and it also delves into the important distinction between the two competing microprocessor design philosophies, called **Reduced Instruction Set Computer (RISC)** and **Complex Instruction Set Computer (CISC)**.

0.5-micron technology

A **semiconductor** fabrication process that enables manufacturers to produce devices, such as **microprocessors**, in which the smallest effective device is one-half-millionth of a meter in width. 0.5-micron technology enables microprocessor manufacturers to create smaller chips that consume less power and generate less heat. In addition, these chips offer improved performance, since the electrical signals within the chip have less distance to travel.

8-bit microprocessor

A **microprocessor** constructed with internal **registers** that are 8 bits wide, so that the **chip** can process only one byte of data at a time. An example of an 8-bit microprocessor is the Zilog Z-80, a pioneering chip widely used in early personal computers that used the CP/M operating system.

16-bit microprocessor

A **microprocessor** constructed with internal **registers** and an **external data bus** that are 16 bits wide, allowing the **chip** to process two bytes of data at a time. An example of a 16-bit microprocessor is the **Intel 8086,** which features 16-bit registers and a 16-bit external data bus. In contrast, the **Intel 8088** chip used in the first IBM Personal Computer (1981) which has 16-bit registers, used an 8-bit external data bus. This compromise allowed IBM designers to use inexpensive, readily-available 8-bit peripherals such as disk drives, at the cost of a substantial performance penalty.

32-bit microprocessor

A **microprocessor** constructed with an **internal data bus** that is 32 bits wide, allowing the chip to process four bytes of data at a time. An example of a 32-bit microprocessor is the **Intel 486DX**. Some 32-bit microprocessors use a compromise design in which the internal data bus is wider than the **external data bus** (such as the 386SX, which uses a 32-bit internal data bus, and a 16-bit external data bus). This is a compromise design that allowss the system to use cheap, readily available peripherals designed for the narrower external bus, but it drastically reduces overall system performance.

64-bit microprocessor

A **microprocessor** constructed with an **internal data bus** that is 64 bits wide, allowing the chip to process four bytes of data at a time. An example of a 64-bit microprocessor is Intel's **Pentium** processor. Today's 64-bit processors typically work with a 32-bit **external data bus**, but this is not so serious a design compromise as a 32-bit processor working with a 16-bit external bus. A "true" 64-bit microprocessor would work with a 64-bit external bus, but such systems will be considerably more expensive than today's high-end PCs because they will require 64-bit peripherals.

680x0

The Motorola architecture that is **binary compatible** with programs written for Apple's Macintosh computers. *See* **Motorola 68000, 68020, 68030, 68040**.

address bus

The circuit within the **microprocessor** that handles the numerical identification (addressing) of specific memory locations. The width of the address bus determines the maximum size of the memory that the microprocessor can use.

In your computer's memory, every storage location must have an address, just as every house on a street must have an address, so that the post office can deliver the mail. Without memory addresses, the microprocessor couldn't figure out where to get program instructions or data, or where to put the results of processing operations.

The address bus is like a freeway, in which the bits of a memory address travel in parallel, one bit in each wire, or "lane." The number of wires determines the maximum width of a memory address, just as the width of a freeway determines the maximum number of cars that can travel side-by-side. Since memory addresses use binary numbers, you can easily calculate a given computer's maximum memory; for example, a 20-bit address bus allows a maximum of 220 memory locations (2 multiplied by itself 20 times, or 1,048,576 bytes)—exactly 1 MB. That's the maximum memory permitted by the **Intel 8088**, the microprocessor used in the first IBM Personal Computer (1981). (The 640KB memory limitation familiar to DOS users stems from a design decision to set aside the remaining memory for video usage and other purposes.)

Advanced Micro Devices (AMD)

The fifth-largest U.S. manufacturer of **integrated circuits**. Focusing on personal and network computers and communication devices, AMD produces **microprocessors** and related devices as well as circuits for telecommuncations and networking applications. With headquarters in Sunnyvale, California, AMD has manufacturing facilities in Austin, Texas; Aizu-Wakamatsu, Japan; Bangkok, Thailand; Penang, Malaysia; and Singapore. The firm has produced more than 70 million microprocessors since 1975.

ALU

See **arithmetic-logic unit (ALU)**

Am386

A **microprocessor** manufactured by **Advanced Micro Devices (AMD)** that is fully compatible with the **Intel 80386.** AMD is the leading 386 supplier in the world and its 386 microprocessors are available in faster clock speeds than competing manufacturers.

Am486

A **microprocessor** manufactured by **Advanced Micro Devices (AMD)** that is fully compatible with the **Intel 486** microprocessor. Like Intel's 486 line, AMD offers a family of microprocessors, including the **clock-doubled Am486DX2** and the **clock-tripled Am486DX4** microprocessors.

Am486DX2

A version of the **Am486,** manufactured by **Advanced Micro Devices (AMD),** that uses **clock doubling** techniques to increase the speed of the **microprocessor,** without requiring the same high speed from the motherboard. Fully compatible with software written for the **Intel 486DX2,** this microprocessor features an on-board **floating point unit (FPU)** for fast numerical calculation, as well as an 8K cache memory. The most recent version of this processor runs at 80 **MHz.**

Am486DX4

A version of the **Am486DX microprocessor,** manufactured by **Advanced Micro Devices (AMD),** that uses **clock-tripling** techniques to achieve a **clock speed** of 75 **MHz** or 100 MHz (the chip runs at these high speeds internally but use a 25 MHz or 33 MHz motherboard). Fully compatible with software written for the **Intel 486DX4,** the Am486DX4 offers an 8K cache memory, smaller than the 16K cache used in the **Intel 486DX4.**

AMD K5

A microprocessor, manufactured by **Advanced Micro Devices (AMD)**, that is designed to be **binary compatible** with the **Pentium** microprocessor manufactured by **Intel**. By no means a "clone" of the Pentium, the K5 diverges radically from the **complex instruction set computer (CISC)** design philosophy taken by Intel's designers. In contrast to the Pentium, the K5 is essentially a **reduced instruction set computer (RISC)** that uses special processing circuitry to decode the Pentium instructions. In addition, the K5 is a **quad-issue processor**, which is capable of initiating the processing of four instructions simultaneously, while the Pentium can initiate only two. Also, unlike the Pentium, the AMD K5 uses **register renaming**, a technique used to overcome the x86 architecture's sharp limit of 8 registers (with register renaming, the K5 implements a total of 40 physical registers). The result of all these design improvements, according to AMD, is a microprocessor that can execute Pentium instructions 30% faster than a given Pentium microprocessor with the same clock speed.

AMD plans a progression of increasingly powerful microprocessors culminating in the K8, slated for 2000, which will top today's Pentium by a factor of 10. The K5 includes 4.3 million transistors, and is manufactured using AMD's 0.5-micron, 3.3 volt **CMOS** process. Not available at this writing, the K5 is projected to be available at clock speeds in excess of 100 MHz. *Compare* **Cyrix M1, NexGen Nx585**

AMD

See **Advanced Micro Devices (AMD)**

architecture

As applied to microprocessors, the chip's overall design, as expressed in choices such as **CISC** vs. **RISC**.

arithmetic-logic unit (ALU)

One of the three major components of a **central processing unit (CPU)**, this is the part that carries out the **control unit's** instructions and processes the data. As the name of this component implies, some of its circuits can perform simple arithmetic operations, such as adding and subtracting, performing logical operations on data, such as comparing two values to see which is the larger. For this reason, the ALU contains **logic gates** as well as circuits designed to perform calculations at high speed. *Compare* **floating-point unit (FPU)**.

benchmark

A standard program, or a set of programs, that can be run on a variety of computer systems to measure overall system **throughput** and provide a frame of reference for meaningful comparisons. Some benchmarks rate the processor's speed at performing integer calculations, while others stress floating-point operations, and still others test the system by running a suite of typical user applications. *Compare* **MIPS, SPEC, Winstone**.

Be aware that manufacturers are naturally prone to select the benchmark that puts their system in the best possible light. For this reason, proprietary benchmarks—benchmarks created by one company for the evaluation of its products alone—should be viewed skeptically. Check out independent benchmarks such as SPEC and Winstone. Remember, too, that overall system performance can be dramatically affected by the type of cache memory used, the choice of the drive controller, the brand and model of video accelerator, and other factors. By themselves processor benchmarks are poor indicators of overall system performance.

binary compatible

 Able to run programs designed to execute on another brand's **microprocessor**. For example the **NexGen Nx585** is claimed to be binary compatible with all the software that will run on Intel's **Pentium** microprocessor. When this term is used with reference to software, it means that a given program will run on a specific brand and model of microprocessor.

brain-dead design

An uncomplimentary slang term used by programmers and system designers to refer to **microprocessors** that incorporate a crippling or frustrating feature that discourages the full realization of the chip's potential. An oft-cited example is the protected mode of the **Intel 80286** microprocessor, which does not allow the operating system to switch from one mode to another without restarting the computer.

branch prediction

A method of predicting the outcome of conditional (branch) instructions in **microprocessors** that employ **superscalar architecture**. In a conditional instruction, one set of instructions is followed if the condition turns out to be true, while another set is followed if the condition turns out to be false. Without prediction, conditional instructions tie up the processor's **pipelines** until the true-false test is completed, and since conditional instructions constitute as many as one fifth of the instructions in a typical program, that adds up to a heavy performance penalty. With branch prediction, the microprocessor can predict the outcome of the test and line up the correct set of instructions so that they're ready to go. Intel's **Pentium** microprocessor incorporates a branch prediction unit that guesses correctly 90 percent of the time.

central processing unit (CPU)

The three core components of a computer: the **control unit,** the **arithmetic-logic unit (ALU),** and the **system clock.** The CPU, **random-access memory (RAM),** and input/output interfaces are connected by a **data bus** and control circuits. Together, these components define a computer's architecture. In personal computers, the CPU is provided by a **microprocessor.**

chip

An **integrated circuit,** such as a **microprocessor** or a **dynamic random-access memory (DRAM)** circuit. The term "chip" is a result of the manufacturing process used to create integrated circuits, which are fabricated on a wafer of silicon.

CISC

See **Complex Instruction Set Computer (CISC).**

clock cycle

The time that lies between two beats of the computer's **system clock,** measured in millionths or billionths of a second.

clock doubled

Designed to operate at twice the speed of the **system clock.** Clock-doubled **microprocessors** include the **Intel DX-2,** which operates at 50 MHz (twice the speed of a 25 MHz motherboard) or 66 MHz (twice the speed of a 33 MHz motherboard).

Don't buy a clock-doubled PC without checking out the reviews in reputable computer magazines such as *PC Magazine*. There is considerable variation in overall system performance. Far more than ordinary 486DX computers: For example, the slowest DX4-based computers, supposedly operating at 100 MHz, were outpaced by the fastest DX2s operating at 66 MHz. These differences are attributable to differences in cache memory (see Chapter 3), video accelerators, and disk drive interfaces, which can markedly affect total system **throughput**.

---

clock tripled

Designed to operate at three times the speed of the **system clock**. Clock-tripled microprocessors include the **Intel DX-4**, which operates at 100 **MHz** (three times the speed of a 33 MHz motherboard).

---

clock speed

The rate at which the computer's **system clock** produces timing signals, typically expressed in millions of cycles per second (MHz).

A given computer's clock speed is one way to determine its processing capabilities, but not the only one. A more advanced microprocessor is faster than its predecessors because it processes information more efficiently (*see* **pipelining, superscalar architecture**). For example, a computer that uses an **Intel 80486DX** microprocessor running at 33MHz is roughly twice as fast as a computer running an **Intel 80386DX** microprocessor at the same speed. An **Intel 80486DX4** running at 100MHz is comparable to a **Pentium** running at 60 MHz.

| CMOS |

See **complimentary metal-oxide semiconductor (CMOS)**

Complex Instruction Set Computer (CISC)

A microprocessor designed with the philosophy that provides special-purpose circuits is justified even if these circuits are infrequently used. *Compare* **Reduced Instruction Set Computer (RISC)**.

No microprocessor manufacturer would willingly claim that its CPUs are CISC—"CISC" is just an uncomplimentary epithet created by the proponents of RISC technology. Moreover, there's no hard-and-fast rule that differentiates CISC from RISC chips; for example, a popular "CISC" microprocessor (the **Intel 486**) recognizes about 150 instructions, while the **PowerPC 601**—a "RISC" chip—recognizes about 220. What differentiates RISC processors from their CISC counterparts is their insistence on simplicity. For example, RISC processors avoid **microcode** and provide plenty of **registers** so that the processor doesn't have to fetch data from memory so often.

> From the user's perspective, what matters most is compatibility with the software that's proven crucial to your business or professional success. And that's the reason people keep buying CISC-based systems, despite the evidence that RISC processors are technically superior. Having a technically superior microprocessor won't matter much if there's not much software for you to run.

complimentary metal-oxide semiconductor (CMOS)

A **semiconductor** manufacturing technique that allows designers to fabricate the two chief types of transistors on the same silicon chip. The result is an **integrated circuit** that func-

complimentary metal-oxide... CPU

tions at significantly higher speeds than the alternative **metal-oxide semiconductor (MOS)** process, while consuming less power and running cooler. Rapid advances in CMOS technology have led to the reduction in the size of chip components to as little as 4 **microns** (4 one-thousandths of a millimeter).

Because today's microprocessors are fabulously complex (Intel's **P6** processor features 5.5 million transistors), the use of CMOS technology has become an indispensable part of microprocessor manufacturing. CMOS chips occupy less space, run cooler, and consume less power than their MOS equivalents.

control unit

One of the three main components of a **central processing unit (CPU)**, the control unit interprets a program's instructions and controls the processing operation. Guided by the precisely-timed pulses of the **system clock**, the control unit fetches program instructions and data from the computer's memory, stores initial and intermediate values in **registers**, and orders the **arithmetic-logic unit (ALU)** to process the data.

core-logic chip set

A set of **integrated circuits** that are designed to integrate a given **microprocessor** with cache memory (see Chapter 3), **random access memory (RAM)** (see Chapter 5), and an **expansion bus** (see Chapter 6).

CPU

See **central processing unit (CPU)**

Cyrix

A small, **fabless** manufacturer of **microprocessors** based in Richardson, Texas, with sales of $294 million in 1994. Dismissed as a minor player as late as 1993, the company fielded an impressive line of 486DX-2-compatible microprocessors. With the **Cyrix M1** processor the company made headlines with its plans to go head-to-head with Intel in the Pentium market. Cyrix subcontracts the manufacturing of its chips to IBM and SGS Thomson.

Cyrix 486DLC

A microprocessor, created by **Cyrix**, that is designed to be **binary compatible** with software written for the Intel 486 series processors. The chip's external connections are exactly compatible with the **Intel 386DX** processor, making the chip ideal for upgrading a 386DX-based machine to the 486 level. However, the 486DLC lacks a **math coprocessor**, so a full 486DX upgrade would require the installation of a Cyrix 83D87 math coprocessor. Designed to emulate the **clock speeds** of the 386DX chips it replaces, the 486DLC is available at speeds of 16 to 33 MHz. A **clock-doubled** version, the Cyrix CX486DRu2, runs at speeds of up to 66 MHz. Reports on the Internet indicate that the Cyrix 486DLC is not compatible with the NeXTStep operating system.

Cyrix 486SLC

A **microprocessor**, created by **Cyrix,** that is designed to be **binary compatible** with software written for the Intel 486 series processors. The chip's external connections are exactly compatible with the **Intel 386SX** processor, making the chip ideal for upgrading a 386SX system to the 486SX level. Designed to emulate the **clock speeds** of the 386SX chips it replaces, the 486SLC is available at speeds of 16 to 25 **MHz**.

Cyrix 486 SLC	Cyrix M1

A **clock-doubled** version, the Cyrix CX486SRu2, runs at speeds of up to 66 MHz. Reports on the Internet indicate that the Cyrix 486SLC is not compatible with the NeXTStep operating system. A **low-power** version is the Cyrix 486SLC/e-V.

Cyrix 486DX2

A **microprocessor**, created by **Cyrix,** that is designed to be **binary compatible** with software written for the Intel 486 series processors. The chip's pin-out design is exactly compatible with the **Intel 486DX2** processor, enabling system designers to employ the less expensive Cyrix chip instead of the Intel part. A **clock-doubled** processor, the Cyrix 486DX2 runs at speeds up to 80MHz. In contrast to the Intel 486DX2 design, which uses a 16KB internal cache, the Cyrix chip offers only 8KB of internal cache memory (see Chapter 3).

Cyrix M1

A **microprocessor**, created by **Cyrix**, that is designed to be **binary compatible** with the **Pentium** microprocessor manufactured by **Intel;** not available at this writing, the chip is expected to cost less than current Pentium models while exceeding the Pentium's performance.

Like the Pentium, the M1 is a **superscalar** processor that can initiate the processing of two instructions simultaneously (under ideal conditions). By using **superpipelining**, in which the normal five stages of **pipeline** execution is expanded to seven, the M1 is claimed to have greater processing efficiency than the Pentium design. Like the Pentium, the M1 is a **dual-issue processor** that can initiate two instructions simultaneously. But unlike the Pentium, which is limited by severe **issue restrictions,** the M1 places fewer restrictions on the types of instructions that can be processed simultaneously.

Additional design innovations reduce the number of **pipeline stalls**. The M1 uses **register renaming** to overcome the x86 architecture's limit of eight **registers**.

Not yet available at this writing, the M1 is projected to be available at clock speeds in excess of 100 MHz. Cyrix claims that the chip will run 30 to 50% faster than existing Pentium processors. The M1 is **pin-compatible** with Pentium designs, allowing a vendor to create a motherboard that can support the M1 as well as the Pentium.

Cyrix ran into extraordinary difficulties in designing the M1 chip, which is physically very large in comparison to its competition. This large size means higher manufacturing expenses and lower yields. As this book went to press, Cyrix announced a scaled-back version of the M1 that would compete directly with existing Pentium designs.

---

data bus

An electronic channel composed of 16 to 64 parallel wires, which connect the microprocessor to the **random access memory (RAM)** and to the computer's **peripherals**. Just as a freeway with more lanes can carry more traffic, the width of the computer's data bus is one of the primary determinants of overall system **throughput**. A computer with a data bus width of 32 wires (32 bits) can process 4 bytes (32 bits) of data at a time, while a computer with a data bus width of 16 wires (16 bits) can process only 2 bytes (16 bits) of data at a time. With some microprocessors, the width of the processor's **internal data bus** (the data bus contained within the physical confines of the processor chip) is greater than the width of the **external data bus** (the data bus that links the processor to the rest of the computer). This is a compromise design that allows the designer to use widely available, inexpensive peripherals designed for the narrower external bus.

data dependency

In a **superscalar architecture**, in which multiple **pipelines** allow the processor to execute two or more instructions simultaneously, a data dependency is a processing operation that requires one step to be completed before the other. For example, suppose you want to obtain the average of the numbers 2, 7, 9, 14, and 28. These numbers must be added, and the number of data items must be counted, before the average can be obtained by dividing the sum by the count. It is not possible to initiate the adding and average operations simultaneously. Data dependencies sharply limit the **throughput** advantages of superscalar designs. *Compare* **false dependency.**

DIP

See **dual in-line package (DIP)**

dual in-line package (DIP)

A standard method used for packaging **integrated circuits**. The circuit is enclosed in a hard plastic package, with pins sticking down in two parallel rows. which are designed to fit into receptacles on the circuit board. Users find it difficult to press DIP packages into their receptacles; for this reason, **zero-insertion force (ZIF)** packages have been developed for user-replaceable circuits.

Figure 4.1 A standard DIP

dual-issue processor

In a **superscalar architecture** that uses more than one **pipeline**, a two-pipeline design that allows the processor to initiate the simultaneous processing of two instructions. Examples of dual-issue processors are Intel's **Pentium** and Cyrix's **M1**. *Compare* **quad-issue processor.**

emulation

The use of a given type of hardware device to mimic the hardware and operating characteristics of another type of device. For example, an Apple Power Macintosh using emulation software can act exactly like an Intel 486-based computer. However, note that emulation comes with a performance penalty of up to 50%.

Emulation is rarely an adequate solution to the problem of running software intended for another computer. SoftPC, a popular emulation package for the Power Macintosh can run Microsoft Windows software—but only in Windows' Standard mode, in which many of Windows' advanced features are not available.

external data bus

A **data bus** that is designed to handle communication between the **microprocessor** and other components of the computer, including the **random-access memory (RAM)** (see Chapter 5). *Compare* **internal data bus.**

fabless

Lacking manufacturing capability. A fabless microprocessor manufacturer must subcontract the chip fabrication to other firms. **Intel**'s leading competitors, **Cyrix** and **Advanced Micro Devices (AMD)**, are both fabless.

false dependency

In a **superscalar architecture**, in which multiple **pipelines** allow the processor to simultaneously execute two or more instructions, a processing operation that requires the result of instructions would have caused problems with the temporary storage of results in **registers** if they had been processed simultaneously. An example of a false dependency is output dependency, in which two instructions cannot be executed simultaneously because they write their results to the same register. The term "false" is meant to contrast with "true" **data dependencies**, in which the result of one operation is needed before another can commence.

A major source of false dependencies in **x86** designs is the built-in limitation to a maximum of eight registers. Studies of processor architectures show that the optimum number is much closer to 32. In an **x86** design such as Intel's **Pentium**, instructions must compete for the limited register space, causing numerous false dependencies and slowing the processor's **throughput**. *Compare* **register renaming.**

floating-point unit (FPU)

 A section of a **microprocessor** that is devoted to handling floating-point mathematical calculations. In a floating-point calculation, the location of the decimal point is not fixed. Instead, it "floats" or moves left or right as needed to ensure precision. In computers, floating-point calculations are needed because all numbers must be stored in a memory location of fixed length; without the ability to "float" or adjust the decimal point's location, the computer might make serious rounding errors when dealing with very small or very large numbers. The inclusion of an FPU substantially speeds the processing of math-intensive operations, and provides greater precision.

FPU

See **floating-point unit (FPU)**

hard-wired

Physically expressed in an unchangable circuit design, rather than implemented in software.

heat sink

A metal plate, usually constructed with fins, that passively dissipates the heat produced by an electronic device such as a **microprocessor**. Heat sinks and fans are required to keep a microprocessor from overheating and destroying itself.

Today's advanced microprocessors run hot—a **Pentium** can heat up to as much as 160 degrees Fahrenheit, 50 degrees more than its predecessor, the **486**. To deal with the heat, designers of Pentium systems have incorporated massive heat sinks and two or more cooling fans.

IBM 486SLC2

A **low-power microprocessor**, made by IBM, that is **pin-compatible** with the rest of Intel's line of 486 microprocessors and offers performance that is comparable to the **Intel 486SX**.

IBM Blue Lightning

A **low-power microprocessor**, made by IBM, that is **pin-compatible** with the **Intel 486DX** microprocessors, and offers performance that is comparable to them. The IBM 486BLX runs at speeds up to 33 MHz; a **clock-doubled** version, the IBM 486BLX2, runs at 66 MHz; and a **clock-tripled** version, the IBM 486BLX3, runs at 100 MHz.

instruction set

 The collection of commands that a specific brand and model of **microprocessor** can recognize and carry out (**Intel's 486** microprocessor recognizes approximately 150 instructions). Programs use these instructions to tell the microprocessor what to do. Each instruction corresponds to a simple operation, such as comparing two values to see which is the larger, adding two numbers together, or simply waiting until the next instruction arrives. Each brand and model of microprocessor has its own, unique instruction set. This is the main reason that a program written for a certain microprocessor will not run on a machine that uses a different microprocessor (*but see* **emulation**). *See also* **complex instruction set computer (CISC), reduced instruction set computer (RISC)**.

integrated circuit

 An electronic circuit that is fabricated by selectively introducing chemical impurities on a wafer (or chip) of silicon or germanium, which enhance or retard the material's ability to conduct electricity. Because these impurities can be produced on a microscopic scale, it is possible to produce tiny electronic devices of amazing complexity. Today's **Pentium microprocessor**, for example, incorporates the equivalent of 3.1 million electronic switches called transistors.

Intel

The leading manufacturer of **microprocessors**, semiconductors, and networking devices; roughly 75 percent of the world's desktop computers employ Intel CPUs. Based in Santa Clara, California, Intel reported first-quarter revenues in 1995 of $3.56 billion.

Intel 386DX

See **Intel 80386**

Intel 386SL

A **low-power** version of the **Intel 386SX microprocessor** designed for use in notebook computers. The chip incorporates **power management** features, including a **sleep mode** in which the chip consumes only a tiny trickle of current to maintain the state in which it was shut down.

Intel 386SX

A "crippled" version of the **Intel 80386**, introduced in June, 1988, that uses a 16-bit **external data bus** instead of the 32-bit data bus of the original 80386 (which was renamed 386DX when the 386SX was released). Unlike the 386DX, which can use up to 4GB of memory, the 386SX can use only 20 MB. Significantly slower than the 386DX, which can manage 6 **million instructions per second (MIPS)**, the 386SX plods along at 2.5 MIPS. The 386SX achieves a **SPEC** rating of 6.2 for integer calculations, and 3.3 for floating-point calculations.

Intel 4004

The world's first **microprocessor**, introduced in 1971. A four-bit microprocessor designed for use in programmable calculators, the 4004 operated at a **clock speed** of 108 KHz (roughly .1 MHz). The chip's four-bit architecture permitted it to work with a maximum of 16 characters—enough for the numbers 0 through 9 and the symbols for the basic arithmetical operations (addition, subtraction, multiplication, and division).

Intel 4004	Intel 486DX

The 4004 stemmed from a request by a Japanese calculator maker for a special-purpose chip, but engineer Ted Hoff had a grander vision—why not create a general-purpose computer on a chip that could be programmed to do different things? In the end, this would lower development costs because new models of the firm's calculators wouldn't require the expensive design and fabrication of new, special-purpose chips. Hoff got the green light, and the microprocessor was born.

Intel 486DX

A **32-bit microprocessor**, introduced in April, 1989. The 486DX has the equivalent of 1.2 million transistors, operates in its original version at a **clock speed** of 25 **MHz**, and can process about 20 **million instructions per second**. Subsequent versions of the 486DX operate at **clock speeds** up to 33 MHz (the **clock-doubled Intel 486DX2** and **clock-tripled Intel 486DX4** operate at speeds of 66 MHz and 100 MHz, respectively). With a 32-bit **address bus**, the 486DX can use 4GB of memory. In addition, the chip can use up to 64 TB of **virtual memory**. The 486DX achieves a **SPEC** rating of 27.9 for integer calculations, and 13.1 for floating-point operations.

The 486 does not represent a revolutionary technical advance over its immediate predecessor, the 80386, in the same way that the 386 did. The improvements are subtler from a technical standpoint, but they're very noticeable to users— the 486DX is significantly faster than its predecessor. The speed improvement is attributable to several improvements, especially the use of **pipelining**, which allows the 486DX to process most instructions within just one clock cycle which is why a 486DX-33 is nearly twice as fast as a 386DX-33, even though the two operate at the same clock speed.) In addition, the 486DX incorporates a **numeric coprocessor** within the silicon confines of the chip itself. For this reason, 486DX is faster than a 386 equipped with a coprocessor located elsewhere on the motherboard; the signals don't have so far to

Intel 486DX	Intel 486DX2

travel, and that counts when you're talking about clock speeds of 66MHz or more. Like the 386DX, the 486DX comes with an **internal cache**—but it's much bigger (8K).

Figure 4.2 Intel 486DX microprocessor

Intel 486DX2

A version of the **Intel 486DX**, introduced in March, 1992, that uses **clock-doubling** techniques to increase the speed of the **microprocessor** (without requiring the same high speed from the motherboard.) The DX2 processor operates internally at twice the speed of the motherboard. (50 **MHz** DX2 works with a 25MHz motherboard; a 66 MHz DX2 works with a 33 MHz motherboard.) The 486DX2 achieves a **SPEC** rating of 32.2 for integer calculations, and 16.0 for floating-point operations.

The faster the microprocessor, the faster the motherboard's support chips must be to keep up with processing operations, which means increased expense. Both DX2 chips offer system designers the appealing prospect of performing simple modifications on existing 25MHz and 33MHz motherboards, yet offering processing speeds of 50 MHz and 66 MHz (respectively).

The performance penalty in this scheme is that a microprocessor that processes data twice as fast as the motherboard will have to wait around for the motherboard to catch up. Designers can offset this problem by using an external cache (see Chapter 3) that's large enough to store the data and instructions for which the microprocessor would otherwise have to wait. With a properly-designed cache, a clock-doubled microprocessor can offer up to 80% of the performance of a system whose motherboard matches the processor's speed.

Intel 486DX4

A version of the **Intel 486DX microprocessor** that uses **clock tripling** techniques to achieve a **clock speed** of 75 **MHz** or 100 MHz (the chip runs at these high speeds internally but use a 25 MHz or 33 MHz motherboard). With a 16K **internal cache**, the DX4 offers twice the internal caching of its predecessors. The 486 DX4 incorporates an important innovation—unlike the other 486DX processors, it operates at 3.3 volts, providing lower power consumption and cooler operation. The 486DX4 achieves a **SPEC** rating of 51 for integer calculations, and 27 for floating-point operations.

Don't buy a 60 MHz or 66 MHz **Pentium** system, unless the price is extremely low indeed—you'll be getting a hot-running 5 volt microprocessor that's technically inferior to the newer 90 MHz and 100 MHz Pentiums. You should be able to find a 100 MHz DX4 system that comes very close to the performance of the lower-end Pentiums, but for significantly less money.

Intel 486SL

A **low-power** version of the **Intel 486DX microprocessor**, designed for notebook computers. The chip incorporates advanced **power management** capabilities, including a **sleep mode** that preserves the exact state the processor was in when you engaged this mode. Compared to its predecessor, the **Intel 386SL**, the 486SL offers roughly twice the processing power at half the power consumption.

Intel 486SX

A "crippled" version of the **Intel 486DX microprocessor**—but not so crippled as the **Intel 386SX**, which compromised the chip's 32-bit architecture by pairing it with a 16-bit **data bus**. The 486SX, introduced in April, 1991, retains a full 32-bit architecture, but omits the **numeric coprocessor**, and can manage 16.5 **million instructions per second** (compared to the 486DX's 20 MIPS). The first version of the chip ran at a **clock speed** of 20 **MHz**; a subsequent version runs at 25 MHz.

Intel 80286

A **16-bit microprocessor**, introduced in February, 1982. The 80286 has the equivalent of 139,000 transistors, operates at a **clock speed** of 8 **MHz**, and can process about 1.2 **million instructions per second**. Subsequent versions of the 80286 operate at clock speeds up to 20 MHz. With a 24-bit **address bus**, the 80286 can use 16 MB of memory. In addition, the chip can use up to 1 GB of **virtual memory**. The 80286 powered IBM's PC AT (short for "Advanced Technology"), which was introduced in 1984.

The key technical innovation of the 80286 microprocessor was its ability to run in more than one mode. The first mode, called the **real mode**, enabled the chip to retain compatibility with operating systems and software designed for the **Intel 8086** and **Intel 8088** microprocessors. In this mode, the 80286 could use only 1 MB of memory, just like its predecessors. In the second mode, called the **protected mode**, the microprocessor could access up to 16 MB of memory.

Another innovation of the 80286 was its ability to use virtual memory, an extension of memory that involves the use of the computer's hard disk as a temporary storage space. With virtual memory, a computer can seem as if it has much more main memory than it really does.

| Intel 80286 | Intel 80386 |

Initially, programmers and system designers simply ignored the 80286's innovative features., as they weren't compatible with existing DOS programs. What's more, the memory above 1MB wasn't an undifferentiated space that programmers can use as they please; was segmented into 64K blocks. Perhaps worst of all, the chip couldn't switch between the protected mode and the real mode; if you wanted to leave protected mode and start a DOS program, you had to reboot the computer. These deficiencies soon led system designers to regard the 80286 as a **brain-dead design**.

Don't buy a used 80286 computer. Although these systems are OK for running older DOS programs that don't require high-speed processors, 80286-based systems cannot take full advantage of the Microsoft Windows operating system or Windows applications.

Intel 80386

A **32-bit microprocessor**, introduced in October, 1985. The 80386 has the equivalent of 275,000 transistors, operates at a **clock speed** of 16 **MHz**, and can process about 6 **million instructions per second**. Subsequent versions of the 80286 operate at clock speeds up to 20 MHz. With a 32-bit **address bus**, the 80386 can use 4GB of memory. In addition, the chip can use up to 64 TB of **virtual memory.** When the **386SX** was introduced, the 80386 chip was renamed **386DX** and was subsequently released in 20 MHz, 25 MHz, and 33 MHz versions. Compaq was the first computer manufacturer to release a 386-based personal computer.

The 386, as it came to be known, directly addressed the deficiencies of the **Intel 80286:** It would switch on-the-fly between the **real mode** and the **protected mode**, and it can work with up to 4 GB of **random-access memory (RAM)**. The 386 also introduced a small (16 byte) **internal cache** (see Chapter 3), a temporary storage place where the next instruction can be kept until it is used. The use of an internal cache helps the microprocessor access memory faster.

An innovative feature of the 386 was its ability to run DOS programs in an **8086** virtual mode, in which the processor simulates one or more 8086 processors. This allows DOS users to run more than one DOS program at a time, so long as they are using an operating system that supports this.

The 386 made Microsoft Windows possible, and in many ways, Windows 3.1 is a full realization of the 386's technical innovations: You start the program with DOS (in the 386's real mode), and switch to the protected mode, which makes all the memory you've installed in your computer available. In this mode, Windows can set up as many "windows" (actually, virtual 8086 processors) for DOS programs as you wish. Or, if you prefer, you can run nothing but Windows applications, which require the protected mode (and lots of memory).

> **Don't** buy a used 80386-16 (or 386DX-16) if the system was constructed before April, 1987—it may have a defective 80386 chip. Early 386-16s came with a bug that wasn't discovered for two years, in which time many systems were built that had the flawed processors. (The flaw doesn't show up if you're using early versions of DOS.) How can you tell if a given 386 chip is flawed? All the 386 chips made after the flaw's correction have a double sigma symbol on the chip's case.

| Intel 8080 |

An early **8-bit microprocessor**, introduced in April, 1974. The 8080 has the equivalent of 8,000 transistors, operates at a **clock speed** of 2 MHz, and can process about one-half **million instructions per second**. With a 16-bit **address bus**, the 8080 can use 64K of memory. The 8080 powered the world's first microcomputer, the Altair.

Intel 8086

The first **16-bit microprocessor**, introduced in June, 1978. The 8086 has the equivalent of 29,000 transistors, operates at a **clock speed** of 4.77 MHz, and can process about one-third **million instructions per second**. With a 20-bit **address bus**, the chip can use 1 MB of memory.

Many microprocessor design experts believe that the 8086's design was fundamentally flawed. Instead of dealing with memory as a single, undifferentiated space, the 8086 divides it into 64K segments. A programmer who wanted to map out a memory segment larger than 64K faced formidable obstacles—not the least of which is that the 8086's segmentation scheme produced some potential addressing overlaps, in which the same memory address could sometimes point to two different physical memory locations.

Despite the 8086's design flaws, its architecture and **instruction set** provided the foundation for approximately 90 percent of the personal computers now in use worldwide, thanks to IBM's decision to employ the **x86** architecture in its first PCs, introduced in 1981. IBM engineers reportedly preferred the **Motorola 68000**, a **32-bit microprocessor** that offered a much better memory access design, but IBM had obtained the right from Intel to manufacture 8086 microprocessors (and their descendants). *See* **Intel 8088.**

Intel 8088

A **16-bit microprocessor**, introduced in June, 1979, with a "crippled" design using an 8-bit **data bus**. The 8088 has the equivalent of 29,000 transistors, operates at a **clock speed** of 4.77 **MHz**, and can process about one-third of a **million instructions per second**. With a 20-bit **address bus**, the 8088 can use 1 MB of memory. The 8088 powered IBM's first personal computer, the IBM PC, introduced in 1981.

The 8088 is essentially an **Intel 8086**, but with one big difference—its 8-bit data bus. This compromise allowed computer system designers to use inexpensive 8-bit **peripherals**, such as disk drives, which were widely available in the early 1980s thanks to the success of 8-bit computers such as the Kaypro and Osborne.

Intel P6

The successor to Intel's **Pentium** processor, not yet available at this writing. Slated to become available in small quantities in mid-1995, the P6 has won early acclaim for its innovative design and fast processing, all achieved without sacrificing downward compatibility with **x86** software.

The P6 is a **superscalar, superpipelined** processor that will be able to initiate the simultaneous processing of three instructions (compared with two for the Pentium and four for the **AMD K5**). Unlike the Pentium, which is a **CISC (Complex Instruction Set Computer)** design, the P6 employs the **RISC (Reduced Instruction Set Computer)** design philosophy. Like the **AMD K5,** the P6 employs on-board hardware translation to convert x486 instructions into RISC instructions.

Early design prototypes used **speculative execution** to optimize processing; Intel claims that analysis of the Pentium's performance revealed that the path to faster processing lies not so much in improving the performance and number of **pipelines** as in doing a better job of predicting how a given instruction should optimally flow through the processsor (*see* **branch prediction**).

The chip contains several other advanced features, including **register renaming** to overcome the x86 architecture's built-in limitation of eight **registers. Out-of-order execution** capabilities ensure that the P6 will not be plagued by the Pentium's frequent **pipeline stalls**. Using a direct, high-speed interface to a secondary cache (see Chapter 3), the P6 will not depend on the slower **throughput** of the **data bus** to access cache memory (see Chapter 3).

Because it's tightly coupled to its secondary cache chip, the P6 is really two chips linked by a high-speed data bus. A full **64-bit microprocessor,** the P6 employs a 64-bit **external data bus** as well as a 64-bit **internal data bus.** Reportedly, the P6 will feature 5.5 million transistors, and will be offered initially at a 133 MHz clock speed. In terms of **SPEC** benchmarks, performance is estimated to be roughly 200 (twice that of the Pentium) in integer calculations.

internal cache

A cache memory (see Chapter 3) that is physically implemented within the **microprocessor** itself. Because the cache is directly connected to the processing circuitry, program instructions and data stored within the internal cache can be accessed at very high speeds. Intel's **Pentium** microprocessor offers a primary cache of 16KB, while the **NexGen Nx586** offers 32KB. *Compare* secondary cache (see Chapter 3).

internal data bus

A **data bus** that is constructed within the confines of a **microprocessor**, and is designed to handle the internal communication among the various components of the microprocessor itself (*compare* **external data bus**). In general, the wider the internal bus, the faster its operation, just as more lanes permit more cars to travel down a freeway. In many microprocessor designs, the internal data bus is wider than the external data bus; this is a compromise design that permits the microprocessor to perform internal processing operations at higher speeds than those at which communications are handled with the rest of the computer. At the same time, the microprocessor can use peripherals designed for narrower external data busses. For example, the Pentium microprocessor employs a

64-bit internal data bus, but is designed to work with a 32-bit external data bus and widely-available 32-bit peripherals.

issue restrictions

In a **superscalar architecture**, in which more than one **pipeline** is available to process information, the set of rules that determine whether a given pair of instructions can be processed simultaneously. Intel's **Pentium microprocessor** can issue instructions simultaneously only under limited circumstances; the Intel **P6,** as well as the various Pentium "clones" now under develoment (such as the **AMD K5**), will offer fewer issue restrictions and should produce significantly better performance.

logic gate

The basic electronic building block of a **microprocessor's** design, a logic gate is an electronic circuit that selectively performs an operation on the data that is fed into it in the form of two input signals. The term "gate" stems from the device's ability to allow current to flow through the gate—or to shut the current off. For this reason, logic gates can only make simple decisions. For example, an AND gate passes on the current only if both of the inputs have current, while an OR gate passes on the current if either of the inputs have current. A microprocessor is a complex array of logic gates that can perform a variety of simple operations, such as adding two values or deciding which of them is the larger (see **instruction set**). Everything that computers do stems from the results of such simple operations carried out at very high speeds. See **arithmetic-logic unit (ALU)**.

low-power microprocessor

A **microprocessor** that is designed to run on 3.3 volts or less. See **0.5-micron technology, complimentary metal-oxide semiconductor (CMOS)**.

math coprocessor

A processor that is optimally designed to carry out mathematical calculations, and to work with a given brand and model of **microprocessor.** For example, the Intel 80387 is the math coprocessor designed to work with **Intel's 80386** processor. Many older PCs were sold without math coprocessors, allowing the user to install the coprocessor, if needed. In more recent microprocessors (Intel's **486DX** and **Pentium**), the math coprocessor circuitry is included on the main processor chip.

Do you need a math coprocessor? If you do a lot of number-crunching with CAD/CAM applications, spreadsheets, and relational databases, a math coprocessor is likely to increase performance, but it won't speed word processing tasks or have much effect on the performance of Microsoft Windows.

megahertz (MHz)

A basic, if somewhat misleading, measurement of a **microprocessor's** speed, one megahertz is one million **clock cycles** per second. A microprocessor with a **clock speed** of 66 MHz cycles 66 million times per second.

The microprocessor's clock speed does not necessarily equal that of the **system clock**, the pulsating crystal that synchronizes all of the computer's components. In a **clock-doubled** system, the microprocessor operates at twice the clock speed of the system clock. (For example, in an **Intel 486DX-2** system, the microprocessor runs at 66 MHz, twice the speed of the 33MHz system clock.) The **Intel DX-4,** which is a **clock-tripled** system, runs the microprocessor at 100 MHz, three times the speed of the system clock.

A 100 MHz processor is not necessarily always faster than a 75 MHz processor. Clock speeds are not comparable when you are comparing different brands or models of microprocessors. For example, Intel's 66 MHz **Pentium**

processor is significantly faster than a 66 MHz 486DX-2, because the Pentium uses more sophisticated processing circuitry. This circuitry allows the newer processor to perform a given operation in fewer steps than a preceding processor, increasing total system **throughput**. A 100 MHz 486 DX-4 runs at approximately the same overall throughput as a Pentium running at 60 MHz.

---

metal-oxide semiconductor (MOS)

A semiconductor device whose electronic characteristics derive from the insulating properties of aluminum oxide, silicon dioxide, or other metal oxides. MOS devices consume little power but they are vulnerable to damage from discharges of static electricity. *See* **Complimentary metal-oxide semiconductor (CMOS)**.

MHz

See **Megahertz**

---

microcode

A method of improving the flexibility of a computer's **central processing unit (CPU)**. Like any other CPU, a CPU equipped with microcode accepts instructions from computer programs, but these instructions do not directly control the hardware inside the CPU. Instead, the instructions activate codes within the **microprocessor**, which in turn, activate the complex physical actions required to carry out the program's instructions.

The use of microcode simplifies programming by allowing programmers to ignore the specifics of how an instruction is actually carried out. However, microcode raises the complexity of a CPU—it takes time to decode the microcoded instructions, and it takes more logic circuitry within the chip to do so. And that means a larger chip, in which internal messages take longer to travel. *Compare* **complex instruction set computer (CISC), reduced instruction set computer (RISC).**

---

micron

A unit of measurement equivalent to one one-millionth of a meter (approximately 0.0000394 inches).

---

microprocessor

 A programmable data processing unit that is crafted on a single **integrated circuit** of fabulous complexity (current technology has pushed the number of transistors on such integrated circuits well into the millions). In personal computers, the microprocessor provides the computer's **central processing unit (CPU)**. More than any one single factor, a given computer's performance depends on the characteristics and brand of its microprocessor.

Factors affecting a given microprocessor's performance are the widths of its **internal data bus** and **external data bus**, the width of its **address bus**, its **clock speed**, and its **architecture** (**CISC** or **RISC**).

A given microprocessor family (such as the Intel **x86** or **Motorola 680x0** microprocessors) is designed to recognize a specific **instruction set**s, programs must intentionally be designed to work with this microprocessor family. Such a program is said to be **binary compatible** with these microprocessors, and cannot run on a microprocessor made by another manufacturer (except through software **emulation**, which exacts a heavy performance penalty).

The dominant force in the microprocessor marketplace is **Intel**, which created the first microprocessor in 1971. Intel supplies the processors for approximately 80% of the IBM PC-compatible computers in use worldwide. However, Intel is facing stiff competition from **Advanced Micro Devices (AMD), Cyrix**, and

NexGen, which are producing microprocessors that are binary compatible with programs written for Intel's **Pentium** processor. Another important player in the microprocessor market is **Motorola,** which makes the 680x0 processors employed in first-generation Apple Macintoshes. Motorola, IBM, and Apple jointly developed the **PowerPC** microprocessor family, a RISC-based design that is not compatible with **x86** software.

millions of instructions per second (MIPS)

A **benchmark** that measures a **microprocessor**'s performance by the number of instructions it can perform within one second. Although a MIPS figure can provide a rough-and-ready index of a computer's processing capabilities, MIPS tests generally involve making the microprocessor perform a simple mathematical operation repeatedly. Most computer experts agree that a given computer system's performance is better indicated by running a variety of typical application programs. By running application programs, you can find out how the whole system performs, not just the microprocessor.

MIPS

See **millions of instructions per second (MIPS)**

Moore's Law

A prediction made by **Intel** co-founder Gordon Moore at the dawn of the semicondutor era that the number of transistors fabricated in **integrated circuits** would double roughly every 18 months. Thus far Moore's prediction has been uncannily accurate.

MOS

See **metal-oxide semiconductor (MOS)**

Motorola

One of the world's leading providers of wireless communications, **semiconductors** and advanced electronic systems and services. Among Motorola's major equipment businesses are cellular telephones, two-way radio, paging and data communications, personal comunications, automotive, defense and space electronics and computers. Motorola semiconductors power millions of communication devices, computers, and consumer products are powered by. With 1993 semiconductor sales of $5.7 billion, Motorola ranks third worldwide in the manufacture of microelectronic components. The company's **68000** series of **microprocessors** power first-generation Apple Macintoshes while the **PowerPC** processors, jointly developed with IBM and Apple, provide the computing horsepower for Apple's **Power Macintosh**.

Motorola 68000

A **32-bit microprocessor**, created by Motorola, that was used in Apple Computer's first Macintosh computer. Using a 32-bit **internal data bus** and a 16-bit **external data bus**, the 68000 offers a compromise design that enabled Apple to use inexpensive 16-bit peripherals at the sacrifice of overall sytem **throughput**. The microprocessor runs at a **clock speed** of 8 **MHz** and can use up to 32 GB of **RAM**.

Motorola 68020

A **32-bit microprocessor**, created by **Motorola**, that was used in Apple Computer's first Macintosh II computers. Unlike the **68000**, the 68020 is a true 32-bit microprocessor—it uses a 32-bit **external data bus** as well as a 32-bit **internal data bus**. The microprocessor runs at a **clock speed** of 16 **MHz**. It is considered inferior to the **68030** and **68040** processors, which incorporate superior memory management features.

Motorola 68030

A **32-bit microprocessor**, created by **Motorola**, that provides the horsepower for Apple's current entry-level Macintosh computers. Comparable to the **Intel 80386DX** in processing capabilities, the 68030 offers improved memory management capabilities and a **clock speed** of up to 50 **MHz**.

Motorola 68040

A **32-bit microprocessor**, created by **Motorola**, that powers many Macintosh computers including most Quadras, and some Centris and Performa models. Analogous to the Intel **486DX**, the 68040 represents an evolutionary advance over the 68030; its chief improvement lies in its inclusion of a **floating-point unit (FPU)** for faster mathematical calculation with math-intensive software. The 68040 achieves a **SPEC** rating of 21 for integer calculations, and 15 for floating-point operations.

nanosecond

One billionth of a second (abbreviated ns).

native application

A program that is **binary compatible** with a given brand and model of **microprocessor**. In almost all cases, a native application runs significantly faster than a non-native application, which can run only through software or hardware **emulation**. For example, most Macintosh programs will run on a Power Macintosh by means of built-in emulation, but only native Power Macintosh applications can take full advantage of the **PowerPC** microprocessor's sophisticated capabilities.

NexGen

A San Mateo, California-based **fabless** manufacturer of **x86** microprocessors. The firm subcontracts with IBM Micro-electronics, Inc., to manufacture its **Nx585** processor, the first microprocessor to offer full **binary compatibility** with Intel's **Pentium** processor. NexGen's fortunes in the Pentium-compatible computer market have been favored by Intel's difficulties with the Pentium's flawed **floating-point unit (FPU)**, as well as by the efforts by major computer manufacturers such as Compaq Computer Corp. to free itself from what these companies see as disadvantageous pricing from **Intel**.

NexGen Nx585

A **microprocessor** created by **NexGen** that is designed to be **binary compatible** with the **Pentium** microprocessor manufactured by **Intel**. The first Pentium-compatible processor to hit the market, the Nx586 boasts Pentium-like **throughput** at reduced expense (some 15% to 27% less than comparable Pentium models, at this writing).

Like the **AMD K5**, another Pentium competitor, the Nx585 is fundamentally unlike the Pentium in its basic design; it is essentially a **RISC (Reduced Instruction Set Computer)** processor that translates x86 instructions so that they can be executed by the Nx585's RISC design. Unlike the Pentium, the nx585 employs **register renaming**, a technique used to overcome the x86 architecture's sharp limit of eight **registers** (with register renaming, the K5 implements a total of 40 physical registers). However, the Nx585 is not significantly faster than Pentium microprocessors, and is not **pin-compatible** with the Pentium, so that designers must create specially-designed **motherboards** for the Nx585 and use NexGen's **core-logic chip set** instead of Intel's. The Nx585 features a total of 3.5 million transistors, and is manufactured by IBM Micro-electronics using a 0-5 **micron**, 4-volt **CMOS** process. The processor is currently available in speeds of 70, 75, 84, and 93 MHz. The company claims that, in terms of overall performance, the 93 MHz chip is fully the equal of the 100 MHz Pentium.

| ns |

See **nanosecond**

| on-board cache |

See **internal cache**

| operating voltage |

The electrical voltage required by a given **microprocessor** to function properly. A microprocessor's operating voltage is of concern to computer designers for two reasons—the higher the voltage, the more power the processor consumes and the more heat it puts out. Typically, microprocessors require 5 volts, but new 3.3-volt designs cut power consumption in half and reduce heat output.

When transistors were first invented, it was arbitrarily decided to run them at 5 volts, which is high enough to deal with the voltage drops introduced by digital circuits but low enough to avoid noise. The rise of portable and notebook computers led designers to come up with low-voltage designs, since every reduction in operating voltage reduces power consumption by the square of the voltage. A 3.3-volt microprocessor, therefore, requires 60 percent less current than a 5-volt chip. With the rise of complex, hot-running chips such as the **Pentium**, which in its 5-volt version reaches operating temperatures as high as 160 degrees Fahrenheit and consumes as much power as a small light bulb, reducing the operating voltage may prove necessary to keep the chips from frying themselves.

optimizing compiler

A program that is designed to translate computer programming **instructions** into code that the computer can carry out in such a way that the program runs as fast as possible on a given brand and model of **microprocessor**. The use of an optimizing compiler is needed to get the maximum performance from any microprocessor designed with a **superscalar architecture**.

OverDrive

A **processor upgrade** designed to upgrade Intel **486SX** and **486DX** systems to the **486DX2** level. OverDrive processors are of two types; the first is designed to fit into an OverDrive receptacle on your computer's motherboard, while the second—for systems lacking such receptacles—is designed to replace your current CPU. Typically, installation is easy, but the performance gains are minimal (overall system performance increases by roughly 20 percent).

OverDrive upgrades are of questionable value; you'd be wiser to save your money for a new **Pentium** system (or better).

part

In the context of computers, an **integrated circuit**, such as a **microprocessor** ("The SupraComp XL uses the **AMD 486DX-2** *part.*") The use of this term in reference to microprocessors has become more common recently, and may reflect the growing prominence of **pin-compatible** microprocessors; one many motherboards, one can use an **AMD, Intel,** or **Cyrix** part interchangeably.

P24T

See **Pentium OverDrive**

P54C

A version of Intel's **Pentium** processor, introduced in late 1994, that features a smaller size and lower **operating voltage** than its predecessors. The P54C, operating a 100 **MHz**, achieves a **SPEC** rating of 100.0 for integer calculations, and 80.6 for floating-point operations.

Pentium

A **64-bit microprocessor**, made by **Intel**, and introduced in May, 1993. The Pentium has the equivalent of 3.1 million transistors, operates in its original version at a **clock speed** of 60 **MHz**, and can process about 112 **million instructions per second**. Subsequent versions operate at 66 MHz, 90MHz, and 100 MHz, with a 150MHz model reportedly in the works. Like the **486DX**, the Pentium uses a 32-bit **address bus**, allowing the microprocessor to use up to 4 GB of memory. Although the Pentium uses a 64-bit data pathway internally, it is designed to work with 32-bit **external data busses**. The initial Pentium offerings, code-named P5, achieved a **SPEC** rating of 67.4 for integer calculations, and 63.6 for floating-point operations. New versions based on 0.4 **micron** technology will be released in mid-to late 1995, with clock speeds of 120 and 155 MHz.

The Pentium incorporates much of the technology that has previously been definitive of super-fast **Reduced Instruction Set Computer (RISC)** microprocessors, which are used for graphics-intensive applications by engineers and illustrators. These features include **pipelining, superscalar architecture**, and **branch prediction**. The Pentium's twin pipelines are designed to process integers, which is an excellent design decision considering the integer-intensive applications that PC users typically run.

As a result of its adoption of RISC design features, the Pentium rivals the performance of RISC chips and, indeed, has so blurred the boundary between **CISC** and **RISC** that many industry experts now believe that the distinction is meaningless.

A Pentium can (under ideal conditions) execute two instructions for every **clock cycle**, turning in a performance that's roughly twice as fast as a comparably-clocked 486DX. Yet the Pentium retains full compatibility with the 386/486 **instruction set**, which means full compatibility with the existing, huge pool of DOS and Microsoft Windows software.

Another important Pentium innovation is a radically redesigned **floating-point unit (FPU)**, which handles number-crunching at up to five times the speed of DX2/66 systems.

The Pentium offers additional innovations which, if less spectacular, nevertheless help account for its stunning performance. In place of the 486DX's undifferentiated 8K **internal cache**, the Pentium offers an 8K cache for instructions and a second 8K cache for data; the two are designed optimally for the job they need to do, speeding the Pentium's performance considerably. The chip's 64-bit data bus permits the processor to gobble up data at unprecedented rates; a burst transfer mode, for example, permits the entire contents of a 528MB hard drive to be transferred in less than one second.

The first Pentium chips, released in March, 1993, attracted a good deal of criticism for their high power consumption and heat output—for example, the 66MHz chip consumed as much power (and puts out as much heat) as a small light bulb. A significant innovation in Pentium technology was the release, one year later, of the 90Mhz Pentium one year later, which is based on an entirely different chip fabrication technology. This processor, code-named **P54C** during its development, has features as small as 0.6 **microns**, which reduce the chip's **operating voltage** to 3.3 volts. This substantially reduces the heat output, as well.

Don't buy a computer based on the 60MHz or 66MHz Pentium, which can run at temperatures as high as 160 degrees Fahrenheit—hot enough to fry themselves in the absence of cooling equipment (such as **heat sinks** and fans). For only $100 or $200 more, you should be able to get a 90MHz or 100 MHz Pentium that uses the 3.3 volt, 0.6-micron technology.

If you're wondering why Pentium and not 586, here's the answer: Intel's many competitors have fought hard in the courts to win the right to manufacture chips called the "386" and "486." The Pentium name, firmly trademarked by Intel, was intended to prevent any further name-cloning—but it's a wicked world out there. In April, 1994, Intel was hit by $11.5 million lawsuit filed by Taiwan's Pan-Technology International Co. Ltd, which claims Intel infringed upon its Chinese-language trademark "Penteng."

The Pentium processor made headlines in late 1994 when a mathematics professor at a small Lynchburg, Virginia college detected a previously-unacknowledged bug in the Pentium's floating-point unit (FPU). A subsequent analysis showed that 1,738 pairs of numbers would, when divided by each other, produce errors. Intel attempted to dismiss the error, saying that the average user would experience such an error only once in 27,000 years, but this position was greeted by intense opposition, particularly among Internet users, who circulated a variety of Pentium jokes (my favorite: Why didn't Intel call the Pentium "586"? Because they added 100 to 486 and came up with 585.9957389). After initially refusing to replace the chip except in cases where users could demonstrate heavy mathematical usage, Intel backed down and offered to replace any flawed Pentium chip with a corrected version.

Figure 4.3 Intel Pentium microprocessor

Pentium OverDrive

An upgrade processor, designed to work with **Intel 486DX2** computers with an **OverDrive** socket, that brings to such systems the performance of Intel's **Pentium microprocessors**.

PGA

See **pin grid array (PGA)**

pin-compatible

Able to fit into the same receptacle as an **integrated circuit** made by another manufacturer. The **Cyrix M1** processor is pin-compatible with the Intel **Pentium**.

pin grid array (PGA)

A semiconductor package, often used for microprocessors, that features multiple rows of pins along the bottom of the package.

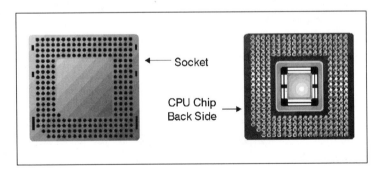

Figure 4.4 Pin grid array

pipeline

Within a **microprocessor**, a pathway through which the processing of a single **instruction** can proceed. In **super-**

scalar architectures, the use of two or more pipelines enables the microprocessor to process two instructions simultaneously.

pipeline stall

In a **superscalar architecture** involving the use of two or more **pipelines**, a pipeline stall is a processing problem that holds up the processing of an instruction. In a in-order execution design, in which all instructions must be executed in a precise sequence, a stall in one pipeline produces a stall in the second pipeline as well, since both instructions must be completed simultaneously. Intel's **Pentium** employs an in-order execution design. In an out-of-order execution design, a stall in one pipeline does not affect the processing of instructions in other pipelines. The **Cyrix M1** claims to offer an out-of-order execution design that dramatically reduces pipeline stalls.

pipelining

A method of improving a **microprocessor**'s performance by pushing more than one instruction through the computer at a time.

Think of a microprocessor's pipeline as if it were an automobile assembly line. At the beginning of the line, the assembly of an automobile starts, and at the end, a new car rolls off the line. Along the way, different workers perform a single, unique task as the automobile passes them. As a result, a new car rolls off the line once every minute, although it takes hours to assemble each individual car.

A pipeline works roughly the same way. On the pipeline, processing tasks are typically divided into five separate jobs— fetching data from memory, decoding program instructions, decoding the data, carrying out the instructions, and writing the results back to the memory. If the processing of each instruction had to be completed before the next instruction could be processed, the computer would need five **clock cycles** to carry out an instruction. With pipelining, a new instruction enters the first stage when the first one moves to the second stage, and so on, so that as many as five instructions are being processed simultaneously. The result is that the computer appears to process one instruction for each tick of its **system clock**.

Pipelining was one of the chief technical innovations of **Reduced Instruction Set Computer (RISC)** microprocessor design, but it has since been shown to be fully compatible with **Complex Instruction Set Computer (CISC)** technology. Intel, the leading manufacturer of CISC microprocessors, uses pipelining in its **Intel 486** and **Pentium** microprocessors.

| plug-compatible |

See **pin-compatible**.

| Power Macintosh |

A line of Apple Macintosh computers that employs one of the **PowerPC** microprocessors, which are based on the **RISC** design philosophy.

| power management |

 A feature built into some **microprocessors** that automatically turns off peripherals, or the entire system, after a period of inactivity. In the resulting **sleep mode**, power consumption can be reduced by as much as 60%, without the loss of data. In the sleep mode, the microprocessor "remembers" the system's exact state, including any messages en route to peripheral devices at the time the system entered the mode. A touch of a key restores the system to full power. Intel microprocessors that offer this feature use the "SL" designation (see, for example, **i486SL**), and other manufacturers mimic it (see **IBM 486SLC**).

Power management is of obvious interest to users of notebook computers; A notebook computer that has an SL- or SL-compatible microprocessor consumes less power, and offers longer battery life, than notebooks that don't have this feature. But it's also of interest to desktop computer users—the U.S. Environmental Protection Agency (EPA) estimates that energy-efficient microprocessors could save 1500 kilowatt-hours of energy per computer system. That adds up to a savings of approximately $160 per year for typical computer users in the U.S.

PowerPC 601

A 32-bit **microprocessor**, jointly developed by Apple Computer, IBM, and Motorola that incorporates many elements of the **RISC** design philosophy. The 601 has the equivalent of 2.8 million transistors, operates at a **clock speed** of 50 MHz. Subsequent versions of the 601 operate at clock speeds up to 100 MHz. A version of the 601 called the 601v employs **0.5 micron** technology to reduce the processor's size and power consumption, and runs at 100 MHz. The 100-MHz 601v turns in a **SPEC** performance (CINT92) of 105.

The PowerPC represents the result of a deliberate and aggressive effort to unseat Intel's dominance of the microprocessor industry. Unlike competing chips from **Advanced Micro Devices (AMD)** and **Cyrix**, the PowerPC chips—led by the 601, the first to appear, seem poised to give Intel a run for its money. With roughly the same processing capabilities as Intel's first **Pentiums**, the 601 costs half as much and consumes less than half as much power (the 601 requires only 3.6 volts). The PowerPC 601 provides the processing horsepower for Apple Computer's initial Power Macintosh offerings.

Not exactly a RISC chip, the PowerPC recognizes a total of 220 instructions, 70 more than an **Intel 486DX,** largely thanks to IBM's insistence that the chip include many of the instructions recognized by IBM mainframes. Motorola countered that programmers should not use the instructions that IBM added and ominously warned that doing so could create processing bottlenecks. In other respects, though the PowerPC embodies the RISC design philosophy. Instructions are **hard-wired** rather than linked to **microcode,** and **pipelining** combined with **superscalar architecture** and **branch prediction** permit the 601 to carry out as many as three instructions for each tick of the **system clock.**

Unlike the **Pentium,** whose superscalar architecture features two pipelines for integer operations, the 601 uses three pipelines—one for integers, another for floating-point (mathematical) operations, and a third for branch operations. For integer-intensive applications, such as most of the applications that PC users typically run, this is far from the best approach. The 601 is less sophisticated than the Pentium in other ways, too—the branch prediction technique isn't as accurate as the Pentium's, and the 601's 32-bit **internal cache** doesn't distinguish between data and instructions (resulting in processing bottlenecks). *Compare* **PowerPC 604.**

There's one point to bear firmly in mind when comparing the PowerPC and the Pentium: The 601's liabilities, such as the use of only one integer pipeline and an undifferentiated internal cache, can be easily corrected, but the Pentium's chief liability—its use of eight data and eight instruction **registers**—cannot. In the Pentium's case, the number of registers is determined by Intel's avowed goal of ensuring downward compatibility with the existing pool of DOS and Microsoft Windows software, which is written with the assumption that the processor will have no more than eight registers. Yet engineering studies have clearly demonstrated that the optimum number of registers is far more than 8; 32 seems to be the optimum number, although some RISC designs employ as many as 64 registers. With additional registers, it's easier to manage pipelining, particularly with the multiple pipelines characteristic of superscalar architectures. Some industry analysts believe that Intel hass bound itself to a fundamentally flawed processor architecture that will eventually prevent the company from competing effectively with the PowerPC.

But the PowerPC doesn't run DOS or Windows programs without **emulation**, which comes with a severe performance penalty. With emulation, a PowerPC can run Windows programs only at **486** speeds. Watch out, though, for hidden perils—for example, existing Windows emulators can't run Windows in the 386 Enhanced Mode, thereby wiping out one of Windows' chief advantages.

Power Macintoshes can't run native Macintosh applications; these are also run through emulation. Unlike the DOS or Windows emulators, however, the Macintosh emulation is excellent—Power Macs run Macintosh programs at the impressive speeds achieved by 68040-based Macs, and hundreds of native Power Macintosh programs are available today. Apple's initial Power Macintoshes look and work just like previous Macintoshes; indeed, they even run a version of the Mac's familiar System 7 operating system. Users of current Macintosh applications can run them with good results on the Power Macintosh, and achieve superior performance using, the Power-PC native versions of these applications..

| PowerPC 602 |

A low-cost **32-bit microprocessor**, jointly developed by Apple Computer, IBM, and Motorola that is based on the **RISC** design philosophy and is designed for consumer and educational applications. The 601 has the equivalent of 2.8 million transistors, and operates at a **clock speed** of **66 MHz.** The PowerPC 602 turns in a **SPEC** rating (CINT92) of 40 (without using a secondary cache).

PowerPC 603

A low-power **32-bit microprocessor**, jointly developed by Apple Computer, IBM, and Motorola, that is based on the **RISC** design philosophy and is designed for notebook computers. The 603 offers much of the **PowerPC 601**'s power at lower cost and with lower power consumption: Requiring only 3.3 volts, the 603 will draw only 2 watts in comparison to the **Pentium's** 17. Advanced **power management** features make the 603 an excellent choice not only for notebook computers, but also for desktop computers that conform to the EPA's Energy Star guidelines. Essentially a simplified version of the 601, the 603 employs a smaller cache (8K each for data and instructions), and employs state-of-the-art 0.5 **micron** technology to produce a fast, compact processor. The 603 has the equivalent of 1.6 million transistors, and operates at a **clock speed** of 66 MHz or 80 MHz. The 80 MHz 603 achieves a **SPEC** rating (CINT92) of 75. A version called the PowerPC 603e offers power-saving modes.

PowerPC 604

A **64-bit microprocessor**, jointly developed by Apple Computer, IBM, and **Motorola**, that is based on the **RISC** design philosophy and is designed to offer high performance for engineering and graphics workstations. The 604 directly addresses many of the design deficiencies of the **PowerPC 601**—for example, it offers superior **branch prediction**. The 604 has the equivalent of 3.6 million transistors, and operates in its original version at a **clock speed** of 100 **MHz**. The 604 achieves a **SPEC** rating (CINT92) of 160.

PowerPC 615

A planned version of the PowerPC **microprocessor**, developed by IBM without the participation of the other two

PowerPC 615   processor upgrade

PowerPC partners (Apple and Motorola), that is rumored to include the circuitry needed to run **x86** software.

PowerPC 620

A **64-bit RISC microprocessor**, jointly developed by Apple Computer, IBM, and **Motorola**, that is designed to offer very high performance for engineering and graphics workstations, local area network servers and **symmetric multiprocessing** systems.(a 133 MHz 620 offers twice the performance of the 100 **MHz PowerPC 604)**. This performance is achieved by using a cache memory that is twice the size of the 604's, a **pre-decode stage** in the **pipeline**, and superior **branch prediction** capabilities. A 3.3-volt design, the PowerPC 620 uses **0.5 micron** technology for reduced size and power consumption. The PowerPC 620 has the equivalent of 7 million transistors and is currently available in a 133 MHz version. The 620 achieves a **SPEC** rating (CINT92) of 225.

---

pre-decode stage

In **superscalar architectures**, a processing stage in which program instructions are categorized in terms of the resources they will require, such as the number of **registers** that will be required to process the operation. Through the use of a pre-decode stage, designers can eliminate an entire stage from the instruction **pipeline**, resulting in faster performance. A **microprocessor** that employs a pre-decode stage is the **PowerPC 620**.

---

processor upgrade

An **integrated circuit** that is designed to fit into existing motherboards and provide enhanced performance. Processor upgrades, such as Intel's **OverDrive** processors, are designed to fit into special receptacles, or to replace the CPU chip itself.

Processor upgrades represent a questionable investment. Upgrading a **386DX**-25 system with 4MB of RAM, for example, would require the installation of additional memory, a new microprocessor, and a faster video accelerator, for a total cost of approximately $700, but overall system performance would still fall far short of a good **486DX2**-66. There are 486DX-2 66 systems on the market for $1100 or less, at current prices.

protected mode

In **Intel 80286** and later **x86** processors, an operating mode in which programs running simultaneously can be assigned to discrete blocks of **extended memory**. Within each block, the program cannot invade any other program's memory space (thus, programs are "protected" from each other). To use the protected mode, your computer must be equipped with memory management software (such as Microsoft's HIMEM.SYS). *Compare* **real mode**.

quad-issue processor

In a **superscalar architecture** that uses more than one **pipeline**, a two-pipeline design that allows the processor to initiate the processing of four instructions simultaneously. The **AMD K5** processor is a quad-issue processor.

random access memory (RAM)

The computer's main internal memory, where program instructions and data are stored temporarily so that they can be speedily accessed by the **microprocessor** (see Chapter 5 for more information).

real mode

In **Intel 80286** and later **x86** processors, an operating mode in which programs directly address the memory. This is the standard memory-management scheme of MS-DOS, and it is unsatisfactory for two reasons. First, in the standard DOS architecture, the computer can use a maximum of 640KB of RAM, which is insufficient for today's applications. Second, programs running in real mode can invade each other's memory space, erasing instructions or data that another program requires in order to complete its processing operations. This is a frequent cause of system crashes under DOS. *See* **protected mode**.

Reduced Instruction Set Computer (RISC)

A design for a computer's **central processing unit (CPU)** that emphasizes simplicity, speed, and efficiency. The design achieves this aim by reducing the number of **instructions** that the **microprocessor** can carry out, as well as by using **pipelining** and **superscalar architecture**. This reduction transfers some of the complexity of information processing to software, but with an impressive net gain in overall system efficiency and speed: RISC designs typically carry out at least one instruction for each tick of the **system clock**. *Compare* **Complex Instruction Set Computer (CISC)**.

Complex CPUs (CISC processors) spend most of their time carrying out a small proportion of the total **instruction set** recognized by the processor. Rather than trying to build circuits to carry out as many as 300 instructions, RISC designers instead concentrate on the instructions that the CPU carries out most frequently. If the circuits that perform these instructions can be made to function at the highest possible speed, the processor will be much faster—even if some complex operations must be carried out by repeating simple ones (for example, multiplication must be performed by repeated addition operations). In general, this theory has proven to be correct, and not just because the chips carry out a few, simple operations at very high speeds. RISC microprocessors tend to be smaller and less complex than their CISC competitors. The more compact the chip, the less distance signals must travel, and the faster the chip is overall.

A reduction in the number of instructions the processor can carry out isn't the only defining characteristic of a RISC microprocessor, and it may not be the most important one. In fact, there is no single, hard-and-fast rule that differentiates CISC from RISC microprocessors. After all, the PowerPC (generally considered to be a RISC chip) recognizes 220 instructions, 70 more than the Intel 486—so which is the "reduced instruction set" processor? Another supposed difference—the ability of RISC chips to process one instruction per clock cycle—has also been equalled, and even surpassed, by the latest CISC technology (*compare* **Pentium**).

In comparison to the most recent high-performance CISC microprocessors, such as Intel's Pentium, what really distinguishes RISC designs are the use of up to 32 **registers** and the avoidance of **microcode**. A register is a temporary storage place, located within the physical confines of the chip, for beginning and intermediate values. To retain compatibility with the existing pool of Intel **x86** software, Intel designers had to limit the **Pentium**—a CISC microprocessor that incorporates certain RISC design elements—to just 8 general-purpose **registers** and 8 floating-point registers which are used for mathematical calculations. In contrast, the **PowerPC 601** employs 32 general-purpose registers and 32 floating-point registers, an optimum number. A design that uses many registers processes data faster because the processor does not have to fetch data from memory, a time-consuming process. In addition, the use of multiple registers enables more efficient **pipelining** by enabling the temporary storage of pipelining data.

Reduced Instruction Set Computer (RISC)

The RISC design's elimination of microcode is another decisive factor in a RISC microprocessor's superior performance. Instead of relaying a code to the microprocessor, which the microprocessor must then decode in order to carry out the requested actions, instructions directly initiate physical actions. This greatly reduces the microprocessor's complexity—and cost. Intel's Pentium microprocessor, a CISC microprocessor with 3.1 million transistors, debuted at a cost of nearly $1,000, while the competing PowerPC 601 (a RISC design) provided equal or better performance at half the cost or less. Another RISC processor, the MIPS R4200, equals the Pentium's performance at one-tenth the cost and one-tenth the power consumption.

RISC microprocessors are all but certain to replace CISC chips eventually for two reasons: First, a massive capital investment will be required to improve the performance of current CISC processors. Second, CISC chips are larger than RISC chips, which means reduced profits for microprocessor manufacturers. According to one report, Intel obtains as many as 187,486 microprocessors from one wafer of silicon, but can obtain fewer than 47 Pentiums from a wafer the same size—and of these 47, as many as 90% may have to be discarded.

In the meantime, Intel keeps pushing the limits of CISC technology. The Pentium microprocessor equals the performance of some of the best RISC processors, and their planned **P6** processor—the Pentium's successor—is designed to hit 250 **MIPS** (millions of instructions per second). Although CISC chips cost more to produce than RISC chips, economies of scale may bring Pentium and P6 prices down to RISC levels and if so, consumers may find little reason to abandon compatibility with the more than 50,000 programs currently available for x86 microprocessors. Rumor has it that the P6's successor will abandon microcode and offer a full RISC architecture.

register

A temporary memory location within the **microprocessor** that is used to hold values (including data and memory locations) while the computer is performing operations on them. Registers get their names from early electromechanical computers that showed numbers in a mechanical display, such as a cash register. A given microprocessor's design specifies the number of registers, and their size, in bits. The larger the register, the more information the computer can process in one operation. *Compare* **8-bit microprocessor, 16-bit microprocessor, 32-bit microprocessor.**

register renaming

In a **superscalar architecture**, in which the use of multiple **pipelines** allows two or more instructions to be processed simultaneously, a means of increasing the number of **registers** (temporary storage places for the results of processing operations) available to **x86**-based software. A major limitation of the x86 architecture is that programs can recognize only eight registers. Studies show that the optimal number is approximately 32 registers. Because programs must compete for limited register space, numerous **false dependencies** occur and **throughput** suffers. In register renaming, a distinction is made between the number of physical registers (the registers that actually exist in the processor's physical architecture), and the number of logical registers (the named registers that are detected by the x86 program). Should an instruction try to use a register that is already in use, the processor can rename a disused physical register and assign it to the instruction that needs it. In this way false dependencies are reduced and overall throughput increases. Intel's **Pentium** processor does not employ register renaming, but its competitors do (*see* **AMD K5, Cyrix M1, NexGen Nx586).**

RISC

See **Reduced Instruction Set Computer (RISC)**

scalar architecture

A **microprocessor** design in which all processing is funneled through a single pathway, called a **pipeline**. A microprocessor that has more than one pipeline is said to have a **superscalar architecture**.

semiconductor

A material whose capacity to conduct electrical current lies between that of an insulator (a material that does not pass current) and a conductor (a material that passes current with little resistance). Two elements—silicon (which is the Earth's second most abundant element, next to oxygen) and germanium—can be made to act as semiconductors. By carefully introducing chemical impurities in various locations on a wafer of a semiconductor material, it is possible to create an electronic circuit. See **integrated circuit**.

sleep mode

In a **low-power microprocessor** designed for power conservation or notebook use, a low-power mode that switches on automatically when the microprocessor detects that the system has not been used for a given period of time. Typically, the system backs up the memory's current contents to the hard disk; when the system is reactivated, the microprocessor reloads this information into the memory, and you can continue working right where you left off.

SPEC

See **Standard Performance Evaluation Corporation (SPEC)**

speculative execution

In **superscalar** processor designs, a method of improving a processor's **throughput** by storing and analyzing as many as 30 or more instructions prior to their execution. Each instruction is analyzed in an attempt to predict its flow through the processor, and is routed and sequenced to optimize processing time. The **Intel P6** processor employs speculative execution to improve processing by as much as 100% compared to previous **Pentium** designs.

Standard Performance Evaluation Corporation (SPEC)

A non-profit corporation, based in California, that seeks, to "establish, maintain and endorse a standardized set of relevant **benchmarks** that can be applied to the newest generation of high-performance computers." While conceding that no single benchmark can be used to compare all computer systems, SPEC seeks to provide a common frame of reference that can be used to compare the performance of computer systems. SPEC is an industry consortium whose members include AT&T/NCR, Auspex, Bull, Compaq, Control Data, Data General, DEC, EDS, Fujitsu, HaL Computer, Hewlett-Packard, IBM, Intel, Intergraph, Kubota Pacific, Motorola, NeXT, Network Appliance, Novell, Olivetti, Siemens Nixdorf, Silicon Graphics, Solbourne, Sun, Unisys, and Ziff-Davis. Currently, there are two standard SPEC benchmarks, one measuring integer computations (CINT92), and a second measuring **floating-point** computations (CFP92). For comparison, an **Intel 486DX2** turns in a CINT92 score of 32.2, while a **Pentium** running at 66 MHz hits 118.1.

superscaler

Having more than one data processing pathway (**pipeline**);
see **superscalar architecture.**

superscalar architecture

A method of improving the efficiency of a **microprocessor**
by providing two (or more) **pipelines** through which processing can take place. The microprocessor's **control unit**
breaks a problem down into pairs that can be worked on
simultaneously by different parts of the microprocessor;
this is called instruction pairing. A microprocessor that has
this capability is called a **dual-issue microprocessor.** The term
superscalar implies that the benefit of this technology go
beyond the impressive gains made by scaling down (shrink-
ing) the physical size of the chip on which the microprocessor is fabricated.

A superscalar microprocessor, such as Intel's **Pentium**, must
manage the job of deciding whether a given instruction
can be separated from the next one so that the two can be
processed independently. A special circuit tests the instructions for **data dependencies**, linkages that require the
instructions to be processed together. If no dependencies are
found, the first instruction is sent down the first pipeline, while
the second is sent down the other pipeling. Under ideal
conditions, then, the Pentium can process two instructions
for each tick of its **system clock**.

One problem that arises in superscalar designs is that conditional instructions—those phrased in the IF/THEN terms
common to programming languages—can hold up both
pipelines until the processor decides the outcome (if the
condition is true, the processor executes one of the waiting
conditions, while if the condition is false, it executes another one). This problem is solved by means of **branch prediction.**
In branch prediction, a special unit of the microprocessor

examines conditional instructions, attempts to predict the outcome of the decision, and lines up the next set of instructions based on the prediction (if it's wrong, there's a penalty of three or four lost clock cycles). In Intel's Pentium microprocessor, branch prediction succeeds 90 percent of the time—and this fact alone accounts for about 25% of the chip's performance gains over its predecessor, the **i486.**

Note that superscalar architectures reach their optimum performance only under carefully controlled conditions. In "real world" processing, involving the use of programs that have not been optimized for superscalar architectures, the gains produced by such architectures may be minimal. *See* **issue restrictions.**

superpipelining

A term used by **Cyrix** to describe its advanced **pipeline** architecture, in which the five basic pipeline stages are increased to seven or more stages. With pipelining, a processor can work on more than one instruction at a time because the instructions are routed through a pipeline, with five basic stages. By increasing the number of pipelining stages, the complexity of each stage's operation is reduced, producing claimed gains in processing speed.

system clock

 An electronic circuit that synchronizes processing operations by emitting timing pulses at fixed intervals—for example, 90 **MHz.** The interval at which the clock emits these signals is called the **clock speed.**

 If it's a computer, it must be accurate, right? For computer purposes, the system clock works just fine, so far as synchronizing your computer's operations goes. But for keeping time meaningful in human terms, system clocks aren't so great. You'll notice that your computer is actually much less accurate than household clocks and watches at keeping time—some computers lose or gain as much as several minutes per week. You'll be wise to set your computer's time by your watch, rather than the other way around.

throughput

The overall rate at which a computer system can perform processing operations, as measured by some recognized **benchmark**, such as **millions of instructions per second (MIPS)** or **SPEC**.

virtual memory

A method of extending the computer's **random access memory (RAM)** by utilizing part of the computer's hard disk as an extension of RAM. Virtual memory must be enabled by specific circuits within the microprocessor.

Winstone

A respected **benchmark** created by Ziff-Davis's PC Labs, and used for *PC Magazine's* extensive system comparisons. The latest version of Winstone employs a suite of application scripts from 13 widely-used Windows business applications, producing a numerical score that reflects the system's performance under real-world conditions. The score is normalized against a reference base of 10, the score of a 386DX-25 Compaq Deskpro.

x86

The Intel processor architecture that is **binary compatible** with MS-DOS and Microsoft Windows software, as reflected in the long series of parts beginning with the 8088 and currently culminating in Intel's **P6**. *Compare* **680x0**.

zero-insertion force (ZIF) package

A receptacle for **integrated circuits** that does not require the user to push the device into a socket. Instead, the socket is designed to be opened by a retainer lever; the circuit can be inserted and, when the retainer is closed, the contacts engage. *Compare* **dual in-line package (DIP)**.

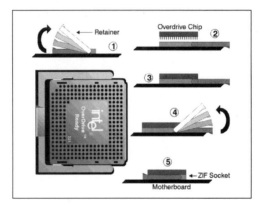

Figure 4.5 Inserting a chip into a ZIF socket

ZIF

See **zero-insertion force (ZIF) package**

Memory

In this chapter, you'll find terms related to the computer's internal memory. Covered are **random-access memory (RAM)**, **read-only memory (ROM)**, the many kinds of **cache memory**, and the various kinds of memory on Intel-based computers (**conventional memory**, **extended memory**, and **expanded memory**).

cache memory

A unit of ultra-fast memory that sortes recently accessed data and frequently used program instructions so that these are more readily available to the microprocessor. If the data or instructions need to be accesssed again, they can be retrieved from the cache much more rapidly than from the computer's **RAM** memory. A cache memory that is built into the microprocessor's circuitry is called a **primary cache**, while a cache memory that is physically separate from the processor is called a **secondary cache**. Cache memories are usually made from **static random-access memory (SRAM)** chips.

Don't even think about buying a computer that doesn't have a cache memory of at least 256KB. A computer that lacks cache memory is up to 30% slower than a comparable machine that has cache memory.

conventional memory

In a computer that employs an Intel microprocessor and runs the MS-DOS operating system, the base memory (maximum: 640K) that can be directly addressed and used in the microprocessor's real mode (see Chapter 4). Microsoft Windows and OS/2 switch the microprocessor into its protected mode, in which **extended memory** becomes available.

direct-map cache

A method of allocating the storage space in a **cache memory**, in which each storage unit in the cache is linked to several storage locations (called blocks) in the main memory. This design is economical. However, it results in frequent cache misses, because there is not enough storage space to link with all the memory locations in each block. When a cache miss occurs, the data required by the CPU is not found in the cache and must be retrieved from the main memory. *Compare* **full-associative cache**, **set-associative cache**.

---

dynamic random access memory (DRAM)

A type of integrated circuit designed to provide **RAM (random access memory)** for personal computers. A DRAM chip cannot store data unless it is re-energized periodically (compare **static randon access memory (SRAM)**), but it is inexpensive and readily available. The DRAM chips in your computer have been matched to your microprocessor's speed demands. Older PCs could use DRAM chips capable of responding within 80 nanoseconds (ns), but today's 486 and Pentium computers require chips that can respond within 70 or 60 nanoseconds. The faster the response time, the more expensive the DRAM.

> How fast should your DRAM be? In general, most 25 MHz and slower motherboards work with 80 ns DRAM, while 33 MHz boards require 70 ns chips. Some 40 MHz boards require 60 ns DRAM, which is the fastest currently available. Check with your motherboard's manufacturer to determine which DRAM speed is required.

DRAM is packaged in **single in-line memory modules (SIMMs)**, which can store 1 or 4 MB of data. *Compare* **static random access memory (SRAM)**.

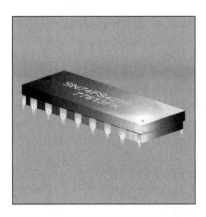

Figure 5.1 *A DRAMM chip*

expanded memory (EMS)

A method of providing additional memory beyond the DOS 640KB limit that uses 64KB memory blocks, which are inserted into **conventional memory** as required. The extended memory specification (EMS) was jointly developed by Lotus, Intel, and Microsoft. With computers based on the Intel 8088 and 8086 microprocessors, expanded memory provides the only means by which programs can use memory beyond the 640KB barrier. Expanded memory is technically inferior to **extended memory**, which became available in the Intel 80286 and later processors. Some DOS games still require expanded memory; these games can be run by configuring your system to set aside part of the extended memory to emulate expanded memory.

extended memory (XMS)

In the standard x86 architecture of IBM PCs and compatible computers, the **RAM** memory above 1MB that is accessible when the microprocessor switches into the protected mode. In its 386 Enhanced Mode, Microsoft Windows switches 80386 and later microprocessors into the protected mode, allowing programs to access up to 16 GB of RAM.

four-way set-associative cache

A **set-associative cache** design that represents the optimal balance between cost and complexity. Four-way set-associative caches surpass the performance of **two-way set associative caches**, and significantly surpass the performance of **direct-map caches**.

full-associative cache

A method of allocating the storage space in a **cache memory** in which each storage unit in the cache can be associated with any storage location in the main memory. This design solves the principal drawback of **direct-map cache** designs, which cannot link to all memory locations and, in consequence, produce frequent cache misses. However, performance is poor because the cache controller must search the entire cache to find the desired data. *Compare* **direct-map cache**, **set-associative cache**.

internal cache

A **cache memory** that is physically implemented within the microprocessor itself. Because the cache is directly connected to the processing circuitry, program instructions and data stored within the internal cache can be accessed at very high speeds. Intel's Pentium microprocessor offers a primary cache of 16KB, while the NexGen Nx586 offers 32KB. *Compare* **secondary cache**.

L2 cache memory

See **secondary cache.**

primary cache

See **internal cache.**

random access memory (RAM)

The computer's main internal memory, where program instructions and data are stored temporarily so that they can be speedily accessed by the microprocessor (see Chapter 4). The term "random access" is meant to suggest RAM's chief technical characteristic: Like a bank of post office boxes, each storage location in RAM is directly accessible. In contrast, sequential access devices such as a tape drive require the computer to wind through the tape until the desired data is reached. Because RAM storage locations can be directly accessed, storage and retrieval operations occur much more quickly than they do on secondary storage devices such as disk drives.

The size of a computer's RAM is measured in megabytes (MB), creating confusion with disk storage figures, which are also given in megabytes. You'll hear people say, "I have a 4MB hard disk and 120MB of RAM," but these figures are reversed: RAM is almost always smaller than hard disk capacity.

How much RAM is enough? That's the question you're sure to ask when buying or upgrading a computer. If you're planning to run Windows, wags might well respond, "You'll never have enough," but the facts attest otherwise. Ostensibly, Windows 3.1 and even Windows 95 will run with just 4 MB of RAM, but you get dramatically improved performance at 8 MB of RAM; at 16 MB, the performance gains level off, so that adding additional memory doesn't do you much good (unless you really want to run a dozen applications simultaneously, which most people won't do).

---

read-only memory (ROM)

A unit of memory that is capable of retaining information when the computer is switched off, and contains programs vital to the computer's operation. ROM-based programs, including the Basic Input/Output System (BIOS), come into play when you start or resstart your computer. They perform diagnostic tests and provide the basic software support needed to integrate your compuer's components. ROM, as the name implies, is a read-only medium, meaning that your computer can take information from ROM, but it can't write information to it. This makes sense, because you wouldn't want to make any changes to these crucial programs. But this makes comptuers difficult and expensive to repair, should the computer manufacturer discover an error in ROM or need to provide a new BIOS to cope with new kinds of peripherals (see Plug and Play). A solution is flash BIOS, which partially replaces ROM with memory circuits that can be rewritten under a special program's direction.

---

secondary cache

A **cache memory** that is positioned outside the microprocessor and designed to improve overall system performance. Don't even think about buying a motherboard that lacks L2 cache memory. A 128K L2 cache might be sufficient for most 486 systems, but you'll need a 256K L2 cache for 486DX4 and Pentium systems. Cache design is also important; the cheapest design is the **direct-map cache**, but **set-associative cache** designs are superior (the best is the **four-way set-associative cache**). In addition, look for a **write-back cache** rather than a **write-through cache**.

set-associative cache

A compromise between a **direct-map cache** and a **full-associative cache** design, in which the **cache memory** is divided into two, four, or eight direct-mapped blocks, called sets. Set-associative cache designs are superior to direct-map caches; **four-way set-associative caches** represent an optimal balance between performance and cost.

single in-line memory module (SIMM)

A hard plastic package that contains from 1MB to 16 MB of **dynamic random access memory (DRAM)** chips, and is designed for easy user installation.

In the late 1970s and early- to mid-1980s, DRAM chips were packaged in dual in-line packages (DIP) that had twin rows of pins that would bend in all directions when the hapless user tried to press them in their sockets. By the late 1980s, **SIMMs** provided a user-friendly alternative, and motherboard designers took note. Early SIMMs had 30 contact pads (commonly, but erroneously, called "pins"); more common today is the 72-pin SIMM, which provides designers with more configuration options.

Wondering how fast your SIMMs are? DRAMs are often marked with their speed after they are tested. Look for a suffix after the part number: a SIMM marked 398739-7 is very likely a 70 ns DRAM.

The cheapest motherboards come with slots for 30-pin SIMMs, but this technology is obsolete. Make sure your motherboard uses 72-pin SIMMs.

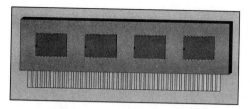

Figure 5.2 A SIMM module

single in-line pinned packages (SIPPs)

A hard plastic package that contains from 1MB to 16 MB of **dynamic random access memory (DRAM)** chips, and—unlike **single in-line memory modules (SIMMs)**—is affixed to the motherboard by means of pins.

static random-access memory (SRAM)

A type of **random acccess memory** that is constructed from static memory circuits, which retain a stored value as long as the current is left switched on. **Dynamic random access memory (DRAM)** chips, in contrast, require the computer to refresh the values they contain at regular intervals. SRAM circuits are more complex, more expensive, and considerably faster than DRAM circuits, so they are used for speed-critical components such as cache memory.

two-way set-associative cache

A **cache memory** design that offers the benefits of a **set-associative cache** at a reasonable cost, and is therefore superior to the **direct map cache**. However, performance is inferior to the more costly **four-way set-associative cache** design.

Video Random Access Memory (VRAM)

 The second most common type of **video memory**, used mainly in high-end display adapters since it is technically superior to **DRAM** but much more expensive. VRAM is dual-ported—two operations can be performed on it simultaneously. The **video controller** can read the VRAM's contents and send them to the **monitor**, while the CPU writes new display information to other memory locations at the same time. Compare **DRAM, VRAM.**

virtual memory

A method of extending the computer's **random access memory (RAM)** by utilizing part of the computer's hard disk as an extension of RAM. Virtual memory must be enabled by specific circuits within the microprocessor (see Chapter 4).

write-back cache

 A **cache memory** design in which the cache records memory writes as well as reads, freeing cache operations from dependence on the slower circuitry of the computer's **random-access memory (RAM)**. *Compare* **write-through cache**, n-way set associative cache.

 For **secondary caches**, write-back cache designs typically score higher on benchmark tests than write-through caches.

write-through cache

A **cache memory** design in which memory reads are cached, but not memory writes, which must be stored in **random access memory (RAM).** This design is inefficient because RAM is much slower than cache memory. *Compare* **write-through cache**, n-way set associative cache.

Expansion Busses

A personal computer's expansion bus lets you add expansion boards, which give your computer new capabilities (such as sound or faxing). Basically a set of wires running in parallel, a bus includes several expansion slots, into which expansion boards can be pressed. More than an electrical socket, the bus provides a host of sophisticated electronic functions that must be synchronized with the microprocessor's functions.

From the standpoint of someone buying or upgrading a system, the key question is "Which bus?" There are a variety of competing standards. Because the situation is still settling out, many motherboards offer more than one bus. In this chapter, you'll find definitions of all the bus options and bus-related terms.

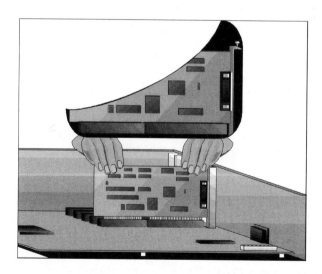

Figure 6.1 Installing an expansion card

| EISA-2 |

See **Enhanced ISA (EISA) expansion bus.**

| EISA |

See **Enhanced ISA (EISA) expansion bus.**

| Enhanced ISA (EISA) expansion bus |

A 32-bit expansion bus design developed by a consortium of nine companies (AST Research, Compaq, Epson, Hewlett-Packard, NEC, Olivetti, Tandy, Wyse, and Zenith Data Systems). Expressly designed to compete with IBM's **Micro Channel Architecture (MCA) expansion bus**, the EISA bus is downwardly-compatible with the previous 16-bit ISA and 8-bit PC bus standards. Running at 8.33MHz, the EISA bus can transfer data at a rate of 33 MB per second. A new version of the EISA specification, called EISA-2, offers data transfer rates of up to 132 megabytes per second. Although the EISA bus has been superseded by the popular **VESA local bus** and the increasingly popular **PCI** expansion bus, the EISA-2 standard offers a very high performance level and is offered in some high-performance LAN server.

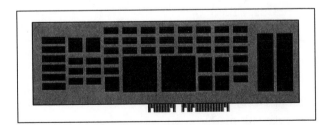

Figure 6.2 EISA Card

expansion bus bottleneck

A barrier to a PC's processing speed created by the slow performance of the older expansion bus standards, such as **ISA**. The expansion bus bottleneck became particularly severe in the early 1990s, when high-speed microprocessors became available. These microprocessors easily outran the processing capacity of the expansion bus, so that the total system could not take full advantage of the new microprocessors' capabilities. The bottleneck was particularly apparent in the display of graphical user interfaces; the graphics information had to be routed through the slow expansion bus, resulting in dreadful performance. *See* **local bus**.

Industry Standard Architecture (ISA) expansion bus

A 16-bit expansion bus design, developed by IBM for its 1984 release of the IBM Personal Computer AT. Designed for downward compability with the original PC's 8-bit expansion bus, the AT's bus uses a supplementary connector to provide 16-bit connections. Running at a speed of 8 MHz, the AT bus could transfer 8 megabytes per second. In 1987, a standards committee affiliated with the Institute of Electrical and Electronic Engineers (IEEE) issued a set of standards, called the Industry Standard Architecture (ISA), that specified all the technical information that was needed to create AT-compatible busses and expansion boards. Since, then, the AT bus has been known as the ISA bus.

> The ISA bus is too slow for today's microprocessors, but it's still nice to have a couple of ISA slots in case you want to use 16- or 8-bit expansion boards.

ISA expansion bus · local bus

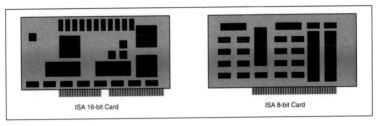

ISA 16-bit Card · ISA 8-bit Card

Figure 6.3 *ISA 16-bit and 8-bit Cards*

ISA

See **Industry Standard Architecture (ISA) expansion bus.**

---

jumper settings

In an expansion card, configuration options that are choosen by physically changing the position of jumpers. A jumper is a small connector that establishes an electrical contact between two upright pins.

---

legacy hardware

An expansion card that does not recognize Microsoft's **Plug and Play** diagnostic procedures. Windows 95 can help you install legacy hardware but you may have to change **jumper settings** manually.

---

local bus

An expansion bus that is a direct extension of the micro-processor's external data bus, allowing the expansion bus to run at the microprocessor's external data bus speed (as much as 33 MHz). The term "local" is used to suggest the intimacy of the connection with the CPU; the local bus is simply part of the close, high-speed connections between the microprocessor and its supporting chip set.

local bus
PCI

In the early 1990s, the **expansion bus bottleneck** encouraged system designers to connect video adapter circuitry to the local bus, and the **proprietary local bus** was born. The video performance gains were so dramatic that the **VESA local bus** standard was quickly developed.

MCA

See **Micro Channel Architecture (MCA) expansion bus.**

Micro Channel Architecture (MCA) expansion bus

A 32-bit proprietary expansion bus design introduced by IBM in 1987 in its line of PS/2 computers. Operating at 10 MHz and offering a peak data transfer rate of 20 megabytes per second, the MCA bus represented a significant technical improvement on the ISA bus. However the MCA bus was not downwardly-compatible with the PC and AT bus, forcing users to purchase MCA-compatible expansion cards. High licensing fees discouraged third-party suppliers for the MCA bus, which IBM itself subsequently abandoned. *Compare* **Enhanced ISA (EISA) expansion bus.**

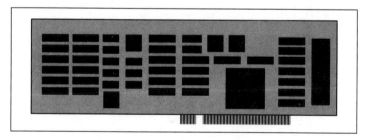

Figure 6.4 MCA Card

PCI

See **Peripheral Component Interface (PCI) expansion bus.**

PCMCIA bus

An expansion bus standard that was originally developed to
provide memory cards for personal digital assistants (PDAs),
the PCMCIA bus has evolved into a standard receptable for
a variety of card-based peripherals, including modems,
sound cards, and even hard disk drives. Although PCMCIA
slots are increasingly found on desktop computers, the standard is still closely associated with notebook computers.
PCMCIA is an acronym for Personal Computer Manufacturer's
Computer Interface Adapter.

Peripheral Component Interface (PCI) expansion bus

A 32- or 64-bit expansion bus based on a design developed
by Intel Corporation in 1992. Not a true **local bus** design, the
PCI bus mediates between the microprocessor's external
data bus and the computer's general input/output bus. This
design allows a PCI bus to run at speeds independent of
the microprocessor's clock speed. What is more, the PCI
design does not tie the use of the bus to a specific microprocessor, as the VESA local bus design was tied to the Intel
486. Also unlike the VESA local bus design, the PCI bus is a
complete expansion bus design that lets system designers dis-
pense with the slow, outmoded ISA bus entirely. (In practice,
motherboard designers usually include an ISA bus so that users
can continue to use their old peripherals.)

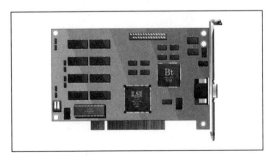

Figure 6.5 A PCI Expansion Card (note: components are on the left side)

In addition, PCI includes provisions for the forthcoming **Plug and Play** standard, which will (finally) allow PC users to install peripheral cards without worrying about port, DMA, and IRQ conflicts.

Plug and Play

A Microsoft-sponsored specification that, if followed completely, enables users to add new expansion cards without worrying about port conflicts and other vexing installation problems. To be fully Plug and Play-compatible, a computer system requires a Plug and Play-compatible operating system (Windows 95), a Plug and Play-compatible BIOS (see Chapter 8), and Plug and Play-compatible expansion cards. If all of these features are lacking, the user must manually configure an expansion card. With Plug and Play support at the operating system level, Windows 95 will guide the user through each step of the installation, but the user may still have to configure the expansion card manually (for example, by changing **jumper settings**). Only when all three features are present is installation automatic.

proprietary local bus

A **local bus** design created by a computer manufacturer for use with its own products only. Avoid proprietary local busses like the plague; if you buy a system with a proprietary local bus, you'll lock yourself into purchasing that company's peripherals, and no others. *Compare* **VESA local bus**.

VESA local bus

A **local bus** design created by the Video Electronics Standards Association (VESA) in 1992. A direct response to **proprietary local busses**, the VESA design provided freely-available specifications for connecting expansion boards to the computer's high-speed external data bus. Originally developed for high-performance graphics video adapters (see Chapter 10), the VESA local bus standard was later used to connect other high-performance peripherals, including network adapter cards. However, it was never designed to replace other expansion buses, so most computers that include a VESA local bus also include an **ISA** expansion bus. With 33 MHz motherboards, the VESA local bus can transfer data at rates up to 107 megabytes per second.

The VESA local bus design is intimately tied to the Intel 486 architecture—so much so, in fact, that it does not work well with Pentium microprocessors. A new version of the VESA standard solves that problem, but in the meantime, the **PCI expansion bus** has come to predominate in the Pentium market. If you're buying a 486, a VESA local bus-based system will perform well, but you may have difficulty finding expansion boards in the future as VESA gives way to PCI. If you're buying a Pentium, there's no contest—get PCI.

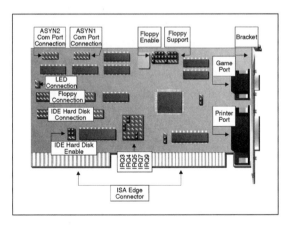

Figure 6.6 *A VESA local bus card*

Ports

This chapter surveys the terminology related to ports, which are the connectors and supporting circuitry that allow information to pass out of the computer to peripheral devices, such as printers, scanners, and modems. All the port-related terms you're likely to encounter when you're shopping for a system, or planning a system upgrade are included.

Computer shoppers rarely think of ports, but there are plenty of reasons to consider them now. A new generation of "smart" peripherals, including modems, printers, and scanners, is on its way. These devices will be able to report their status to your computer—but only if your system is equipped with the new, smarter ports that enable **bidirectional communication**.

16450

An integrated circuit that provided the **Universal Asynchronous Receiver/Transmitter (UART)** for the IBM Personal Computer AT, introduced in 1984. Although the 16450 is an improvement over the **8250**, it is too slow to work with today's fast microprocessors and produces **overrun errors** because it can't up with the pace at which fast microprocessors dish out data. *See* **16550A**.

16550A

An integrated circuit that provides the **Universal Asynchronous Receiver/Transmitter (UART)** for today's fast computer systems. Unlike the obsolete **8250** and **16450** UARTs, the 16550A has a much larger temporary storage buffer, thus eliminating the **overrun errors** that plagued the earlier chips.

8250

An integrated circuit that provided the **Universal Asynchronous Receiver/Transmitter (UART)** for the original IBM PC, the IBM PC XT, and early internal modems. This chip is too slow to keep up with today's computers, which can dish out data faster than the 8250 can handle it, resulting in **overrun errors.** *See* **16550A**.

bidirectional communication

In a parallel port, the capacity of the port to handle two-way communication between the computer and the attached peripheral, such as a printer. Not well supported in the original (Centronics) parallel port standard, bidirectional communication is a worthwhile feature of the new generation of **EPP/ECP ports**. Printers that are enhanced to take advantage of EPP can send informative messages to the computer regarding their status, including paper out, paper jam, and low toner.

bidirectional parallel port

A two-way parallel port for printers and other peripherals that conforms to the Institute of Electrical and Electronics Engineers (IEEE) standard 1284. This standard incorporates two proprietary standards, the Xircom/Zenith/Intel **Enhanced Parallel Port (EPP)** and the HP/Microsoft **Extended Capabilities Port (ECP)** standard. In contrast to the slow, one-way communication allowed by the **Centronics** standard parallel port, a bidirectional parallel port transfers data to the printer at up to 10 times the speed, and allows the printer to send detailed messages to the computer. Several printer manufacturers have announced printers confirming to the **IEEE 1284** standard, and it is expected to replace the standard Centronics parallel port in coming years.

Centronics port

See **parallel port**.

dongle

A physical device that plugs into a port, such as a parallel port or serial port, and adds some kind of functionality. A common but much-despised dongle is a copy-protection device employed by many high-end computer programs, such as professional animation packages. The program checks for the presence of the dongle; if it's absent, the program won't run. Other, less-despised dongles provide infrared interfaces, network connectivity, and PCMCIA ports.

ECP

See **Extended Capabilities Port.**

Enhanced Parallel Port (EPP)

A standard, jointly developed by Intel, Zenith Data Systems, and Xircom in 1991, that improves the speed of the **standard parallel port** and provides **bidirectional communication.** EPP parallel ports can transfer data at a rate of about 2 MB per second, a significant improvement over the 200KB/second rate of standard parallel ports. On desktop systems, this standard and a competing one, called the **Extended Capabilities Port (ECP)**, are supported by widely-used chip sets.

 Does your computer have an EPP/ECP support? Find out with a free utility called PARA14.ZIP, which is widely available on FTP software archives on the Internet.

Enhanced Serial Port (ESP)

A high-speed **serial port** developed by Hayes Microcomputer Products. The port uses a microprocessor and a bank of random-access memory (RAM) to improve serial port performance.

EPP

See **Enhanced Parallel Port.**

EPP/ECP port

 A **parallel port** that supports both the **Enhanced Parallel Port (EPP)** and **Extended Capabilities Port (ECP)** specifications, as well as the standard (Centronics) parallel printer interface. EPP/ECP-capable printer ports are supported by Windows 95. By using a special, high-speed cable, Windows users will be able to use the EPP/ECP port to create connections that operate as fast as Ethernet network connections.

| ESP |

See **Enhanced Serial Port**.

| Extended Capabilities Port (ECP) |

A standard, jointly developed by Microsoft and Hewlett-Packard, that improves the speed of the **standard parallel port** and provides **bidirectional communication**. ECP is technically superior to EPP. Owing to Microsoft's support of ECP in Windows 95, it is likely to become the prevailing standard for bidirectional parallel ports. *See* **bidirectional parallel port, IEEE 1284.**

| game port |

An indispensable component that lets you connect a joystick to your computer. Without it, you won't be able to play Flight Simulator, Doom, or Heretic, and you might actually get some work done.

> Don't have a game port? If you're planning to add a sound card to your system, look for one that includes a game port (many do). You'll get the game port for little or no extra expenditure.

| IEEE 1284 |

A standard developed by the Institute of Electrical and Electronics Engineers (IEEE) that specifies the operation of **bidirectional parallel ports**. *See* **Enhanced Parallel Port (EPP), Extended Capabilities Port (ECP).**

infrared port

A port, usually created by attaching a **dongle** to a serial port, that enables a desktop PC to exchange data with infrared-equipped notebook computers. With infrared transmission, which is similar to the transmission used to exchange signals between your hand-held remote control and your TV, no cabling is necessary. A standard created by the Infrared Data Association allows data to be transmitted at speeds close to 115.2K bps

I/O adapter

An expansion board, designed to fit into one of your computer's expansion slots, that provides a variety of ports, typically including a high-speed **bidirectional parallel port**, a **16550A**-based **serial port**, and a **game port**. Such an adapter is worth having only if your computer's motherboard does not make these ports available—a fairly rare situation unless you purchased a "build-it-yourself" mail-order motherboard.

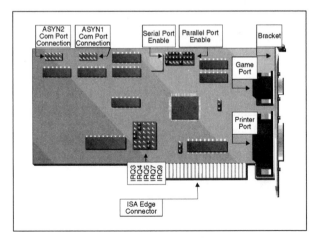

Figure 7.1 *A standard I/O adapter*

overrun error

In a **serial port**, an error—resulting in lost data—that occurs when the computer sends data faster than it can be handled by the **Universal Asynchronous Receiver/Transmitter (UART).**

parallel port

A port that can create a multiple-wire (parallel) connection between the computer and a peripheral device. Unlike a serial port, which transforms the parallel data stream within the computer to a one-after-the-other, single-line series, a parallel port provides enough wires so that all eight bits in a byte of data can travel side-by-side, like cars on a super-wide freeway. Parallel ports are thus inherently faster than serial ports. What's more, they are easier to connect, since no translation circuitry is needed to process the outgoing and incoming signals. The **standard parallel port**, found on most IBM PCs and compatibles, dates back to a standard created by Centronics, an early printer manufacturer. This firm also invented the odd clamping plug (the Centronics plug) that is found on the printer end of parallel printer cables.

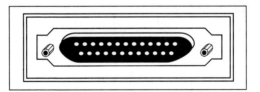

Figure 7.2 *Parallel port*

PCMCIA card reader

A device, designed to fit in an empty drive bay, that enables you to use the PCMCIA peripheral cards developed for notebook computers. These cards include memory cards, modems, sound cards, and even wafer-thin hard drives.

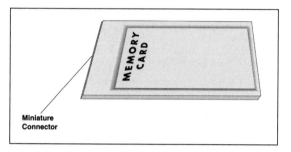

Figure 7.3 *A PCMCIA Expansion Card*

---

port conflict

 A system error caused by two incorrectly configured peripheral devices attempting to access the same port at the same time. Each device should have its own port—for example, connect a serial mouse to COM1, and a modem to COM2.

 Don't try to install more than two serial ports (COM1 and COM2) on any IBM or IBM-compatible computer. If COM3 and COM4 are present, disable them. You may be able to do this by using your computer's SETUP program (see Chapter 8).

RS232C port

See **serial port.**

---

serial port

 An asynchronous port, conforming to the RS-232C standard of the Electronics Industry Association (EIA), that transforms the parallel bit stream within your computer into a single-file, one-after-the-other series that can be transferred by a two-wire connection. The serial port is called *asynchronous* because it does not rely on a synchronization signal, as some serial devices do, to synchronize the single-file stream of data bits. Instead, each byte of data is demarcated by markers (called a start bit and a stop bit) that differentiate one byte from the rest. A serial port consists of a serial connector and a **Universal Asynchronous Receiver/Transmitter (UART)**. *Compare* **8250, 16450, 16550A.**

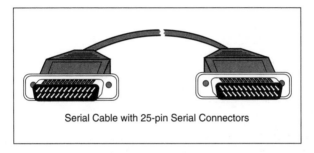

Serial Cable with 25-pin Serial Connectors

Figure 7.4 *Serial Cable with 25-pin Serial Connectors*

standard parallel port

The earliest, Centronics-compatible printer port for the original IBM PC, the PC XT, and the PC AT. This parallel port, which uses a 25-pin D connector, could transfer data at a rate of about 200 KB per second (a glacial pace by today's standards). Communication occurs in one direction only, from computer to peripheral.

UART

See **Universal Asynchronous Receive/Transmitter (UART).**

Universal Asynchronous Receiver/Transmitter (UART)

An integrated circuit that provides the key processing functionality of a **serial port**, namely, transforming the parallel bit stream of the computer into a single-file, one-after-the-other series of data bits. In addition, the UART decodes incoming streams of serial data into a parallel bit stream that the computer can recognize and use. Specific UART chips found on IBM PCs and compatibles are the obsolete **8250** and **16450,** and the **16550A**.

The Basic Input/Output System (BIOS)

This chapter surveys the terms related to BIOS, a set of
essential programs that determine the nitty-gritty details
of the computer's operation. Contained in the computer's **read-
only memory (ROM)**, BIOS determines the computer's ability to cope with hardware advances, such as **Plug and Play**.
For this reason, you'll be wise to prefer a computer that
employs an easily-upgradable **flash BIOS**.

advanced setup options

In the **setup program,** a series of **CMOS** options that permit you to choose settings for ports, hard disk interfaces, PCI interrupt settings, and additional options.

Do not experiment with the advanced setup options. These should be altered only when a new system component is installed by a qualified service technician.

Basic Input/Output System (BIOS)

A set of low-level system programs that are encoded in the computer's **read only memory (ROM),** and automatically fed into the computer on system startup (also called **cold boot**) and system restarts (also call **warm boot**). After the startup or restart, the BIOS performs a **power-on self-test (POST)** and **memory check,** If these diagnostic tests do not reveal any problem, BIOS directs the computer to search for the computer's operating system (see **boot sequence**). One function of BIOS is to provide the **setup program**, a menu-based program that allows you to choose basic system configuration options. **Advanced setup options** include many options that novice users should not attempt to change, including the **cache settings** and **wait state**. Desirable BIOS features in new computer systems include **flash BIOS** and **Plug and Play BIOS.**

boot

To start the computer. The start-up process takes place under the direction of the **firmware** code, and generally involves a **memory check** and the initial loading of programs vital to the computer's basic functions, such as displaying characters on the screen and handing the timing of communication among the computer's various devices. There are two ways to boot—a **cold boot** occurs when you switch on the power, while a **warm boot** occurs when you press a restart key sequence (on IBM PCs and compatibles, this is Ctrl + Alt + Del).

boot sequence

The order in which your computer attempts to access the disk drives installed in your system. By default, IBM PCs and compatibles first attempt to access Drive A (the floppy disk drive), and then attempt to access Drive C (the hard disk drive).

You can speed your system's startup procedure by using the **setup program** to change the access sequence so that the computer accesses Drive C first. This also prevents the system from reporting an error if you try to boot with a floppy disk in the disk drive. Should your hard disk fail, you can reset the boot sequence so that Drive A is accessed first.

cache settings

In the **setup program,** the options that permit you to enable or disable the computer's secondary cache. For more information on secondary caches, see Chapter 5.

Some games are designed to run on 486 computers. On a Pentium, they run too fast. If this happens, you can slow down your computer to 486 speeds by disabling the secondary cache. Just don't forget to enable it again after you've finished playing the game!

CMOS reset jumper

A connector, located on the computer's motherboard, that you can reposition in order to reset the computer's **CMOS** settings. This procedure may become necessary if your computer will not operate because you have incorrectly modified your **advanced setup options.**

CMOS

See **complementary metal-oxide semiconductor (CMOS)**.

complementary metal-oxide semiconductor (CMOS)

 An integrated circuit, or chip, that consumes less power (but costs more) than chips fabricated with the usual silicon-based techniques. In the BIOS context, CMOS refers to a battery-powered CMOS chip that contains a **real-time clock** and stores vital system configuration settings while the power is switched off.

cold boot

A system startup that begins by turning on the power. *Compare with* **warm boot**.

firmware

The program instructions stored in **read-only memory (ROM)**.

flash BIOS

 A programmable chip used to store the computer's **Basic Input/Output System (BIOS).** The advantage of buying a system with flash BIOS is that it's easier to update—the computer manufacturer sends you a disk with the new BIOS and the update program. After you run this program, your computer has a new BIOS. Without a flash BIOS, you would have to return the computer to have the ROM chip physically replaced.

memory check

In most personal computers, a routine diagnostic check of the computer's memory originated by the **firmware** code, that is performed every time you switch on the computer. If an error is found, the memory check program displays the location of the memory chip containing the error. The memory check is part of the **power-on self-test (POST)** routine.

> If your computer fails the power-on memory test, make a note of the memory location displayed on the screen. This number will probably include letters as well as numbers. When you take your computer for servicing, give the memory location to the service technician.

Plug and Play BIOS (PnP BIOS)

A BIOS that conforms to Intel's Plug and Play specification, which allows automatic configuration of expansion boards. Although Windows 95 enables many Plug and Play capabilities without a corresponding PnP BIOS, the PnP BIOS is desirable because it automatically configures the boot sequence and other vital start-up functions. Note that the current Plug and Play specification cannot deal with all of the more than 10,000 manually-configured ISA expansion boards in existence, so the use of Plug and Play (whether at the operating system or BIOS levels) cannot guarantee that your system will be free from interrupt or port conflicts. For more information on Plug and Play, see Chapter 6, The Expansion Busses.

> If you're shopping for an IBM or IBM-compatible computer, look for Windows 95 compatibility. This will mean (among other things) that the system is fully compatible with Intel's Plug and Play specification (look for capital letters; "plug and play" systems may not precisely conform to Intel's specification).

PnP BIOS

See **Plug and Play BIOS**.

POST

See **power-on self-test (POST)**.

power-on self-test (POST)

A set of diagnostic procedures, initiated by the computer's **BIOS**, that determine whether the computer's internal circuitry, keyboard, and disk drives are functioning normally. If any of these components fails the test, an error message is displayed on-screen.

read-only memory (ROM)

A special type of memory chip that can retain information when the power is switched off. ROM chips are used to store a computer's **firmware**, including the BIOS.

real-time clock

An accessory circuit, usually provided on an expansion board (see Chapter 6), that does not rely on the computer's internal clock to keep the time and date accurately.

ROM

See **read-only memory (ROM)**.

setup program

A system configuration program that is encoded in the computer's **BIOS** and stores your configuration choices in

setup program	wait state

CMOS. To initiate the setup program, you press a special key combination when the computer is starting. An on-screen menu is displayed that guides you through choices, including altering the **system time, system date,** disk drive configuration, size of the installed memory, **cache settings, wait states,** shadow ROM, and the **boot sequence.** A well-organized setup program makes your computer easier to use and configure.

---

shadowing

Copying all or part of the computer's low-speed **read-only memory (ROM)** into the significantly faster RAM memory, resulting in faster system operation.

---

system date

In the **real-time clock**, the current date setting. You can change this by using the **setup program**.

---

system time

In the **real-time clock**, the current time setting. You can change this by using the **setup program**. Some computers offer a feature that automatically adjusts the time for daylight savings time.

---

wait state

A setting that determines how many cycles of the computer's internal clock must pass after the processor attempts to access data stored in memory. In some computers, wait states are required because the microprocessor operates much more quickly than the memory.

| wait state | warm boot |

 If you set the wait state setting too low, your system may become unreliable. Don't change the wait state setting unless you're willing to suffer system crashes.

| warm boot |

A system restart. *Compare* **cold boot**.

Input Devices

In this chapter, you'll find terms covering all the devices you can use to get information into the computer, including the **keyboad**, the **mouse** (including variations such as **track-balls**), **scanners**, **video capture cards**, **voice recognition**, and more.

101-key keyboard

Synonymous with extended **keyboard**. A keyboard introduced by IBM with later models of its IBM Personal Computer AT. Departing from the original AT keyboard, the 101-key Enhanced Keyboard (as IBM termed it) featured a single row of function keys (numbered F1 through F12) along the top of the keyboard, a dedicated cursor pad, additional control keys (Home, End, Insert, Delete, Page Up, Page Down), and—unfortunately—a smaller Enter key.

83-key keyboard

A **keyboard** design used by the first IBM Personal Computer, introduced in 1984. The keyboard was widely criticized for its nonstandard key layout (which departed from that of the firm's hugely successful Selectric typewriters), the small size of the Enter key, and the lack of indicators for toggle keys (Caps Lock, Num Lock, and Scroll Lock). The keyboard has two vertical rows of function keys along the left edge of the keyboard, and includes a numeric keypad.

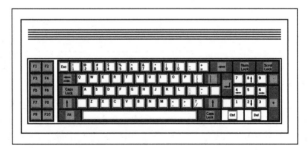

Figure 9.1 *An 83-key keyboard*

84-key keyboard

A **keyboard** design used by the IBM Personal Computer AT, introduced in 1984. In response to criticisms of the origi-

84-key keyboard	charge-coupled device

nal **83-key keyboard**, this design has a larger Enter key, a keyboard layout that closely resembles that of Selectric electronic typewriters, and indicators for toggle keys.

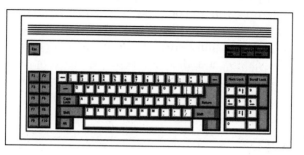

Figure 9.2 *Note the larger Enter key on this 84-key keyboard*

---

audible feedback

In a **keyboard**, the capacity to provide an audible signal indicating that the key has been depressed sufficiently to send the appropriate signal to the computer. Microsoft's Natural Keyboard comes with user-selectable audible feedback, including manual and electric typewriter sounds. *Compare* **tactile feedback**.

---

bus mouse

A **mouse** that is designed to connect to your computer by means of an expansion board, which fits into one of your computer's available expansion slots. A bus mouse may be required if your computer has no **mouse port** and no available serial ports.

---

charge-coupled device (CCD)

In a **scanner**, a light-sensitive receptor that emits electricity when exposed to light. Scanners digitize images one line at

| charge-coupled device | digital camera |

a time, using a tightly-packed row of CCDs. A scanner's true resolution (its **optical resolution**) is physically limited by the number of CCDs in the row. A scanner's resolution is usually expressed by indicating the horizontal resolution first, followed by the vertical (as in "300 x 600"). A scanner with a horizontal resolution of 300 dpi packs 300 CCDs into the row, while a scanner with a horizontal resolution of 600 dpi squeezes 600 smaller and more expensive CCDs into a row. (The scanner's vertical resolution is determined by the number of lines it captures per inch; this is generally 300 or 600.)

| color depth |

In a **scanner**, the number of bits with which the scanner can represent and process colors scanned from the original artwork. Scanners that use 24 bits to represent colors can depict 16.7 million colors and 256 levels of gray, while 30-bit scanners can represent more than 1 billion colors and 1,024 levels of gray.

| color scanner |

A **scanner** that can capture colors as well as shades of gray. The quality of a color scanner's output is directly related to its **color depth**, the number of bits used to represented the captured color information. 24-bit color scanners can represent 16.7 million colors.

| digital camera |

A battery-powered, portable camera that captures digitized images, which can then be downloaded to a computer for display, further processing,and printing. Digital cameras aren't poised to replace optico-chemical systems anytime soon; they're expensive, and the quality isn't that great; Apple's QuickTake 150, for example, lists for $749 at this writing, and can capture only 16 high-quality images (24-bit color at a resolution of 640 x 480). However, a digital camera makes excellent sense for applications in which the images will wind up in the computer anyway via a **scanner**; taking digitized pictures cuts out time-consuming and expensive film processing and scanning steps. To download the images to your computer, you connect the camera to your computer's serial port (see Chapter 7), and save them to your hard disk using the software included with the camera.

Dvorak keyboard

A **keyboard** layout advocated in 1936 by August Dvorak and William L. Dealey, and said to be optimal for fast typing. In his enthusiasm for promoting the design, Dvorak overstated the advantages of the Dvorak keyboard. If you have already learned how to touch-type with the standard QWERTY keyboard layout, there is little justification for learning Dvorak.

dynamic range

In a **scanner**, one of the fundamental determinants of the quality of the scanned image. The greater the dynamic range, the more contrast the original artwork can have before vital information is lost from the scan. A scanner with a high dynamic range can capture a wide range of tones from very dark to very light.

enhanced 101-key keyboard

See **101-key keyboard**.

ergonomic keyboard

A **keyboard** that has been designed to reduce the wear and tear on nerves passing through the carpal tunnel, a tiny pas-

ergonomic keyboard   full-travel keyboard

sageway in the wrist that is stressed by the normal typing position. By orienting the two halves of the keyboard at an angle that more nearly resembles the natural angle of the hands as they sit on the keyboard, stress on the carpal tunnel is reduced. Carpal tunnel injuries make up a significant proportion of repetitive strain injuries (RSI), the fastest-growing category of work-related injuries in the U.S.

extended keyboard

See **101-key keyboard**.

flatbed scanner

A **scanner** that is designed to accept flat reflective art (such as printed illustrations or photographs), generally no larger than 8.5 by 11 inches. Some scanners can also accept transparencies and slides with additional equipment. Flatbed scanners vary in the number of **scanning passes** they make, their **dynamic range**, their **color depth**, and their **optical resolution**.

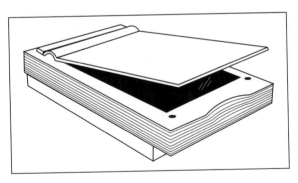

Figure 9.3 *A typical flatbed scanner*

full-travel keyboard

In a **keyboard**, a design that lets the user depress the key at least one-eighth of an inch. According to ergonomic studies, typists achieve the highest speeds and lowest error rates with full-travel keyboards.

game port

A port (see Chapter 7) that is specifically designed to accommodate a **joystick**. Game ports are not normally provided on PCs. You can add a game port in two ways: by buying a sound card (Chapter 14) that contains a game port, or by buying a special expansion card that contains one or more game ports.

grayscale scanner

A **scanner** that digitizes an image using 256 shades of gray. Grayscale scanners are less expensive than **color scanners**.

hand-held scanner

A **scanner** that is designed to be held in the hand; to capture the scan, you physically move the scanner over the artwork. Hand-held scanners are less expensive than **flatbed scanners** because no mechanism is required to move the lens over the artwork. However, hand-held scanners generally are not wide enough to capture an entire 8.5-inch-wide page, limiting their use to smaller photographs and artwork. (Some units come with "stitching software" that claims to be able to piece multiple scans together.) Due to this limitations, and to the rapidly-falling prices of flatbed printers, hand-held scanners are best avoided.

interpolated resolution

In a **scanner**, a method of increasing the apparent resolution of a scan by adding additional dots among those actually scanned, which normally do not achieve a resolution higher than 300 dpi or 400 dpi. The interpolation, which is normally carried out by software, colors the new dots by averaging the values of adjacent dots. The result is an improved image with a resolution of up to 1,600 dpi, but interpolation can never match the quality of an actual scan at that resolution.

Note that one scanner's 1,600 dpi may actually look worse than another scanner's 1,200 dpi. The reason is the differences in the algorithms employed to interpolate the additional dots. Before buying a scanner, be sure to preview samples of the type of artwork you're planning to scan.

joystick

An input device, designed for use with games, that enables the user to guide on-screen activity using an upright, movable lever. A joystick requires a **game port**, which is not normally included with most PCs. For flight games, a variety of sophisticated joysticks are available that are intended to simulate the flight controls of actual aircraft.

If you want to connect a joystick to your PC, look for a sound card (see Chapter 14) that contains one—many do.

keyboard

A bank of electromechanical switches, each of which is designed to input a specific, numerically-coded character (a letter, number, punctuation mark, or control character) into the computer.

mechanical mouse

A **mouse** whose movements are detected by two metal rollers (one horizontal and one vertical), which are rotated by the mouse's rubber ball as the mouse is moved. The advantage of a mechanical mouse is that the mouse may be

| mechanical mouse | mouse |

used on virtually any surface; the disadvantage is that the rollers and ball tend to become dirty and require periodic cleaning. *Compare* **optical mouse**.

| microphone |

An input device commonly found on Macintosh computers but rarely attached to PCs, even though most sound cards have microphone inputs. Voice recordings can be used for a variety of purposes, including recording new system sounds that play when certain system events occur (such as opening documents). A practical use: Microsoft Word and many other applications provide provisions for including voice annotations within documents, which play a recorded sound file when the user double-clicks the annotation icon.

| mouse |

A computer control device that displays a pointer on the screen; as the user moves the mouse on the desktop, the pointer mirrors the device's movements. By pointing at on-screen objects and using the mouse button or buttons, the user can initiate control and editing functions, such as choosing an item from a menu or selecting a word or sentence for deletion.

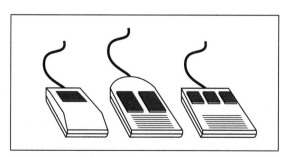

Figure 9.4 *Examples of several types of mice*

mouse port

Synonymous with PS/2 mouse port. A round receptacle, located on the back of the computer, that is designed to accept the plugs of mice that are compatible with IBM's PS/2 computer line. The advantage of a PS/2-compatible mouse port is that it is not necessary to tie up a serial port to plug in the mouse.

optical character recognition (OCR)

In a **scanner**, the transformation of optically-detected text into computer-readable ASCII text files, which can be edited with a word processing program. OCR requires software that performs the analysis and translation. OCR isn't perfect; even under the best conditions—generally, an original typescript with a generic typewriter font—you will encounter errors; however, these can be detected and corrected with a spell-checking program. Some OCR programs rely on intelligent algorithms that attempt to guess an unknown word from its context. Most scanners have OCR capabilities and come with OCR software, although the best OCR programs are expensive and aren't bundled with scanners.

optical mouse

A **mouse** whose movements are detected by means of a light beam moving across a grid. The grid is provided by a special mouse pad. The advantage of an optical mouse is that no periodic cleaning is required; the disadvantage is that the mouse cannot be used on any surface other than the mouse pad that contains the necessary grid.

optical resolution

 The degree of density, measured in dots per inch (dpi), with which a **scanner** can digitally reproduce an image. A scanner's optical **resolution** is physically limited to the number of optical detection devices (called **charged-coupled devices**) that are available to scan the art work; in scanners costing less than $2,000, this limitation generally restricts the scanner's resolution to 300 dpi or 400 dpi. Scanners claiming higher resolution are using **interpolated resolution**, an image-enhancement technique.

pointing stick

An input device, introduced with IBM's Think Pad notebook computers, that is located between the "G" and "H" keys of the standard **keyboard**. Resembling a tiny **joystick**, the pointing stick lets you use an index finger to move the mouse pointer on-screen.

PS/2 mouse

A **mouse** that is designed to connect to your computer by means of an IBM PS/2-compatible **mouse port**, a round connector specifically designed for this purpose. With a PS/2 mouse port, it is not necessary to use one of your computer's serial ports to connect the mouse to your system.

PS/2 mouse port

See **mouse port**.

resolution

In a **scanner**, the ability of the scanning hardware and software to resolve fine details in the source artwork.

scanner

An optical input device that scans source artwork, such as a photograph or drawing, and transforms the image into a digitized representation. Accompanying software saves this digitized information into a standard graphics file, which you can import into an image-processing program such as Adobe Photoshop. Many scanners are also capable of **optical character resolution (OCR)**, which can transform clearly-printed text (especially typescript) into an ASCII file that can be edited with a word processing program. There are several types of scanners in a wide range of prices, ranging from inexpensive, **hand-held scanners**, the more expensive **flatbed scanners**, and top-of-the line **sheet-fed scanners** designed for heavy duty work. Overall, **grayscale scanners**, which can capture only shades of gray, are less expensive than **color scanners**, which can create color graphics files from colored artwork. Scanners vary in the **optical resolution** at which they capture artwork; physical limitations prevent resolutions greater than 600 dots per inch (dpi), but a technique called interpolation overcomes this limitation and produces effective resolutions as high as 1,200 dip

| scanning pass |

The movement of the scanner's optical detectors over the surface of the artwork or photograph being scanned. Increasingly popular are **single-pass scanners**, although they are not necessarily faster than **triple-pass scanners**.

| serial mouse |

A **mouse** that is designed to connect to your computer via a standard serial port. A serial mouse poses no problems as long as your computer has a serial port avaiable for its use.

| sheet-fed scanner |

A **flatbed scanner** that is equipped with a sheet feed mechanism for high-volume work.

single-pass scanner

A **scanner** that scans the source artwork with a single **scanning pass**. The advantage of a single-pass scanner is that there is less wear and tear on the scanner's motorized mechanism; however, single-pass scanners are not necessarily faster than **triple-pass scanners**.

tactile feedback

In a **keyboard**, the capacity of the keyboard to provide a tactile signal (perceptible by your sense of touch) that the key has been depressed and the appropriate signal sent to the computer. The simplest type of tactile feedback is the pressure generated by the key "bottoming out" at the end of the keystroke. Because this design tends to tire the fingers, some keyboard designers prefer using **audible feedback**, in which a beep or click signals when the key has been depressed sufficiently to send the signal.

trackball

An input device that resembles an upside-down **mouse**: The case stays put, and the user manually rotates the ball to move the pointer on-screen. The trackball's advantage is that it is not necessary to move your entire arm to move the on-screen pointer, as is necessary with a mouse; the disadvantage is that the pointer can seem somewhat harder to control.

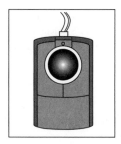

Figure 9.5 *A trackball can be used as an alternative to a mouse*

transparency adapter

In a **scanner**, an optional accessory that allows the scanner to scan 35mm color slides and transparencies.

triple-pass scanner

A scanner that scans the source artwork with two or more **scanning passes**. One scan is made for each of the three primary colors. After all three scans are complete, the separate scans are superimposed to create the final image. *Compare* **single-pass scanner**.

video capture card

An expansion card (see Chapter 6) that enables you to connect a VCR or VHS-compatible video camera and record full-motion video (at least 30 frames per second). The purpose of the video capture card is not only to digitize the incoming signal, but also to compress it, since an uncompressed video input produces 27 MB of digitized data per second. To get video files down to a manageable size, video capture cards use lossy compression techniques (such as Motion JPEG), which remove information in such a way that the eye doesn't notice the loss, and reduced image size (at 30 frames per second, the maximum resolution of most video capture cards is 320 x 240, played in a small on-screen window). And don't expect miraculous quality: output is "VCR quality," at best. Still, video capture cards are now available for less than $400, and may prove invaluable for educators, trainers, and others who need to develop multimedia presentations.

voice recognition

The perception by a computer system of the distinct, meaningful words in a spoken human voice, such that the computer can act on these words or transform them into ASCII text. Computers have one of the same drawbacks as people: They talk better than they listen. Voice synthesis (the synthesis of a human voice from a text file) is well within the reach of the relatively simple programs packaged with many sound cards. Voice recognition is another matter. Equipped with a **microphone** and voice-recognition software, computers can be trained to detect a few hundred words with reasonable accuracy; if you so desire, you can equip your system with a voice-command system that enables you to give Windows commands (such as "Maximize"). Only recently available for personal computers are voice-dictation systems that enable you to dictate text to be transformed into a text file, and they're not cheap: IBM's Personal Dictation System lists for $995. The program has a 20,000-word vocabulary and enables you to add up to 12,000 words of your choice.

Display Adapters

This chapter surveys terms related to the most important part of your computer's display system, the **display adapter**. One of the expansion boards that fits into your computer's expansion bus (see Chapter 6), the display adapter must be designed to work with the type of bus your computer uses (in Chapter 6, see ISA bus, PCI bus, and VESA local bus). Your display adapter's capabilities determine the two most important characteristics of overall image quality, the refresh rate and resolution, which are defined in the next chapter.

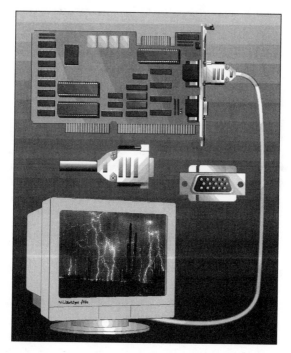

Figure 10.1 *Video adapter with monitor and cabling*

128-bit display adapter

A **display adapter** that offers an internal data path 128 bits wide, enabling the adapter to process 16 bytes of data simultaneously. The wider the data path, the better the adapter's performance. A 128-bit display adapter is strongly recommended for graphics-intensive applications, such as desktop publishing.

32-bit display adapter

A **display adapter** that offers an internal data path 32 bits wide, enabling the adapter to process 4 bytes of data simultaneously. Considered obsolete, 32-bit display adapters are too slow to display Windows applications at high resolutions (such as 1280 x 1024).

64-bit display adapter

 A **display adapter** that offers an internal data path 64 bits wide, enabling the adapter to process 8 bytes of data simultaneously. The wider the data path, the better the adapter's performance. For use with Microsoft Windows and at high resolutions (such as 1280 x 1024), a 64-bit display adapter is considered the practical minimum.

6845

A **video controller** chip, first used in the IBM **MDA** display adapter, which all modern **display adapters** either use or simulate with more recent chips. The 6845 is so versatile—and has survived so long—because it is completely programmable. Programs called **video drivers** can change all characteristics of the video signal sent to the monitor by the 6845 and the other hardware on the display adapter by altering the values in the 6845's 18 registers (Chapter 4).

8514/A

An early 1024-by-768-pixel display standard adopted by IBM in 1987 and used in high-end IBM **display adapters** for about three years. Designed for use with IBM's 8514 monitors, 8514/A adapters suffered from slow refresh rates and compatibility with IBM's ill-fated Micro Channel bus (Chapter 6) technology. Though it survived for a while as part of the **XGA** standard, 8514/A is effectively dead.

color depth

The number of colors a **display adapter** can handle simultaneously. The basic **VGA** standard allows 256 simultaneous colors, while improvements upon it allow more than 16.7 million simultaneous colors. Since the number of bits used to represent colors determines the maximum number of colors that can be represented, color depth is commonly referred to as bit-depth. An 8-bit color representation system can handle only 256 colors; 24-bits of storage are required for 16.7 million color.

Color Graphics Adapter (CGA)

A defunct **video standard** that replaced the eerie green text of the first IBM PC displays with crude graphics and 16 colors. Introduced by IBM in 1982 as an alternative to **MDA,** CGA was the first PC video standard to incorporate color.

The CGA standard defines a pixel array of 640 pixels by 200 pixels, and allows each character a box only eight pixels square. In comparison, high-quality modern **monitors** and **display adapters** can generate displays with resolutions of 1280 pixels by 1024 pixels and better.

CGA monitors and adapters are virtually impossible to find, except in used-hardware markets. They are sold new only to handle large-screen text-display tasks in which resolution and graphics capability are unimportant. Don't even consider buying a CGA adapter unless you have such a unique need. **VGA** adapters are the modern minimum standard.

D-shell connector

The standard plug on the **display adapter** end of a monitor cable, named for its resemblance to the letter "D." There are two kinds of D-shell connectors: 15-pin, used on **VGA** and **Super VGA** monitors; and 9-pin, used for earlier video standards.

display adapter

 An expansion board that allows a computer to communicate information via a monitor. Display adapters convert a central processing unit's (Chapter 4) output into a signal that can be interpreted by a monitor, much as a cable television box prepares signals coded on a wire for display on your television. Display adapters are often called **video cards** or display cards. In some computers, the display adapter circuitry is found on the motherboard.

A variety of **video standards** emerged as computer designers determined new ways to display computer information on screens. These standards—including **CGA, EGA, VGA** and the now-popular **Super VGA**—are one means by which display adapters are differentiated. If you have a VGA monitor, you need a VGA display adapter.

Display adapters typically include a **Random Access Memory Digital-to-Analog Converter (RAMDAC)** chip, a clock synthesizer, and some video memory (typically between 512KB and 4MB). Newer display adapters include the RAMDAC and clock synthesizer on a single chip, reduc-

ing adapter size and complexity, and incorporate faster
video memory.

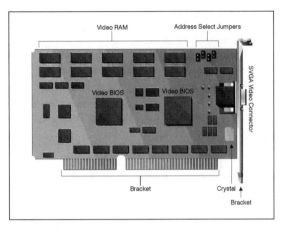

Figure 10.2 Display adapter

---

display card

See **display adapter.**

DRAM

See **Dynamic Random Access Memory (DRAM).**

---

dynamic random-access memory (DRAM)

One of the two types of video memory in common use.
Unlike the more expensive **VRAM**, DRAM is single-
ported, which means it provides data access either to the
graphics controller ot the **RAMDAC**, but not to both at
once. As a result, display adapters that use DRAM
cannot process video data as fast as adapters using
VRAM chips.

dynamic random-access...   graphics accelerator

A DRAM-equipped adapter may not be able to display 1280 x 1024 resolution at a **refresh rate** high enough to avoid **flicker**.

Enhanced Graphics Adapter (EGA)

A **video standard** that offers better resolution and graphics capability than **MDA** and **CGA**. The EGA standard replaced the CGA standard in 1984 and remained in vogue for about three years. EGA offered 640-by-350-pixel resolution and supported graphics on monochrome screens.

When shopping for a computer, don't consider less than a **VGA** monitor and **display adapter**. Few modern software packages support the EGA standard.

Extended Graphics Array (XGA)

Extended Graphics Array, the **video standard** IBM introduced in 1990 to replace its unpopular **8514/A** standard. Unlike 8514/A, XGA allows for both interlaced and non-interlaced monitors. XGA also was the first video standard to include many features that are common on **graphics accelerators** today, including hardware-based bit-block transfers and a hardware sprite. XGA has not caught on as a video standard, mainly because it was designed to work with IBM's ill-fated Micro Channel bus.

graphics accelerator

A **display adapter** that includes either special chips to handle specific graphics tasks or a **graphics coprocessor**. The graphics accelerator relieves the CPU (Chapter 4) of many display-related tasks. By freeing the CPU from mundane video jobs, the CPU is free to spend time on other tasks. A good graphics accelerator can dramatically increase a PC's apparent processing speed.

graphics adapter

See **display adapter.**

graphics board

See **display adapter.**

graphics card

See **display adapter.**

graphics coprocessor

The microprocessor (Chapter 4) chip that handles graphics tasks on certain types of **graphics accelerators,** relieving the central processing unit (Chapter 4) of the need to do them. For example, a graphics coprocessor can be used to keep track of various windows in a graphical operating environment or support hardware panning. The Weitek W5086 and W5186 and the 86C911 of S3, Inc. are commonly used graphics coprocessors.

hardware windowing

A method of dividing video memory into sections and assigning each an on-screen window, as an area of the display dedicated to a particular program's workspace is called. **Graphics accelerators** that incorporate hardware windowing (most do) free the central processing unit (Chapter 4) from having to keep the various windows under control, and thereby increase a computer's apparent processing speed.

Hardware windowing also reduces the time required to update the display, since it allows the **display adapter** to work with only the video memory assigned to a particular window and ignore the rest of the display. Graphics accelerators that use hardware windowing don't need to redraw the entire screen every time something changes in a single window—only that window, a small part of the whole displayed image, needs to be redrawn.

Hercules graphic adapter

An improved version of the **MDA** video standard that features some graphics capability. Released in the early 1980s the HGA uses the same 6845 processor as MDA, but uses a special memory scheme to handle 720-by-348-pixel graphics.The card was especially appealing to users of Lotus 1-2-3, who could display charts and graphics in the HGA's graphics mode.

MCGA

See **memory controller gate array.**

MDA

See **monochrome display adapter.**

Memory Controller Gate Array (MCGA)

A **video standard**, based on **VGA**, used in early 286-class IBM PS/2 computers. MCGA was supposed to reduce costs by eliminating most of the VGA memory requirements, but eliminated much of VGA's image quality in the process. MCGA, like the 286-class computers in which it appeared, is obsolete.

Monochrome Display Adapter (MDA)

The earliest PC **video standard**, incorporated into the first IBM PCs in 1981. MDA supports only **monochrome displays** and allows no graphics other than the crude block graphics included in the IBM Extended Character Set. MDA was obsolete by 1983, but the **6845 video controller** it used is still a part of **display adapters** today.

monochrome display and parallel printer adapter

See **monochrome display adapter.**

Random-Access Memory Digital-to-Analog Converter (RAMDAC)

In a **display adapter**, an integrated semiconductor chip that combines the three color signals (red, green, and blue) into a single, combined output for an analog monitor (see Chapter 11). The RAM memory module is needed to store color information temporarily before it is combined into the output signal.

screen memory

See **video memory.**

Super VGA

An improvement of the **video graphics array (VGA) video standard** that allows for 800-by-600-pixel **resolution**. Super VGA is the most popular video standard today, and variations of the basic specification give resolutions of 1280-by-1024 pixels with more **color depth** than human beings can perceive.

Though Super VGA **display adapters** can be purchased inexpensively, consider buying a **graphics accelerator**. They can increase a computer's apparent processing speed by as much as 30 percent and usually provide more resolution options than a basic adapter.

video accelerator

See **graphics accelerator.**

video adapter

See **display adapter.**

video board

See **display adapter.**

video card

See **display adapter.**

video controller

The microprocessor (Chapter 4) that regulates the flow of information from the video memory to the monitor. Essentially, the video controller reads data from video memory addresses in sequence, arranges the data into a coherent stream, inserts some synchronization signals to allow for vertical and horizontal retrace, and sends it to the monitor.

video driver

A program that serves as an intermediary between applications and the **display adapter.** The video driver determines how a program appears on the display, and sometimes includes a user interface that allows you to choose resolution and other display characteristics.

Video Graphics Array (VGA)

 A **video standard** introduced in 1987 in IBM PS/2 PCs. The modern minimum standard for display adapters and monitors, VGA supports 640-by-480-pixel resolution and 256 colors. Display adapter manufacturers have pushed the VGA specification beyond its original limits to establish **Super VGA**, capable of 800-by-600-pixel resolution, and even more advanced standards that support displays of 1280-by-1024 pixels.

VGA monitors and display adapters are standard on modern PC systems, and likely will remain the standard for some time. VGA is very flexible, allowing display adapter and monitor makers to develop useful modifications of the basic standard, and it is well suited to the needs of desktop computer users— there's only so much detail you can see on a 15-inch monitor from 18 inches away.

When shopping for display adapters, don't just get a VGA card if you plan to use a graphical operating environment like OS/2 or Windows. Instead, get a **graphics accelerator**, which relieves the CPU (Chapter 4) of video tasks and frees it to do more "real" work.

| video memory |

In a display adapter, a bank of memory chips that holds display information before the video controller sends it to the monitor. The CPU (Chapter 4) writes image information to the video memory. Later, the **video controller** reads it and sends it to the monitor for display. Certain types of video memory, such as **VRAM**, allow both read and write operations to occur at the same time. *Compare* **DRAM and VRAM**.

Most modern display adapters have between 512 KB and 4 MB of video memory. Get as much video memory as you can afford—it makes things easier for your computer's CPU and display adapter and is one of the most cost-effective ways to improve your computer's apparent processing speed. For use with Microsoft Windows, at least 2 MB of video memory is recommended.

| video standard |

Any protocol for communicating video information from
the **display adapter** to the monitor and showing it on a display. Video standards specify resolution, color depth, vertical and horizontal retrace rates, and can be followed by
many manufacturers of video hardware. **MDA, CGA, EGA,
VGA** and **Super VGA** are all video standards. Some so-
called video standards are not standards at all—for example,
IBM's **XGA** specification was used only in IBM machines.

| Video Random Access Memory (VRAM) |

 The second most common type of **video memory,** used
mainly in high-end display adapters since it is
technically superior to **DRAM** but much more expensive.
VRAM is dual-ported—two operations can be performed
on it simultaneously. The **video controller** can read the
VRAM's contents and send them to the monitor, while
the CPU writes new display information to other
memory locations at the same time. Compare **DRAM,
VRAM.**

| XGA |

See **Extended Graphics Array.**

| Windows accelerator |

See **video accelerator.**

Monitors

Surveyed in this chapter are the **monitor**-related terms you're likely to encounter when you're buying or upgrading your system. Bear in mind that a crucial determinant of your monitor's performance is the display adapter (see Chapter 10) that drives the monitor; even the best monitor on the market will display noticable **flicker** if it's driven with a slow, unaccelerated display adapter.

14-inch monitor

A **monitor** that offers a (claimed) diagonal tube measurement of 14 inches; the actual figure is less (from 12.8 to 13.5 inches). 14-inch monitors are standard equipment in most computer systems today, but their small size is incompatible with the high **resolution** displays made possible by today's display adapters, which are capable of displaying 1280 horizontal lines by 1024 vertical lines. On a 14-inch monitor, text displayed at this resolution will be difficult to read.

15-inch monitor

A **monitor** that offers a (claimed) diagonal tube measurement of 15 inches; in reality, the tubes measure 13.3 to 14 inches diagonally. 15-inch monitors offer some improvement over the entry-level monitor in most PC systems today, the **14-inch monitor**, but the emerging standard—and highly recommended—is the **17-inch monitor**.

17-inch monitor

 A **monitor** that offers a (claimed) diagonal tube measurement of 17 inches, 28 percent greater than the image area of **15-inch monitors**. The actual viewable image of a 17-inch display ranges from 15.4 to 16.6 inches, producing an image area of approximately 155 square inches.

17-inch monitors are well on their way to becoming the standard, and for good reason: At high resolutions (such as 1280 x 1024), a 15-inch monitor displays text that is too small to read comfortably. On a 17-inch monitor, the same text is readable. In addition, more room is available for opening additional windows, and that's a plus now that so many users are running two, three, or more applications simultaneously.

21-inch monitor

A **monitor** that offers a claimed diagonal tube measurement of 21 inches, although the actual measurement is 19 inches. 21-inch monitors are ideal for desktop publishing applications because they enable the display of two full document pages.

active matrix

A type of **LCD**, also called thin-film transistor or TFT. An active matrix display uses a transistor to control each of its pixels, allowing on-screen images to be brighter than those generated by **passive matrix** and **dual-scanned passive matrix** LCDs. The transistors also allow the computer to update its display more frequently than passive-matrix displays, creating a screen that doesn't flicker.

> If you're buying a portable computer, get one with an active-matrix display. Such LCDs cost $200–$300 more than passive-matrix displays, but you'll find the high refresh rate and greater brightness worth it.

addressability

A misleading term used by some **monitor** manufacturers to describe their products' quality. Addressability describes the number of screen locations to which electrons from a monitor's **electron guns** can be directed, but ignores the fact that the **shadow mask** obscures many of those points. A monitor's addressability describes the highest-quality video signal it can handle, but has little to do with the actual appearance of the display.

> If a monitor's sales literature specifies only addressability, make sure you get more relevant information such as **dot pitch, resolution**, and **refresh rate**. Addressability is not an important point of comparison among monitors.

analog monitor

 A **monitor** that accepts analog video input. In this kind of video input, the strength of the incoming signal determines the brightness of the resulting electron beam. For this reason, analog monitors can display an unlimited number of colors. All video standards since VGA call for analog monitors. *Compare* **digital monitor**.

anti-glare

Any treatment of a **monitor** to reduce annoying reflections of outside light sources. Glare can make the **display** hard to see or cause eyestrain, reducing productivity. Anti-glare treatments may be as simple as turning your monitor slightly or relocating a lamp in your computer room, but more often involve modifying the display itself. The simplest anti-glare fixtures are essentially nylon screens stretched over the display; others involve special light-damping chemical treatments.

 Be aware that anti-glare fixtures often reduce the **brightness** of the display on which they are installed. To reduce glare problems, make sure you put your monitor directly behind your keyboard, instead of on a corner of your desk where you must look at the display at an angle. Also, try to locate your desk either perpendicular to windows or with the back of the monitor facing them.

aperture grille

The functional equivalent of a **shadow mask**, used in Sony **Trinitron** monitors and **CRTs** of similar design. Instead of using a perforated sheet of metal to direct an electron gun's beam to **phosphors** of a particular color, aperture grille designs rely on closely-spaced vertical wires behind the screen to accomplish the same thing. The result, overall, is a screen that's noticeably sharper and a monitor that's less susceptible to heat-related degradation (a common problem of shadow mask designs).

In Trinitron and similar monitors, phosphors are "painted" on the inside of the screen in vertical stripes. The wires of the aperture grille only allow **electron guns** to fire at the correct phosphors—for example, the blue gun shoots electrons at the blue phosphors, but the grille shades the red and green phosphors from blue gun electrons.

While **dot pitch** describes the fineness of standard monitors' resolution, **slot pitch** and screen pitch serve the same function in Trinitron-type monitors. Slot pitch is the space between aperture grille wires and screen pitch is the spacing of the phosphor stripes on the screen. Screen pitch is usually slightly larger than slot pitch, since the electron beams widen after they pass through the aperture grille.

| aspect ratio |

The relationship between the width and height of an image on a **display**. Modern monitors have aspect ratios of 1.33:1, meaning the screen is one-third wider than it is tall. (This proportion is often described as 4:3.)

Of course, you can use a **monitor's** vertical and horizontal amplification controls to adjust the aspect ratio, since the aspect ratio of the displayed image does not have to be the same as that of the screen. For example, you may have to adjust the aspect ratio to prevent an **EGA** image from appearing distorted on a **VGA** display.

| autosizing |

The ability of a **monitor** to display an image of constant dimensions regardless of the **resolution** of the video signal it receives from the display adapter. Autosizing automatically adjusts the **aspect ratio** of a displayed image so it fills a specific portion of the **display**, which you can often adjust with monitor controls.

backlighting

A way of making **LCDs** easier to read. Since LCDs rely on creating dark spots on a screen, there must be a light source to serve as contrast. Many LCD designs incorporate back-lighting, in which light shines at the LCD from behind. Backlighting is especially important if you plan to use your LCD outside, where sunlight can easily wash out displayed images. *Compare* **reflective LCD, edgelighting.**

bandwidth

A measure of how much information a **monitor** can accept from the display adapter. Usually expressed in megahertz (MHz), greater bandwidth in **monochrome** monitors denotes higher **resolution** and faster **refresh rates**.

In color monitors, however, **dot pitch** is more important than bandwidth. It doesn't matter how much information a monitor can take in if it doesn't have the ability to display it.

brightness

A **CRT** control that regulates the intensity of the electron beams emitted by the cathode ray tube (CRT). A high bright-ness setting makes the electron beams stronger and the displayed image brighter, while a low brightness setting has the opposite effect.

cathode ray tube (CRT)

The most common **display** mechanism for desktop computers. CRTs offer high-resolution display capability at relatively low cost, since they are mass-produced by

cathode ray tube (CRT)

scores of manufacturers and were used in televisions decades before the advent of personal computers.

CRTs consist primarily of a glass tube filled with an inert gas at low pressure. One end of the tube holds three **electron guns**—three cathodes, one each for red, green, and blue. The cathodes emit negatively charged electrons when directed by the monitor hardware and the **display adapter**. The electrons fly through the tube to the other end, which is positively charged. There, they strike **phosphors**, which glow when hit by electrons.

If the electrons emitted by the cathodes traveled unimpeded to the phosphor end of the tube, all you'd see would be a tiny dot in the center of the display. So, powerful electromagnets steer the flying electrons, directing them to scan the entire surface of the screen many times each second. A typical **Super VGA** CRT scans horizontally 48,000 times per second and vertically 72 times per second.

Even at such high scanning frequencies, one part of the screen would appear dark while another part was being scanned. To counteract this problem, phosphors have a brief **persistance** time (the time they continue to glow after being struck by electrons). A phosphor's decay time allows the electron guns to scan the rest of the screen and return to that phosphor before it goes dark.

While CRTs generate high-resolution images, they use a lot of electricity and generate potentially harmful electromagnetic fields. Look for monitors that satisfy the **MPR II** standard and are **Energy Star**–certified. MPR II is a set of criteria established by the Swedish government

for to reduce electromagnetic radiation emissions. Energy Star–certified monitors satisfy the U.S. Environmental Protection Agency's standards for reduced power consumption, and typically feature a **sleep mode** in which the display is shut off during periods of non-use.

CGA

See **Color Graphics Adapter (CGA)** in Chapter 10.

contrast

A **display** control that regulates the way in which a monitor differentiates between bright and dim images. The contrast control, whether a knob or a pair of pushbuttons, determines how bright high-intensity images are in comparison to low-intensity images. Contrast is especially important when using your computer in bright light, which can wash out all but the most high-contrast images.

convergence

The ability of the three electron beams in a color **CRT** to aim precisely at the same **pixel**. Convergence is measured in millimeters (mm), and describes how far one electron beam may stray from another at a particular place on the screen. Convergence numbers are often bigger than **dot pitch**, particularly at the corners of a display, so in those areas the convergence is the effective sharpness. Because **monochrome** monitors have only one **electron gun**, they are immune to convergence problems.

Poor convergence is easiest to spot at the edges of a display, where it appears as a multicolored halo around displayed images. More serious convergence problems cause text characters to appear as three-color blobs. Adjusting convergence is a job for a computer technician, so expect to pay dearly if your monitor has this kind of problem.

 Convergence varies from one screen location to another—it's usually small at the center of the screen and larger at the corners. Make sure a convergence measurement specifies where on the screen it was taken.

CRT

See **cathode ray tube.**

daisy-chaining

Joining several **monitors** together in series to show the video output of a single computer. It may be useful to daisy-chain monitors if you want to show a computer's output to a large crowd of people, perhaps spread throughout a convention hall, when it is not practical to use a single giant monitor.

Many monitors feature output jacks linked directly to their inputs, which means you can plug one monitor's input into the output of another almost indefinitely without image degradation. Such monitors are also useful because the output jack can be used as an input if the main input is damaged, since it connects directly to the input.

Bear in mind that some monitors loop video signals through a **video amplifier** before sending them to the output. This design eliminates the possibility of using the output jack as an emergency input, and may result in image degradation when several monitors are daisy-chained together.

deflection yoke

See **yoke.**

digital controls

In a **monitor,** a set of controls for brightness, contrast, and image size that is set by adjusting digital (numerical) displays. The monitor can remember your settings for each of a series of resolutions or **refresh rates,** saving you the trouble of readjusting these settings if you switch video modes. If you commonly switch from one screen resolution to another, digital controls can save you the time you'd otherwise spend fiddling with the controls to adjust the screen image.

digital monitor

A **monitor** that accepts digital video input. In this kind of video input, the number of colors that can be displayed is limited by the number of bits set aside for color representation. **CGA** monitors can display only 16 colors, while **EGA** monitors can display up to 64 colors. Since these numbers are insufficient for today's multimedia and desktop publishing applications, more recent video standards (VGA and up) require **analog monitors**.

display

The **CRT, LCD**, or whatever other device is used to generate images from a video signal. Don't use "display" and "monitor" interchangeably—while the two are often confused, they're not the same. The monitor includes the display, its support circuitry, and the cabinet in which the whole assembly is contained. *Compare* **monitor**.

Display Power Management Signaling (DPMS)

A sophisticated power conservation method that requires a compatible display adapter. A DPMS monitor follows the commands of a DPMS-capable display adapter to power down using three levels: Standby, Suspend, and Off. In Standby mode, the monitor uses 30 percent less energy, and the image can be restored at the touch of a key (or the nudge of a mouse). To allow instant screen regeneration, a heater keeps the cathode guns warm. In suspend mode, power consumption is further reduced by shutting down the monitor's internal heater. In the off mode, virtually everything is shut down except the monitor's master control circuits, which consume only 1 or 2 watts per hour. *Compare* **screen blanking**.

A DPMS-compatible monitor won't do you much good unless your display adapter knows how to "talk" to it. Check with your display adapter's manufacturer to find out whether the adapter can issue DPMS commands.

---

dot pitch

The most important measure of a color **CRT's** sharpness. Dot pitch is the distance, in millimeters, at which the **pixels** on the inside of a CRT are spaced. Typical dot pitches for modern monitors are 0.19, 0.28, and 0.31. The smaller the dot pitch, the sharper the monitor appears.

> Don't buy a desktop monitor with a dot pitch greater than 0.28. Monitors with large dot pitches can look grainy, and are likely to be found at the bottom of a manufacturers line. As low-end products, they may have several other substandard features.

---

double-scanned passive matrix

See **dual-scanned passive matrix.**

DRAM

See **Dynamic Random Access Memory (DRAM)** in Chapter 10.

---

dual-scanned passive matrix

A type of **passive-matrix LCD display** that scans twice as fast as normal passive-matrix screens. Dual-scanning improves **brightness** and **contrast**, but still lags behind **active-matrix** LCDs' vertical **refresh rates**. Synonymous with double-scanned passive matrix.

dynamic astigmatism control

See **dynamic beam forming.**

dynamic beam forming

In a **monitor,** an advanced cathode gun control system that adjusts the shape of the electron beam so that it is precisely circular when it strikes the surface of the screen. Since the beam originates from the center of the monitor, it is circular only when directed at the center of the screen. Without dynamic beam forming, the beam would become elliptical when directed toward the edges of the screen, producing degraded sharpness away from the screen's center. Dynamic beam forming ensures that the beam remains circular at all screen locations. Synonymous with dynamic astigmatism control.

edgelighting

One of several ways of making **liquid-crystal displays (LCDs)** more readable in bright light conditions. Edgelighting works by shining light at an LCD from around its borders, thereby providing contrast to the dark images on the LCD. Though not as effective as backlighting, edgelighting can prevent an LCD from becoming washed out and unreadable in bright sunlight. *Compare* **reflective LCD, backlighting.**

EGA

See **Enhanced Graphics Adapter (EGA)** in Chapter 10.

electron gun

A cathode in a **CRT** that emits electrons when directed to do so by the display adapter and **monitor** circuitry. The **yoke,** also under the control of the display adapter and monitor circuitry, steers the electrons from the electron gun to their destinations on the **display.**

Color monitors have three electron guns—one each for red, green, and blue—while **monochrome** monitors have only one. Even color monitors with so-called one-gun tubes have three electron guns; in such monitors, the three cathodes are bundled into a single physical assembly.

electromagnetic radiation

Low-frequency **monitor** emissions that some scientists and computer experts say are harmful to computer users, particularly pregnant ones. Some say Extremely Low Frequency (ELF) and Very Low Frequency (VLF) radiation such as that generated by the power-handling systems in **CRTs** (and electric blankets, too), can promote cancer and alter fetal development.

There's no way to be sure who's right in this debate, but it's not a bad idea to invest in a monitor that's **MPR II-** or **TCO-** certified. These monitors are specially shielded and tested to greatly reduce emissions of electromagnetic radiation.

Energy Star

A standard established by the U.S. Environmental Protection Agency that rewards energy-conserving **monitors** with special certification. To win the certification, the monitor must not consume more than 30 watts when deactivated in **sleep mode**. Energy Star-certified monitors carry an identifying sticker and can save their owners hundreds of dollars in electrical costs each year.

Energy Star–certified monitors typically have a sleep mode in which their screens go blank after a certain period of non-use, dramatically reducing electrical use. In the power conservation technique called **screen blanking**, the power reduction is kicked in by your saver program, as the monitors go blank when the screen saver kicks in. The display comes back on almost immediately when you press a key or move the pointing device, since the monitor uses some electricity to keep the **electron guns** warm while in sleep mode. A more advanced power management technique, called **Display Power Management Signaling (DPMS)**, requires a DPMS-compatible video adapter.

Some monitors feature an "off" mode that goes into effect after a certain period of "sleep." Off mode does not use electricity to keep the **CRT** warm, saving more electricity than sleep mode but requiring that you wait a few seconds for warm-up when you press a key to reawaken your monitor.

| flat tension-mask |

A Zenith design that produced the first truly flat color display. Flat tension-mask monitors use a special **shadow mask** to eliminate the distortions that plague spherically or cylindrically curved displays. The first flat tension-mask monitors exacted a high toll in electrical costs and desktop real estate in exchange for their distortion-free images, and annoyed their users with the noise of a cooling fan. Newer flat tension-mask monitors are free of many of the problems of the earliest models, but are still very expensive. *Compare* **flat-square, vertically flat.**

| flat-square |

A misleading term attached to **CRTs** that have comparatively gentle spherical curves, but are really neither flat nor square. Most displays are spherically curved to ensure electrons from the **electron guns** must travel approximately equal distances to all parts of the screen, and so that the tube can resist the crushing force of atmospheric pressure. So-called flat-square CRTs feature broader-than-typical curves, but are curved nonetheless. So far, only the very expensive Zenith flat shadow-mask design has spawned a saleable flat color screen. *Compare* **vertically flat.**

flicker

An annoying, eye-straining defect in a monitor's screen display caused by an inadequate **refresh rate**, the rate (measured in cycles per second [Hz]) at which the monitor repaints the screen. Flicker becomes noticable at refresh rates lower than 70 Hz, particularly when data is viewed against a white background. If you're planning to use the high-resolution modes of today's display adapters, such as 1280 x 1024, avoid display adapters (see Chapter 10) and **monitors** with refresh rates lower than 72 Hz. In addition, avoid **interlaced** monitors.

frame buffer

The video memory that stores an electronic replica of the image shown on the **display**. The frame buffer serves as sort of a middle ground between the central processing unit (Chapter 4) and the video controller. The CPU writes to the frame buffer, then the video controller reads from it and sends data to the **monitor**. Newer types of video memory, such as **VRAM**, allow the CPU to write to the one part of the frame buffer while the video controller reads from another.

When a display adapter includes more video memory than the frame buffer requires, the excess memory may be used to accommodate hardware panning or other advanced features.

frame rate

See **vertical frequency.**

gas-plasma

A type of **display**, most often used in portable computers that don't need to run on battery power for long periods. Gas-plasma displays work by using high voltage to change the

chemical properties of a gas, usually neon, causing it to
give off light. Though relatively inexpensive to manufacture
and capable of very high **resolution**, gas-plasma screens are
rarely used on battery-operated portable PCs because their
appetite for electricity drains a typical battery in about an hour.
Compare **LCD**.

glare

Light, generated by a lamp or window, that reflects from
a monitor's surface directly into your eyes, causing eyestrain
and making the monitor more difficult to read. If you can't
reduce the light that's causing the glare, a simple—if somewhat unaesthetic—solution is to construct a monitor hood
out of cardboard. Anti-glare screens are less desirable
because they reduce the monitor's effective brightness.

hardware panning

The ability of a display adapter to use extra video memory
to simulate a **display** larger than the one physically attached
to a computer. While part of the video memory serves as a
frame buffer, the rest of the memory stores image information that is not immediately sent to the **monitor**. When you
drag your mouse pointer to the edge of the display on a
hardware-panning system, the display adapter changes
the part of video memory designated as the frame buffer and
scrolls more image onto your display.

While hardware panning simulates a larger display
than you own, it's not a substitute for a large monitor.
Hardware panning is fine for occasional work, but if
you find yourself constantly dragging your mouse pointer around, trying to find the right part of the image,
consider investing in a larger monitor.

rhardware sprite

A portion of display adapter resources reserved for a small graphical element, such as a cursor or mouse pointer, that overlays the rest of the displayed image. The sprite enables the element to be moved around with simple commands, without redrawing the rest of the screen. IBM's **XGA** was the first video standard to include a hardware sprite.

horizontal frequency

The measurement of the number of times per second a **monitor** draws a horizontal line on its **display**. Typically measured in kilohertz (KHz), horizontal frequency is rarely an issue in comparing monitors. *Compare* **vertical frequency**.

horizontal retrace

The process by which the **yoke** directs a **CRT's** electron beam from the end of one scan line to the beginning of the next. Though it occurs very fast, horizontal retrace time cannot be ignored by the display adapter because the yoke requires an instant to adjust its magnetic field.

interlaced

A method of screen drawing in which the **electron guns** scan every other horizontal line from top to bottom, then return to the top and scan the lines that they missed on the first pass. This scheme is a somewhat sneaky way of doubling the monitor's apparent **frame rate**, but your eyes may not fall for the trick. To some people, interlaced monitors seem to flicker, causing eyestrain and headaches. *Compare* **non-interlaced**.

While not everyone sees flicker in interlaced monitors, such monitors have a reputation for it. Try to buy a non-interlaced monitor, or at least try out any interlaced monitor you're considering buying.

LCD

See **liquid-crystal display.**

LED

See **light-emitting diode.**

---

light-emitting diode (LED)

An electronic device that emits light when current flows through it. Though LEDs are often used as indicators and warning signals, a marketable LED **display** for portable computers has not yet been developed because LEDs require much more electricity than **LCDs.**

---

line rate

See **horizontal frequency.**

---

liquid crystal display (LCD)

The **display** found most frequently in portable PCs. LCDs are popular because they can generate sharp images with high **contrast** while using very little electricity.

An LCD consists of two sheets of plastic, holding a special liquid between them. The liquid is comprised of rod-shaped "nematic" molecules that darken when a current is applied to them. The **monitor** hardware sends electricity to individual **pixels** by a variety of means—**passive matrix, dual-**

| liquid crystal display (LCD) | MPR II |

scanned passive matrix, or **active matrix**—which darkens the liquid in a particular pattern.

To enhance the contrast of an LCD, display designers use special lighting schemes, including **backlighting** and **edgelighting**, which make it easier to see an LCD, especially in sunlight or other bright conditions.

| monitor |

The **display** and its attendant hardware. Don't use "monitor" and "display" interchangeably—while the two are often confused, they're not the same thing. The display is solely the **CRT, LCD**, or whatever other device is used to generate images, while the monitor includes the display, its support circuitry, and the cabinet in which the whole assembly is contained. *Compare* **display**.

| MPR I |

A standard adopted by the government of Sweden to limit **electromagnetic radiation** emissions—thought by some scientists to be harmful—from monitors. The more stringent **MPR II** standard replaced MPR I in 1990.

Some monitor manufacturers claim their monitors satisfy the "Swedish standard" when they meet only MPR I rules. Make sure the monitor you buy satisfies MPR II specifications, or, better still, **TCO** rules.

| MPR II |

A stringent Swedish standard for limiting **electromagnetic radiation** emissions from monitors. MPR II measures x-radiation, static electricity, and electrical and magnetic fields at a variety of locations around the monitor. MPR II-compliant monitors are well-shielded to prevent possibly dangerous rays from escaping.

Though MPR II-compliant monitors typically cost more than other monitors, the extra expense may be worth it. Be sure to get an MPR II-certified monitor, though. Some manufacturers will claim compliance with the "Swedish standard" when their products comply with only **MPR I**. Better still, look for monitors that comply with **TCO** standards, which are even more stringent than MPR II.

monochrome

A term used to describe **monitors** that are capable of displaying only one color. Early **MDA** adapters showed only green or amber text on a black background. Some low-end portable PCs still feature monochrome displays, but color monitors are standard on modern desktop computers and very common on portables.

Though you may be able to save as many as a few hundred dollars by buying a portable PC with a monochrome screen, seriously consider buying one with a color display. Graphical environments such as Windows and OS/2 rely on colors to help differentiate on-screen information.

multiscan monitor

A **monitor** that is able to detect the **refresh rate** generated by the video adapter (see Chapter 10), and adjust itself automatically in response. See Figure 11.1.

non-interlaced

A method of screen drawing in which the **electron guns** scan each line from top to bottom, then return to the top and scan the lines sequentially again. Non-interlaced **monitors** are less likely to flicker than **interlaced** monitors.

Non-interlaced monitors are worth the premium price they command. A screen that flickers quickly leads to eyestrain and headaches.

overscan	passive matrix

Figure 11.1 *Multiscan monitor*

---

overscan

The margin by which an image generated on a **CRT** display is larger than the frame created by the **monitor** housing. A little bit of overscan may be desirable for a couple of reasons. First, image **brightness** and **resolution** are easier to control at the center of a CRT image than at the edges, and hiding the fuzzy and distorted edges behind the monitor case may make the image look better. Second, CRT images tend to shrink over the years, and some overscan in a new monitor may disappear in time. *Compare* **underscan.**

> Make sure you know a monitor's image size as well as its screen size. A monitor with excessive overscan is wasteful and hard to use.

---

passive matrix

A variety of LCD that features a conductive grid with a **pixel** at each intersection of a vertical and horizontal wire. The pixels darken when current flows through both conductors.

Passive matrix LCDs are inferior to **active matrix** designs because of their slow vertical refresh rates—often fewer than 15 screen redraws per second—but they are inexpensive. *Compare* **dual-scan passive matrix**.

pel

See **pixel**.

persistence

The length of time **phosphor** continues to glow after it is struck by an electron beam. Persistence lets a display appear uniformly bright to the human eye. Without it, the **display** would appear bright in the area recently scanned by the electron beam and dark everywhere else.

phosphor

A chemical powder placed on the inside of a **CRT display**. Phosphors have **persistence**, which allows a display to appear uniformly bright to the human eye.

Different types of phosphor give off light of different colors when struck by electrons. Color CRTs have three different kinds of phosphor: one for red, one for blue, and one for green. The three kinds are painted on the inside of the display with great precision—usually in three-dot clusters called color triads but sometimes, in Trinitron-type monitors, in vertical stripes. The light emitted by the different phosphors blends and creates the variety of colors that appear on a display.

picture element

See **pixel**.

picture tube

See **cathode ray tube**.

pixel

The smallest element of a displayed image; often abbreviated to pel. When operating at its highest possible resolution, a pixel in a color **display** consists of a cluster of three **phosphors**, each of which glows a different color when struck by electrons. A pixel can comprise several clusters if the monitor is operating at less than its maximum resolution. In a typical color **CRT**, pixels are composed of phosphors that glow red, green, and blue.

Under direction from the display adapter and **monitor** circuitry, **electron guns** selectively shoot electrons at the phosphors in pixels. The pattern in which the electrons strike the phosphors and cause them to glow creates the color that appears on the display. For example, an image of a cherry would be made up of pixels with their red phosphors energized.

reflective liquid-crystal display (reflective LCD)

A **liquid crystal display** that uses no special lighting scheme to enhance its contrast and instead relies only on light from outside sources to differentiate dark pixels from light ones. Reflective LCDs are hard to see in brightly lit environments, so be sure to get **edgelighting** or **backlighting** if you plan to use your portable computer with a reflective LCD outdoors.

refresh rate

The speed, measured in cycles per second (Hz), at which a monitor's cathode guns re-energize the **phosphors** that generate the screen display. The higher the refresh rate, the lower the risk that you'll see eye-straining **flicker**. A monitor that displays a resolution of 1280 x 1024 at a refresh rate of at least 72 Hz will appear to be flicker-free.

resolution

 A measure of the fineness with which a **display** can show image details. Resolution is typically measured in **pixels**, as in "640-by-480 pixel resolution," which means a display can show an image containing 640 pixels horizontally and 480 pixels vertically. You should consider both display size and **dot pitch** along with resolution specifications, since a 21-inch monitor with 640-by-480-pixel resolution will either have severe **underscan** or very large dot pitch. Likewise, a 14-inch monitor with 1,024-by-768-pixel resolution will display That is too small to read comfortably.

scan rate

See **refresh rate.**

screen blanking

A minimal power conservation method that initiates a **sleep mode,** in which the screen is blanked, at the point that a screen saver utility kicks in. Although this power conservation method is inferior to the **Display Power Management Signaling (DPMS)** standard, it does not require a DPMS-compatible display adapter.

shadow mask

A perforated metal plate inside a **CRT** display that prevents each electron beam from striking incorrect **pixels.** CRT manufacturers carefully align the holes in the shadow mask—which is typically made of Invar, an alloy that expands very little as it heats—to allow the electrons from the blue **electron gun** to hit only **phosphors** that glow blue, for example. Although **aperature grill** designs are said to deliver crisper foccus. Shadow masks are prefered by some designers because the pixels they generate are precisely round (rather than cylindrical, as in the case of aperature grills.

sleep mode

In an **Energy Star**-compliant **monitor** that conserves power using **screen blanking** or **Display Power Management Signaling (DPMS)**, a low-power mode in which the monitor blanks the screen after a period of disuse. However, the monitor keeps its cathode guns warm, so that the image can be restored instantly at the press of a key.

slot pitch

The distance by which the wires in the **aperture grille** of a **Trinitron**-type monitor are separated. **Screen pitch** is a more accurate measure of the fineness of a Trinitron monitor's resolution.

snow

See **video noise**.

TCO

The Swedish labor union for white-collar workers, which has developed a standard for reduced **electromagnetic radiation** emissions even stricter than **MPR II**. The TCO standard makes the same measurements as MPR II and requires the same readings, but at a distance of 30 centimeters from the monitor instead of 50 centimeters as for MPR II. Few monitors sold in the United States are TCO-certified, but TCO's standards for electromagnetic radiation emissions are the strictest in the world.

tensioning wire

One of two or three thin wires that run horizontally across the **aperture grille** of a **Trinitron**-type **monitor** to keep the grille wires aligned. Though tensioning wires are extremely fine, their shadows can sometimes be seen on the screen, most easily in pure white images. Be sure to check for tensioning wire shadows before you buy a Trinitron-type monitor.

TFT

See **active matrix.**

thin film transistor (TFT)

See **active matrix.**

three-gun tube

The sort of tube found in a color **CRT**. Each of the three **electron guns** emits electrons that are directed toward **phosphors** that glow in a particular color— red, green, or blue. Even color monitors with so-called one-gun tubes really have three-gun tubes. Their three guns are combined into a single assembly, but they operate independently.

transistor-transistor logic (TTL) monitor

The earliest type of **monochrome** PC **monitor**, TTL monitors accept only digital video signals and are compatible only with **MDA** and Hercules display adapters. Some low-end computers use TTL monitors with Hercules adapters today, but you should avoid them in favor of the sharper and more versatile **VGA** or Super VGA video specifications.

Trinitron

A type of **CRT** that uses an **aperture grille** instead of a **shadow mask** to prevent electron beams from striking incorrect **phosphors**. An invention of the Sony Corporation, Trinitron monitors were designed to have brighter screens than traditional shadow-mask monitors. In reality, Trinitron monitors are no brighter than other types of monitors, but they do not have the problems of unevenly bright displays that plague shadow-mask monitors. On the other hand, Trinitron monitors have **tensioning wires** that can cause unwanted shadows on the screen.

Sony's patents on Trinitron technology began expiring in 1991, and other manufacturers began working with the technology immediately. Mitsubishi manufactures Diamondtron monitors that use aperture-grille technology.

See also **slot pitch**, screen pitch.

TTL monitor

See **transistor-transistor logic monitor.**

underscan

The margin by which a monitor's image size is smaller than its screen size. Underscan creates the black borders that commonly appear around images on **CRT** displays. Underscan represents a mixed blessing, since it ensures that the entire displayed image can be seen, but it leaves the image edges in view, which are sometimes distorted and dark in comparison to the center of the image. Since CRT images shrink as monitors age, underscan may be more pronounced in older monitors. *Compare* **overscan.**

Since CRT images shrink over time, be sure you actually see a used monitor in operation before you buy it. You don't know how pronounced the underscan is without checking.

vertical frequency

The number of times per second a **monitor** redraws its displayed image, scanning all its horizontal lines in sequence from top to bottom. Typically measured in Hertz (Hz), vertical frequency has a great deal to do with a monitor user's comfort. Monitors with vertical frequencies of less than 70 Hz can appear to flicker, especially under fluorescent lighting, and cause headaches and eyestrain. *Compare* **horizontal frequency.**

vertical refresh rate

The rate, measured in cycles per second (Hz), at which a monitor repaints the screen from top to bottom. In practice, it is the vertical refresh rate (not the horizontal) that determines the monitor's ability to display data without noticable **flicker.**

vertical retrace

The process by which the electrons from the **electron guns** in a **CRT**, after completing a scan, are directed from the bottom of the **display** to the top in preparation for another scan. Though the guns do not actually move, the **yoke** needs time to adjust its magnetic field. During vertical retrace, blanking is in effect to prevent an unwanted diagonal streak from appearing on the screen.

vertically flat

A characteristic of **Trinitron**-type and some other **CRTs**. Vertically flat monitors, instead of being curved along two axes like a sphere, are curved along only one, like a cylinder. Vertically flat monitors offer slightly reduced distortion. *Compare* **flat-square, flat tension-mask.**

video amplifier

Part of the **monitor** hardware that boosts the low-voltage signals received from the **display adapter**. The low-voltage signals must be strengthened in order to drive the **electron guns** that actually create the image on the **CRT**. **Monochrome** monitors have only one video amplifier, while color monitors have three carefully balanced amplifiers, one for each electron gun.

video noise

Often called "snow," video noise appears as white dots in random locations on a **display**. Video noise can occur when the **display adapter** sends information about a **pixel** to the **monitor** while the **video memory** address that handles that pixel is being updated by the CPU (Chapter 4).

Though it is rarely a problem in modern PCs, video noise occurred frequently in **CGA** monitors when the user scrolled the screen faster than the CPU could update the video memory.

VGA

See **Video Graphics Array** in Chapter 10.

XGA

See **Extended Graphics Array (XGA)** in Chapter 10.

yoke

In a **CRT**, the group of electromagnets that steer electrons from the **electron guns** to their destination on the **display**. The circuitry inside the **monitor**, under direction of the display adapter, controls the yoke.

The yoke is one of the monitor's most crucial components; properly adjusted, it assures sharp focus and good **convergence**. But the yoke's magnets are glued in place. Rough shipping can dislodge them. If you order a monitor by mail, insist on a 30-day money-back guarantee.

Disk Drives

This chapter surveys the terms you're likely to encounter when your considering storage media—floppy disks, floppy disk drives, hard disk drives, and tape backup units. (CD-ROM drives are covered in Chapter 13.) Of crucial concern are a prospective hard disk drive's **interface standard**, its **average access time**, and its capacity (the bigger, the better).

The good news is that hard disk drives are easier to install, faster and bigger, and cheaper than ever before. If you're shopping for a system, don't settle for anything less than 1 GB (one billion characters) of hard disk storage.

| 2 1/2-inch floppy disk | 3 1/2-inch floppy disk |

2 1/2-inch floppy disk

A **floppy disk** with a 2 1/2-inch diameter and a 720 KB capacity. Contained in a plastic **shell** like the more-popular 3 1/2-inch floppy disk, Zenith introduced 2 1/2-inch floppy disks in one of its portable computers in 1989. The disks did not win acceptance in the marketplace because no other manufacturer adopted the standard, leaving users of the Zenith portable unable to exchange data on disk with anyone else.

3 1/2-inch floppy disk

 A **floppy disk** with a diameter of 3 1/2 inches and a capacity as high as 2.88 MB. Because of their high capacity, durability and convenient size (really cool PC users walk around with several disks stuffed in their breast pockets), 3 1/2-inch floppy are the most popular floppy disks today. Since they are contained in a sturdy plastic **shell** with a sliding metal door to protect the recording **medium**, you don't need to keep 3 1/2-inch floppy disks in a special sleeve like **5 1/4-inch floppy disks**.

 Don't buy a PC without a 3 1/2-inch **high-density floppy disk drive**. Though many data-transfer jobs can be handled by **modem** or **CD-ROM** (Chapter 13), there's no substitute for saving files on a disk for mailing or storage.

Also, don't forget that although Macintosh computers and PCs both use 3 1/2-inch floppy disks, the two encode data onto them in different ways. Without special software, a PC cannot use a Macintosh disk and a Macintosh cannot use a PC disk. The Macintosh includes the necessary software, however PCs do not.

| 3 1/2-inch floppy disk | 5 1/4-inch floppy disk |

Figure 12.1 *A standard 3.5-inch floppy disk*

| 5 1/4-inch floppy disk |

An obsolete type of **floppy disk**. Although the earliest PCs used 5 1/4-inch floppy disks, the disks' awkward size and special handling requirements caused the **3 1/2-inch floppy disk** to gain favor. Though two floppy-disk drives—one 5 1/4-inch, one 3 1/2-inch—were standard equipment on computers in the late 1980s and early 1990s, most new computers now have only a 3 1/2-inch **high-density floppy disk** drive.

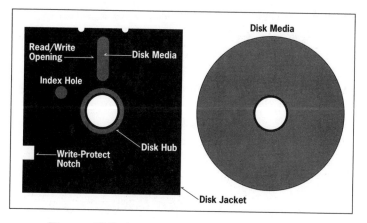

Figure 12.2 *A standard 5.25-inch floppy disk*

765

A controller chip that handles the grunt work of **floppy disk** operation in a **floppy disk controller**. The 765 regulates the flow of data between the disk and the central processing unit (see Chapter 4). Because it can be programmed with Basic Input-Output System (BIOS) (see Chapter 8) instructions, the 765 has been used in floppy disk controllers for more than a decade.

8-inch floppy disk

An ancient type of **floppy disk**, similar in appearance to the **5 1/4-inch floppy disk**, in which the recording medium is fused to a circle of plastic eight inches in diameter. Introduced in 1971 and popular for most of that decade, 8-inch floppy disks hold one megabyte of data.

access time

See **average access time**.

active termination

A means of ending a chain of **Small Computer System Interface (SCSI)** devices. Active termination can reduce electrical interference problems in a long chain of SCSI devices. *Compare* **passive termination, forced perfect termination**.

actuator

See **head actuator**.

Advanced SCSI Programming Interface (ASPI)

A means of defining how of **Small Computer System Interface (SCSI)** devices interact with one another and the rest of a PC developed by the Adaptec Corporation. ASPI uses driver software for each device and ASPI driver software that controls the devices' access to the SCSI interface adapter and is the most popular means of controlling SCSI devices on an IBM-compatible PC.

areal density

A measure of how much information can be packed onto the surface of a **hard disk** or **floppy disk**. Typically expressed in megabits per square inch (Mb/in^2), areal density is determined mainly by the smoothness of the disk surface and the size of the recording-medium particles. Modern hard disks have areal densities of between 100 and 200 Mb/in^2.

ASPI

See **Advanced SCSI Programming Interface (ASPI)**.

AT Attachment (ATA)

Synonymous with **Integrated Drive Electronics (IDE)**.

ATA Packet Interface (ATAPI)

A standard for attaching a **CD-ROM drive** (Chapter 13) to an **Integrated Disk Electronics (IDE)** interface. For more information on ATAPI, see Chapter 13.

ATA-2

See **Enhanced IDE**.

ATA-3

A scheme—still deep in the planning stages—for attaching **hard disk drives**, CD-ROM drives (Chapter 13), **tape**

backup unit, and other recording media to PCs. ATA-3, which probably won't be standardized until late 1995 or early 1996, will replace **Enhanced IDE** and should vastly improve the **throughput** of recording devices.

ATAPI

See **ATA Packet Interface (ATAPI)**.

automatic head parking

A feature of modern **hard disk drives** that moves the **read/write head** to the **landing zone** when power is cut off and holds it there until the disk stops spinning, preventing the head from crashing into the recording medium somewhere it shouldn't. Older drives require you to issue a command to move the head to the landing zone.

average access time

The average time a **hard disk drive** requires to begin transferring data to the computer. This time equals the **average seek time** plus the average **latency** (the time it takes for the disk to spin to the place where the data is stored). Expressed in milliseconds (ms), lower average access times are better than higher ones. Older hard disk drives have average access times of about 120 ms; newer models have average access times that are less than 10 ms.

Don't confuse average access time with **average seek time**, a figure that some manufacturers use in an attempt to portray their drive's performance in the best possible light. Always compare drives using average access time.

average seek time

The average time a **hard disk drive** requires to move the **read/write head** from one location above the **platter** to another. This is an incomplete measurement of drive performance because it does not include **latency**.

bad sector

A **sector** on a **hard** or **floppy disk** that contains a manufacturing error preventing it from storing data accurately. Low-level formatting usually identifies bad sectors and marks them as unusable in the **File Allocation Table (FAT)**, reducing disk capacity slightly but saving you the hassle of lost data. Many disks have bad sectors; a disk with one or two of them is not defective.

bad track

A **track** on a **hard** or **floppy disk** that contains a **bad sector**. Bad tracks are marked as unusable in the disk's **File Allocation Table (FAT)** during formatting and usually cause no trouble, unless track 0 is bad. A disk with a bad track 0 is unusable and must be replaced.

band-stepper actuator

A mechanism that moves the **read/write head** of a **hard disk drive** one **track** at a time from the center of the **platter** to its edge and back again under direction of a **hard disk controller**. Band-stepper actuators rely on a **stepping motor** and a track, called the band, to position the read/write head over the recording medium. Band-stepper actuators are less common than **servo-voice coil actuators** in modern hard disk drives.

Bernoulli box

A disk drive manufactured by Iomega Corporation that uses airflow to hold a spinning flexible disk near a

read/write head. Bernoulli drives, named after the Swiss mathematician who figured out the physics behind aircraft, sustain less damage from head crashes than traditional **hard disk drives**, but tend to wear out relatively quickly.

bias field

A magnetic field generated by a **read/write head** that alters the magnetic character of a disk's recording medium. The **disk controller** alters the head's bias field.

binder

The "glue" that holds a recording **medium** such as ferrous oxide in place on the surface of a disk. Before the advent of **thin-film magnetic media**, disk manufacturers mixed particles of recording medium, and often a lubricant, with binder. A thin layer of this slurry was then applied to the **substrate**, often by **sputtering**.

buffer

A cache memory unit, built into a **hard disk drive**, that stores frequently-accessed data so that it does not have to be retrieved from the hard disk again. A buffer of 32K or 64K can greatly improve a drive's performance.

certified

Warranted by the manufacturer to hold a certain amount of data with accuracy. A disk might be certified to hold 1.44 MB of data.

closed-loop actuator

A mechanism that moves the **read/write head** of a hard disk drive and sends signals to the **hard disk controller** to confirm that it has moved. Since the controller circuitry of a **hard disk drive** with a closed-loop actuator can tell where the read/write head is with greater accuracy than drives with **open-loop activators**, it can pack data closer together. Drives with closed-loop actuators, nearly universal on modern hard disk drives, have higher **areal densities** than those with open-loop actuators.

---

cluster

The smallest piece of disk space a file can occupy under the MS-DOS operating system. Clusters consist of four **sectors**. Some operating systems, including the High Performance File System (HPFS) of OS/2, do not use clusters. Instead, they use sectors as their basic storage units.

---

coercivity

The resistance of a recording medium to changes in its magnetic character. Measured in oersteds, coercivity indicates how quickly a magnetic medium will allow information recorded on it to fade. Typical **hard** and **floppy disks** have coercivities of about 600 oersteds, while **magneto-optical disks** have coercivities 10 times higher, making them well-suited for archiving data. **CD-ROM** disks (Chapter 13) do not have coercivity measurements because they rely on optical signals, not magnetic signals, to store information.

---

common command set

A software control protocol for recording devices, first included in the **SCSI-2** interface standard. The common command set helps of **Small Computer System Interface (SCSI)** devices from different manufacturers work well on a single daisy chain.

constant angular velocity (CAV)

A disk-reading method in which the **platter** spins at a constant rate. Since the speed of rotation is constant, the linear velocity (the speed at which the recording medium passes under the read/write head) varies with the head's location.

The linear velocity is higher when the head is near the perimeter of the platter than when it is near the center. To get an idea of how linear velocity varies in a constant angular velocity recording, imagine you're holding an old-fashioned vinyl record album. Think about putting your finger on the edge of the label and dragging your finger around it, taking one second to complete the circle. Now imagine putting your finger on the edge of the album and taking a second to drag your finger around the record's circumference. You had to move your finger a lot faster when it was near the outer edge than when it was near the label, even though you completed both revolutions on the same amount of time.

Even though constant angular velocity recording does not maximize **hard disk drive** capacity—constant linear velocity recording would allow more sectors to fit on the outer tracks—it keeps down **latency**. If a disk had to change speed for the read/write head to do its work, it would take much longer for the disk to access data. *Compare* **constant linear velocity recording**.

constant linear velocity (CLV)

A disk-reading method in which the **platter** spins faster as the **read/write head** nears the **spindle**, ensuring that the same amount of recording medium passes under the head in a given amount of time regardless of how far the head is from the spindle. *Compare* **constant angular velocity recording**.

Constant linear velocity recording allows efficient use of disk space since it can pack more sectors into the outermost tracks than constant angular velocity can. CD-ROM disks (Chapter 13) and a few kinds of magneto-optical (MO) disks use constant linear velocity recording to maximize their capacities. On the other hand, constant linear velocity recording does not suit hard disk drives because too much time is required to accelerate or decelerate the platter. This would increase **average access time** to levels that are unacceptable for a read/write medium in nearly constant use by the computer.

contact head

A variety of **read/write head** that, instead of flying at low altitude over the recording medium of a **hard disk**, scoots across the disk's surface on a thin film of lubricant. The advantage of a contact head is twofold. First, a read/write head moving across the surface of a disk cannot crash into the recording medium—it's already there. Second, a read/write head moving directly on the disk improves **areal density**, since it can pack as much information onto the disk as the recording medium can handle. Contact heads are rare, but because of their advantages over traditional disks, they may become more common in the future.

controller

The circuitry that operates a **hard** or **floppy disk drive**, usually mounted directly to the drive mechanism. *See* **hard disk controller, floppy disk controller.**

Curie temperature

The temperature at which a material's **coercivity** changes dramatically. **Magneto-optical (MO) disk drives** use the Curie temperature phenomenon to encode data on their recording media. At room temperature, the coercivity of the recording medium of an MO disk is very high—several thousand oersteds. It is nearly impossible to change the magnetic character of MO media at room temperature. But when a laser heats a tiny patch of the material past its Curie temperature, the coercivity drops to a few hundred oersteds, and the **read/write head** can easily change the magnetic characteristics of the medium.

cylinder

An element of hard disk **geometry** that consists of all the **tracks** of a given number on all a **hard disk drive's platters**. For example, the outermost tracks on each of four platters, taken together, comprise a cylinder. Typical hard disks have between 312 and 2048 cylinders, and always have the same number of tracks per platter.

DASD

See **Direct Access Storage Device (DASD)**.

data striping

Dividing data among several different **hard disk drives**. A data-striping scheme might put half of each byte in a data file on one disk and half on another, or put one bit of each byte on each of eight hard disk drives. Data striping, especially when individual bits are written to more than one disk, can help protect against drive failure and is key to **Redundant Arrays of Inexpensive Disks (RAID)**.

data transfer rate

The speed at which, in theory, a **hard disk drive** can transfer recorded information to the PC in which it is installed. Measured in megabits per second (Mbits/sec), megahertz (MHz), or megabytes per second (MB/sec), a higher data transfer rate is better than a lower one.

Data transfer rate is a theoretical specification only. It is calculated by engineers to indicate how well a disk *could* work under perfect conditions that can't exist on any real-life PC. **Throughput**, rather than data transfer rate, is a better measurement of how well a hard disk drive works under realistic conditions.

Direct Access Storage Device (DASD)

IBM's term for a **hard disk drive** installed in a mainframe computer.

disk drive

A **random-access** data-storage device that records information on a round surface covered with recording **medium**. Several types of disk drives exist, including **floppy disk drives**, **hard disk drives**, **magneto-optical (MO) disk drives**, **floptical disk drives**, and CD-ROM drives (Chapter 13).

diskette

A **floppy disk**, usually a **5 1/4-inch** or **3 1/2-inch** model. The term "diskette" was first applied to the 5 1/4-inch floppy disk, which looks petite in comparison to the once-ubiquitous **8-inch floppy disk**.

double-density floppy disk

An obsolete type of **floppy disk** that eliminates the synchronization bits from **single-density** recording techniques and lets you pack about 720K of data onto a disk. **High-density floppy disks**, which require a special **floppy disk drive**, have replaced double-density models, so be sure your PC has a high-density 3 1/2-inch floppy disk drive.

double-sided floppy disk

A **floppy disk** with two recording surfaces, one on each side of a circle of flexible plastic. Though a few obsolete **5 1/4-inch floppy disks** recorded data on only one side, all modern **3 1/2-inch** and 5 1/4-inch floppy disks, including **double-density** and **high-density** models, can record data on both of their sides.

drive activity indicator

A light, usually mounted on the case's front panel, that glows when a disk drive is doing work. Drive activity indicators in **floppy disk drives** turn on whenever the disk is spinning. Indicators in **hard disk drives**, in which the disk spins whenever the computer is turned on, illuminate only when a read or write operation is underway. (Indicators for hard disk drives are usually on the case of the PC and are connected directly to the hard drive.)

drive arrays

Groups of **hard disk drives** that work together to improve speed or offer data protection. Drive arrays may divide files' data among two or more disks, mirror the data on one disk to another, or some combination of the two. *See* **Redundant Array of Inexpensive Disks (RAID)**.

DMSR

See **Dual-Stripe Magneto-Resistive (DSMR) head**.

dual-actuator hard disk

A hard disk with two **read/write heads,** each of which moves over the recording medium by its own actuator. First developed by Conner Peripherals, dual-actuator hard disks can cut **average access time** in half because the needed data is never more than half a revolution away from one of the heads. Dual-actuator hard disks also allow simultaneous read and write operations. Unfortunately, few operating systems take advantage of this capability.

Dual-Stripe Magneto-Resistive (DSMR) head

A recently-introduced variation on **magneto-resistive (MR) head** technology that reduces a **hard disk drive's** susceptibility to electrical interference from the outside environment. The result is a 75 to 100 percent improvement in a hard drive's real capacity. The term "dual stripe" refers to the fact that the head is composed of separate read and write elements, each optimized for its function.

ESDI

See **Enhanced Small Device Interface (ESDI).**

elevator seeking

An advanced hard-disk data-hunting technique, often used with drive arrays, that reduces **average access time.** A **hard disk controller** that uses elevator seeking organizes seek requests from the central processing unit (Chapter 4) to minimize jumping among **tracks.** It instructs the **read/write head** to get data from the innermost tracks first and progress to the outer tracks, then tells it to handle other seek requests in order as it heads back to the innermost tracks.

Enhanced ATA

See **ATA-2.**

Enhanced IDE (E-IDE)

A standard for connecting **hard disk drives** and CD-ROM drives (Chapter 13) to PCs. The Enhanced IDE standard allows the use of high-capacity hard disk drives (the **Integrated Drive Electronics (IDE)** standard limits drives to 528 MB) and enables the user to connect four hard disk drives to a single host adapter, a **master** and a **slave** disk on each of two cables. The maximum capacity of a Enhance IDE drive is 8.4 GB. *Compare* **Integrated Device Electronics (IDE), Small Computer System Interface (SCSI).**

Enhanced IDE has all but supplanted SCSI now that high-capacityE-IDE drives are available. SCSI drives are often slower, and more expensive, than their E-IDE counterparts. To get the most out of E-IDE, you need an E-IDE controller that is designed to work with a VESA local bus or PCI bus (see Chapter 6).

Enhanced Small Device Interface (ESDI)

An improvement on the **ST412/506 hard disk drive** interface protocol developed by the Maxtor corporation. ESDI uses control signals similar to, but not exactly compatible with, those of ST412/506. Like ST412/506, the ESDI standard calls for a data cable and a control cable between the hard disk drive and the **host adapter**. The ESDI standard is faster than the ST412/506 standard, but it has been outmoded by the **Integrated Drive Electronics (IDE)** and **Small Computer System Interface (SCSI)** specifications, which are even faster.

extra-high-density floppy disk

A **floppy disk** designed to work in a drive with two heads—a traditional **read/write head** and a special erase head that prepares the recording **medium** for the read/write head. Extra-high-density floppy disks (all of which have diameters of 3 1/2 inches) have a theoretical capacity of 4 MB, but hold 2.88 MB when formatted to work with MS-DOS. *Compare* **single-density floppy disk, double-density floppy disk, high-density floppy disk**.

Fast ATA

Synonymous with **Enhanced IDE**.

FAT

See **File Allocation Table (FAT)**.

File Allocation Table (FAT)

Information about file locations and **cluster** usage recorded on any disk used by the MS-DOS operating system. The FAT, recorded on track 0 of a disk, prevents DOS from overwriting clusters that contain useful data and directs the **read/write head** to the information requested by the central processing unit (Chapter 4).

---

fixed disk

IBM's favored term for a **hard disk**.

---

floppy disk

A **random-access storage medium**, comprised essentially of a circle of flexible plastic covered with magnetic recording medium, that may be removed from a **floppy disk drive** for storage or transport. In comparison to **hard disks**, floppy disks store very little data, but they are inexpensive and can easily be moved from one computer to another.

| floppy disk | floptical disk |

Floppy disks for PCs come in two sizes, **3 1/2-inch** and **5 1/4-inch**, and in two data densities, **double-density** and **high-density**. The larger disks are quickly losing popularity, and many new computers have only one 3 1/2-inch floppy disk drive.

floppy disk controller

The circuitry that receives instructions from the **host adapter**, handles the tedious work of moving the **read/write head** of a **floppy disk drive** to find the needed data, and sends the data to the host adapter. The floppy disk controller is usually mounted directly on the floppy disk drive mechanism, and is based on the **765** controller chip.

floppy disk drive

A mechanism for reading and writing information on **floppy disks**. Floppy disk drives consist of a **spindle**, a **spindle motor**, and a **read/write head**. The two common types of floppy disk drive are **5 1/4-inch floppy disk** drives and **3 1/2-inch floppy disk** drives. Each handles only floppy disks of a particular size.

Floppy disk drives also have density capabilities. **High-density floppy disk** drives have narrower read/write heads that let them pack lots of data onto high-density disks. Older drives could handle only **double-density** disks or even (horrors!) **single-density** disks.

Make sure your PC has a high-density 3 1/2-inch floppy disk drive. All other floppy disk drives are obsolete, so don't pay for them unless you have a special need.

floptical disk

A **floppy disk**, almost identical in appearance to standard **3 1/2-inch floppy disks**, that uses an optical-alignment scheme

| floptical disk | forced perfect termination |

to pack data tracks much closer together than standard floppy disks. Floptical disks, which require a special **floptical disk drive**, can hold up to 21 MB of information. By comparison, standard **high-density** 3 1/2-inch floppy disk drives hold only 1.44 MB of data.

The "optical" part of the floptical's name refers only to the optical alignment feature, not to the way in which the disk stores data. Floptical disks store data as magnetic pulses, just like traditional floppy disks. The optical alignment, however, lets the floptical disk drive place data closer together, increasing **areal density** and disk capacity.

| floptical disk drive |

A disk drive that supports the optical alignment feature of **floptical disks**. A floptical disk drive can move its **read/write head** over the recording medium more precisely than a traditional floppy disk drive, allowing it to fit more tracks, and therefore more data (21 MB), onto each disk.

Though the name is somewhat misleading, floptical disk drives do not record data by means of light pulses. Floptical disk drives use optics only to orient their read/write heads on the disks, but actually encode information as magnetic pulses. In fact, floptical disk drives can read from and write to double-density and high-density 3 1/2-inch floppy disks, but without improving the capacities of those disks.

Though floptical disk drives sound like the ideal removable storage medium, they are not popular among PC users. The high cost of floptical drives and diskettes makes them less economical than traditional floppy disk drives.

| forced perfect termination |

An unusual means of ending a chain of **Small Computer System Interface (SCSI)** devices. Forced perfect termination uses diodes to indicate the end of a SCSI daisy chain. *Compare* **active termination, passive termination**.

form factor

A **hard** or **floppy disk drive's** physical size, usually expressed in terms of height. A 5 1/4-inch floppy disk drive fits into a half-height drive bay, while a **hard disk drive** or 3 1/2-inch floppy disk drive fits into a half-height drive bay. The fractions refer to the size of drives in the earliest PCs.

geometry

The physical layout of a **hard disk's** surface. Geometry comprises disk capacity, the number of **tracks**, the number of **sectors** per track, and the **landing zone** location. Disk **setup parameters** include disk geometry figures.

green

Having special electricity-conservation features. Since **hard disk drives** use very little power to begin with, not many are called green. Those that are typically use a certain amount of electricity when reading or writing, a smaller amount when idle, and almost none when they have gone unused for several minutes. The green designation is more important to monitors (Chapter 11), which use a great deal of electricity. *See* Energy Star (Chapter 11).

hard disk

Technically, the solid **platter** that is permanently enclosed within a **hard disk drive**; in practice, the term "hard disk" card "hard disk drive" are used interchangeably. *See* **hard disk drive**.

hard disk card

A **hard disk drive**, **hard disk controller** and **host adapter**, all combined onto a single expansion card (Chapter 1). You can plug a hard disk card into one of your computer's expansion slots (Chapter 3) and avoid the trouble of mounting a hard disk drive in a drive bay and installing cables. However, hard disk cards usually cost more and don't perform as well as separate components, and occupy a valuable expansion slot.

hard disk carrier

A device that gives any **hard disk drive** the advantages of a **removable hard disk** drive, without the performance or expense drawbacks. A hard disk carrier consists of a mount that fits inside a drive bay and an adapter that you attach to your hard disk drive. With a hard disk carrier installed, you plug a drive into its mount before starting your PC and remove it after shutting down. This way, you can keep the hard disk drive in a safe for security or use it in another computer.

hard disk controller

The circuitry that receives instructions from the **host adapter**, handles the tedious work of moving the **read/write head** of a hard disk drive to find the needed data, and sends the data to the host adapter. The hard disk controller is usually mounted directly on the hard disk drive itself. You must configure hard disk controllers on **Integrated Drive Electronics (IDE)** hard disk drives to act as **masters** or **slaves**, depending on your PC's setup.

hard disk drive

A type of **random-access** magnetic storage device in which the magnetic **medium** cannot be removed from the PC case. Hard disk drives store lots of program and data files—typically between 200 MB and 500 MB worth—and can send them to the central processing unit (Chapter 4) quickly. All modern PCs have at least one hard disk drive, and hard disk drive operation greatly benefits overall system performance.

Mechanically, hard disk drives consist of several **platters**, coated with recording medium and mounted on a **spindle**. A **spindle motor** makes the platters spin whenever your PC is on, unlike **floppy disk drives**, which spin only when the CPU needs to read data from or write data to the disks they contain. A special motor called an **actuator** moves several **read/write heads**, one for each side of each platter in most designs, in a straight line from the spindle to the outer edges of the platters. All the heads move together, so they are always in a column with the platters between them.

The recording medium would quickly wear out if the read/write heads actually dragged across their surfaces. Instead, the heads are shaped like tiny airplane wings. The spinning platters create subtle currents of air, on which the heads "fly." They hover within a few microinches of the recording medium, which is close enough to do their work but far enough away for safety. A few hard disk drives have platters coated with viscous lubricant, across which **contact heads** slide.

Under direction from the **hard disk controller**, the heads move to specific **sectors** and **tracks** to read or write data. To read data, the heads sense magnetic signals encoded on the magnetic medium and pass them along to the controller, which sends them to the host adapter. To write data, the heads do just the opposite and they generate their own **bias fields**, which become signals in the magnetic medium.

Several specifications describe hard disk drive performance. Most important among these is **average access time**, which describes how long it typically takes a particular hard disk drive to find the data the CPU asks for. Other important figures include **data transfer rate**, **throughput** (which takes into account the performance of the host adapter), and **latency**.

hard disk drive	head

One of a hard disk drive's most important characteristics is which hard disk drive interface it's designed to work with. The largest drives connect to **Small Computer System Interface (SCSI)** or **SCSI-2** interfaces, but they are often expensive. Less expensive drives connect to the **Enhanced IDE** interface. The least expensive drives connect to the **Integrated Drive Electronics (IDE)** interface, the most common interface today. Older drives attach to the **Enhanced Small Device Interface (ESDI)** or **ST412/506** interfaces.

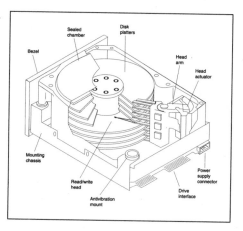

Figure 12.3 Interior view of typical hard drive

hard drive

See **hard disk drive**.

Hardcard

See **hard disk card**.

head

See **read/write head**.

head access aperture

The hole in a **floppy disk's shell** through which the **read/write head** reaches the recording medium. In **3 1/2-inch floppy disks**, a metal shutter covers the head access aperture, but it is exposed in **5 1/4-inch floppy disks**. You should never open a 3 1/2-inch disk's protective shutter, and you should take care that nothing touches the recording medium of a 5 1/4-inch disk.

head actuator

The mechanism that moves the **read/write head** across the surface of a disk. The operation of the head actuator affects **areal density, track-to-track seek time,** and **average access time.** *See* **open-loop actuator, closed-loop actuator, servo-voice coil actuator, band-stepper actuator, dual-actuator hard disk.**

head parking

Moving the **read/write head** of a **hard disk drive** to a point above its **landing zone.** Head parking prevents the read/write head from digging a trench in important data when you turn off the power to your PC. Older hard disks require you to type a command to park the head, but newer ones, with **automatic head parking**, park their heads without instructions from you.

high-density floppy disk

A **floppy disk** designed to work with a narrow **read/write head** to pack extra **tracks**—and thus more data—onto the recording medium. High-density **3 1/2-inch floppy disks** hold as much as 1.44 MB of data, while high-density **5 1/4-inch floppy disks** hold 1.2 MB. *Compare* to **single-density floppy disk, double-density floppy disk, extra-high-density floppy disk.**

host adapter

Circuitry that serves as an interface between a **hard** or **floppy disk drive controller** and the rest of a PC. Some computers have host adapter circuitry built into their motherboards, but most use a special card that plugs into an expansion slot (Chapter 3).

The host adapter, which conforms to an interface standard such as **Integrated Device Electronics (IDE)**, **Enhanced Small Device Interface (ESDI)**, or **Small Computer System Interface (SCSI)**, tells the hard or floppy disk controller what data the central processing unit (Chapter 4) needs, receives the data from the disk controller, and passes it on to the CPU. Many host adapter expansion cards handle both **hard disk drive** and **floppy disk drive** interfaces.

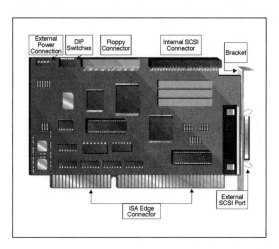

Figure 12.4 A SCSI host adapter

hub ring

On some **5 1/4-inch floppy disks**, the ring of plastic or Teflon that protects the recording medium from wear by the **spindle**. Not all 5 1/4-inch floppy disks, (particularly **high-den-**

sity ones) have hub rings, since they can push a disk out of alignment if applied improperly

---

IDE

See **Integrated Drive Electronics (IDE)**.

---

index hole

The small hole just outside the **hub ring** of a **5 1/4-inch floppy disk**—the equivalent of a human vestigial appendix in the floppy disk world. The original specifications for the 5 1/4-inch floppy disk called for a light in the **floppy disk drive** to shine through the index hole and give the drive controller a reference point as the disk spun. Though a few early drives followed that plan, most relied on magnetically-defined **sector** boundaries and didn't use the index hole at all.

---

indexing

The means by which a **floppy disk drive** places its **read/write head** over the proper **track**. When indexing, the head moves all the way to the outer edge of the disk, then moves back toward the disk's center one track at a time until it reaches the proper one.

Integrated Drive Electronics (IDE)

 An **interface standard** for **hard disk drives**. Sometimes called the AT Attachment interface, IDE requires only two connections to each hard disk drive—a power cable and a data cable. IDE is attractive to computer buyers because it combines low cost and a respectably high **data transfer rate**, and is the most common interface standard on computers a year or more old. As the name implies, the drive includes the control electronics, so IDE drives do not require an expensive adapter card (as **SCSI drives** do).

Unlike **Enhanced IDE** or the **Small Computer System Interface (SCSI)**, IDE allows only two hard disk drives to be connected to a **host adapter**. One of these drives is configured as a **master**, the other as a **slave**. Once you have configured each drive according to its manual—which usually isn't too hard —you can quickly hook them up to the host adapter and get down to business.

IDE is far faster and more flexible than its predecessors, **ST412/506** and **Enhanced Small Device Interface (ESDI)**. However, IDE itself has been outmoded: most new computer systems use the Enhanced IDE interface standard, and some use SCSI or **SCSI-2**.

| interface standard |

A set of specifications that describe how a **hard disk**, **hard disk controller**, and **host adapter** interact with one another and the rest of the PC. ST412/509, **Enhanced Small Device Interface (ESDI)**, **Integrated Drive Electronics (IDE)**, **Enhanced IDE**, and the **Small Computer System Interface (SCSI)** are interface standards.

| interleave factor |

The ratio of **sectors** on a **hard disk drive** that are skipped for each one that is actually used. Interleaving is a method of slowing down a hard disk's peformance so that it doesn't outrun the **microprocessor**. With today's fast microprocessors, interleaving generally isn't required. A disk without **interleaving** has an interleave factor of one (sometimes expressed as 1:1), while a disk that skips 5 sectors for every one that is read has an interleave factor of 6:1. Most modern hard disk drives without **track buffering** have interleave factors of two, while those with track buffering have interleave factors of one.

Don't mess with your computer's hard disk interleave
factor. If you set it too low, you'll lose data.

interleaving

A way of distributing data on a **hard disk drive's** recording
media so the drive does not outrun the rest of the system. Interleaving places the **sectors** of a hard disk in non-sequential order
so there is a pause between sectors, allowing the drive's
electronics and the microprocessor sufficient time to process
the previous sector and prepare for the next. The **interleave
factor** describes the amount of interleaving in a hard disk drive.

Kerr effect

The physical phenomenon that allows **magneto-optical
(MO)** disks to work. The Kerr effect is the tendency of **polarized** light reflected from a magnetized surface to shift its orientation slightly—as much as 7%. The **read/write heads**
of MO drives sense the Kerr shift in the polarized light and
use it to encode data.

landing zone

An area of a **hard disk's** surface designated for physical
contact with the **read/write head**. The read/write head is
parked, either automatically or with a command, over the
landing zone before you shut off the PC. This way, it drifts
to a landing on an unused portion of the recording medium
instead of damaging useful data. See **head parking**.

latency

The time required for the needed piece of data to appear
beneath the **read/write head** of a **hard disk drive**. If a par-

ticular bit has just passed under the head when the **hard disk controller** hears from the central processing unit (Chapter 4) that that bit is needed, the controller must wait for the disk to complete a full rotation before it appears under the head again. A drive's average latency plus its **average seek time** equals the **average access time**, an important measure of a drive's performance.

On average, the latency is half the time required for the disk to complete a revolution—about 8.3 milliseconds on most hard drives, 5.6 milliseconds on some advanced models. **Dual-actuator hard disks** have inherently lower latency because there are two heads to read data, and the needed data is always within half a revolution of one of the two.

LED indicator

See **drive activity indicator**.

liner

The cloth jacket that separates the magnetic **medium of** a **floppy disk** from its **shell**. The liner reduces friction between the medium and the shell and helps sweep dust from the recording surface.

magneto-optical (MO) cartridge

A removable storage device designed for use in a **magneto-optical (MO) drive**. MO cartridges come in two sizes: 5 1/4 inches, which hold up to 1300 MB of data and 3 1/2 inches, which hold up to 230 MB. Like **floppy disks**, cartridges of a particular size may be used only in MO drives of the same size.

magneto-optical (MO) drive

A type of **disk drive** that uses laser technology to increase the **areal density** of a recording **medium**. The recording medium of MO drives has very high **coercivity** making it extremely hard to change its magnetic characteristics. MO disk drives come in two sizes: 5 1/4 inches to handle up to 1300 MB cartridges, and 3 1/2 inches to accommodate 230 MB.

MO drives write data by heating a tiny section of medium past its **Curie temperature** with a laser, changing the magnetic characteristic of that section with a **read/write head**, and letting it cool. As it cools, the coercivity of the section increases again. The high coercivity lets MO drives pack magnetic signals close together, increasing areal density and therefore capacity, and ensures that the information encoded on MO cartridges will not soon fade; experts say it may last 15 years or more.

MO drives read data with help from another useful physical phenomenon, called the **Kerr effect**. Instead of reading the magnetic signals on the recording medium directly, MO drives focus a beam of **polarized** laser light on the recording medium and analyze the light reflected back. The drive interprets the changes in the light's polarization, caused by the Kerr effect, to decode stored information.

Because of their high coercivity under normal conditions, MO technology is great for archiving information. Purely magnetic media, such as tape, floppy drives, and hard disks, may lose data when stored for prolonged periods. The trade-off is performance, since MO drives have poor **throughput** and **average access times** relative to permanent **hard disk drives**.

magneto-resistive (MR) head

A type of **read/write head** with separate reading and writing portions. MR heads, which are used on very fast, high-capacity **hard disk drives** in network servers, significantly increase a disk's **areal density** and **throughput**, and reduce power consumption. MR heads are coated with a special alloy, which behaves more precisely than traditional head materials and allows the drive **controller** to place **tracks** very close together. MR heads are often used with **Partial-Response Maximum-Likelihood (PRML) read-channel technology.**

| master |

The first **Integrated Drive Electronics (IDE) hard disk drive** in a group of two attached to an IDE interface cable. "Master" is a somewhat misleading term, since the master drive does not control the **slave** drive. Instead, the master drive interprets signals from the **host adapter** and sends them along to the slave drive.

When installing two IDE hard disks on an IDE cable, it is important to configure the two drives properly. You must configure the master disk to send commands to the slave disk, and you must configure the slave disk to receive information from the master disk, not the host adapter. Check your drives' manuals for instructions on configuration. Note that you'll have the best chance of getting this to work if both drives are made by the same manufacturer.

| mean time between failures (MTBF) |

A measure of a **hard disk drive's** reliability. Expressed in hours, mean time between failures describes how long a drive will live. A longer MTBF indicates a higher-quality hard disk drive.

Most MTBF ratings are between 200,000 and 1 million hours—22.8 and 114 years, respectively. But don't take this too seriously—MTBF estimates are based on statistical analyses that don't reflect real-world conditions. In practice, you can expect at least five years of continuous service from a good drive—maybe less, maybe more

---

medium

The actual material on a **hard** or **floppy disk** on which the **read/write head** records signals. The first disks used ferrous oxide—rust, essentially—to record magnetic signals. Newer magnetic disks use **thin-film magnetic media** like barium ferride that increase **areal density** and **coercivity**. Other media include **magneto-optical (MO) disks** and **floptical disks**.

MO drive

See **magneto-optical (MO) drive**.

MTBF

See **mean time between failures (MTBF)**.

MR head

See **magneto-resistive (MR) head**.

Multiple-Zone Recording (MZR)

A way to compensate for the inefficient use of recording **medium** capacity in **hard disk drives** that use **constant angular velocity** recording. MZR drives increase the frequency at which they record data near the edge of hard disk platters, packing more data into these areas and increasing drive capacity.

MZR

See **Multiple-Zone Recording (MZR)**.

---

open-loop actuator

A mechanism for moving the **read/write head** across the recording **medium**. Unlike a **closed-loop actuator**, an open-loop actuator gives no feedback to the **hard disk controller** to confirm its location. Therefore, the disk controller has less precise control over the read/write head's location, meaning a drive with an open-loop actuator has lower **areal density** than a closed-loop actuator drive.

Open-loop actuator drives are obsolete. Never buy a drive without a closed-loop actuator.

Partial-Response Maximum Likelihood (PRML) read-channel technology

A **hard disk drive** technology that improves **areal density** and **throughput** by making tracks narrower and speeding up the flow of data between the **read/write head** and the drive **controller**. Typically used in conjunction with **magneto-resistive head** technology, PRML technology is new and expensive, and is found only in network-server hard disk drives with capacities of a 1 gigabyte or more.

---

partition

A division of a **hard disk drive**, created with software for purposes of organization or compatibility with older programs.

partition   platter

A single physical hard disk drive may be divided into several partitions, each with its own drive letter, with an MS-DOS utility called FDISK. "Partition" is also a verb, meaning to create two or more partitions on a single physical disk.

Before version 4, MS-DOS could not support hard disk drives larger than 32 MB, so people had to partition large hard disks into 32 MB pieces. Newer versions of MS-DOS handle large hard disks without trouble, but some people still choose to organize their disks by partitioning them. Partitioning a disk allows you to run more than one operating system, or to set aside part of the disk for encrypting data as a security safeguard.

passive termination

A means of ending a chain of **Small Computer System Interface (SCSI)** devices. Passive termination is the oldest way of ending a SCSI daisy-chain, and works best when there are four or fewer devices in series. *Compare* to **active termination, forced perfect termination**.

plating

A means of coating a **hard disk platter** with a **thin-film magnetic medium**. Plating a platter is similar to galvanizing a nail—the uncoated platter is charged electrically and submerged in liquid that contains molecules of the **medium**. The electric charge attracts the molecules, and they coat the **substrate** evenly. *Compare* **sputtering**.

platter

A disk of metal **substrate** coated with recording **medium**, on which a **hard disk drive** records data. A typical hard disk drive has three to six platters, all mounted on a **spindle** and turned by a **spindle motor**.

polarization

A process by which light waves are made to vibrate in one direction only. You're probably familiar with polarized sunglasses, which cut glare by filtering out light that travels parallel to the ground, such as that reflected from water.

Magneto-optical (MO) drives use polarization to encode and read data. Using the **Kerr effect**, which alters polarization, MO drives can write data to disks and read it back later.

PRML read-channel technology

See **partial response maximum likelihood (PRML) read-channel technology**.

QIC-wide

A **quarter-inch cartridge (QIC)**, used in **tape backup units**, that employs .32-inch wide tape (instead of .25-inch wide tape) for a maximum capacity of 850 MB.

quarter-inch cartridge (QIC)

A cartridge containing 0.25 inch magnetic tape that is used in **tape backup units**.

RAID

See **Redundant Array of Inexpensive Disks (RAID)**.

RAID level 0

Once, RAID level 0 meant no RAID scheme at all, just one or more hard disks with no **data striping**. Now, the term describes a data-striping scheme with no redundancy. Such

| RAID level O | RAID level 3 |

a configuration may improve data-retrieval performance, but offers no protection against physical disk failure.

RAID level 0 & 1

See **RAID level 10.**

RAID level 1

An array of two identical disks, each containing the same data. RAID level 1 allows one disk to fail without data loss, but it is inefficient and uneconomical: you can effectively use only half the physical disk space you have paid for.

RAID level 2

An array of as many as several dozen disks, on which **data striping** occurs. Additionally, RAID level 2 systems have several disks with copies of the striped data that are used to catch and correct errors. RAID level 2 is one of the fastest and safest RAID schemes.

RAID level 3

A scheme similar to RAID level 2 that requires fewer disks but imposes a slight performance penalty. RAID level 3 employs **data striping** like RAID level 2, but its extra disks can only identify errors, not correct them. The array must read the faulty data again, requiring 17 extra milliseconds. Luckily, errors occur infrequently enough in modern **hard disk drives** that the performance penalty occurs rarely. Saving the cost of the extra drives is usually worth the occasional slowdown.

RAID level 4

Instead of using **data striping** of bits as RAID levels 2 and 3 do, RAID level 4 distributes copies of sectors across an array of **hard disk drives**. Like RAID level 3, RAID level 4 requires uses one drive to identify, but not correct, errors in the data stream. RAID level 4 updates the information on its error-checking drive each time data is written to the array, adding some time to write operations.

RAID level 5

The most popular form of RAID protection, RAID level 5 is very similar to RAID level 4, but does not require a dedicated error-checking drive. Instead, RAID level 5 distributes the function of the error-checking drive across all the drives in the array. Because it does not need a special error-checking drive, a RAID level 5 array can contain as few as two **hard disk drives**.

RAID level 6

Essentially, a RAID level 5 array with two separate sets of error-checking information distributed across the array. RAID level 6 allows two **hard disk drives** in the array to fail without any loss of data. Because they maintain two sets of error-checking data, write performance on RAID level 6 arrays is abysmal, but read performance is superb.

RAID level 10

Sometimes called RAID level 0 & 1, RAID level 10 combines the attractions of **RAID level 0** and **RAID level 1**. Like RAID level 0, RAID level 10 employs **data striping**. Like RAID level 1, RAID level 10 maintains two copies of all its data to protect against drive failure.

RAID level 10   read/write head

RAID level 10

RAID level 10 arrays are very fast, since there are two sets of data to work with independently of one another. On the other hand, RAID level 10 arrays are expensive, since they allow you to use only half the disk space you've paid for.

RAID level 53

A combination of **RAID level 0** and **RAID level 3**. A RAID level 53 array uses **data striping** on two RAID level 3 arrays, combining the speed of a RAID level 0 array with the safety of a RAID level 3 array.

random-access storage media

Any storage device, that allows the **read/write head** to work on any part of the data at any time. **Hard** and **floppy disk drives** are examples of random-access media, since their heads can reach any bit they contain almost instantly. Tape devices such as **tape backup units**, on the other hand, are not random-access media because their read/write heads must wait for the proper portion of the tape to appear, a process that could take several seconds.

read/write head

An electromagnet that alters (writes) or senses (reads) magnetic signals on a disk's magnetic **medium**. Under instructions from the **drive controller**, the read/write head flies just above the medium, reading and writing information at particular locations on the disk.

Most **hard** and **floppy disk drives**, have at least two read/write heads, one for each side of the disk. Most hard disk drives have several **platters** on a single **spindle**, and have read/write heads for each side of each platter. *See* **contact head**, **closed-loop actuator**, **open-loop actuator**.

redundant array of inexpensive disks (RAID)

A collection of **hard disk drives** designed to work together to protect data from loss due to equipment failure and improve performance. Originally described in a 1988 paper by three researchers at the University of California at Berkeley, RAID relies on **data striping** and multiple copies of data on several different physical disks to protect against data loss. Array management software handles the mechanics of distributing the data. Since "inexpensive" is a relative term, RAID setups are used mainly on large networks for which tape backups are too slow or otherwise impractical.

There are several RAID schemes, called levels. Each uses a different protocol to protect data while wasting as little space as possible. *See* **RAID Level 0** through **RAID Level 53**.

removable cartridge drive

A hard disk that may be removed from its drive and transported or stored much like a **floppy disk**. Removable hard disks have all the advantages of floppy disks, and can hold more than 100 MB of data. They're not as fast as permanent **hard disk drives**, however, since their read/write heads must be especially bulky to accommodate removable cartridges. Syquest and Bernoulli are two makers of removable cartridge drives.

A removable cartridge drive is a great idea if you're working with sensitive data—you can remove the cartridge and lock it up when you're away from the computer.

SASI

See **Shugart Associates Standard Interface (SASI)**.

SCSI

See **Small Computer System Interface (SCSI)**.

SCSI-2

An improvement on the **Small Computer System Interface (SCSI)** standard, SCSI-2 reduces conflicts between devices and improves **throughput**. SCSI-2, introduced in 1991, includes the **common command set**, which allows devices from different manufacturers to operate together smoothly.

SCSI-3

A standard, still under development, that will increase the potential number of devices in a **Small Computer System Interface (SCSI)** daisy chain to 16. It will also change the way devices use the **common command set** and will allow fiber optic cable connections between devices. SCSI-3 likely will replace **SCSI-2** when it is completed.

sector

The smallest physical division of a disk's surface recognizable by the **read/write head**. Defined by characteristics of the magnetic **medium**, even the tiniest files can occupy no less than one sector on a disk. A **track** is comprised of a number of sectors, though the number of sectors in a track varies based on the disk's physical size.

Operating systems like OS/2, with its High Performance File System (HPFS), can manage disk space sector-by-sector. Other operating systems, including MS-DOS, can't handle individual sectors. MS-DOS combines sectors into groups of four, called **clusters**, and uses the groups as the smallest amount of disk space it can allocate to files.

sector interleaving

See **interleaving**.

See **average access time**.

servo-controlled DC motor

The type of **spindle motor** found in modern **hard disk drives**. Unlike its predecessor, the **synchronous motor**, servo-controlled DC motors are small and inexpensive. They rely on sensors to keep the **platters** spinning at a constant rate, since the speed of servo-controlled DC motors is not tied to the frequency of electrical power from an outlet, they can be as fast or as slow and the design engineers want.

servo-voice coil actuator

A type of **head actuator** that uses an electromagnet pulling against a spring to move the **read/write heads** across the surface of a **hard disk drive's** recording medium. As part of a **closed-loop actuator** system, servo-voice coil actuators constantly receive information about the heads' positions and can adjust their placement with precision. Servo-voice coil actuators are the most popular kind of head actuators in use today.

setup parameters

The information about a **hard disk drive** recorded in a Basic Input-Output System (Chapter 8). Setup parameters include disk capacity, number of **tracks**, **cylinders**, and cylinders at which **write precompensation** should begin.

shell

The cover that protects the recording **medium** of a **floppy disk**. **3 1/2-inch floppy disks** have a fairly rigid plastic shell with a metal shutter to protect the **head access aperture**. **5 1/4-inch floppy disks** have more flexible plastic shells with an unprotected head access aperture, and must be kept in protective sheaths when not in use.

Shugart Associates Standard Interface (SASI)

The progenitor of the **Small Computer System Interface (SCSI)**. Developed by Shugart Associates and NCR in 1981 to link PCs and hard disk drives, SASI served as the seed from which the SCSI standard grew.

single-density floppy disk

An obsolete type of **floppy disk** that requires a synchronization bit to accompany each bit of data. Single-density **5 1/4-inch floppy disks** held 360 KB of data. **Double-density floppy disks**, and later **high-density floppy disks**, made the single-density recording **medium** into museum pieces.

single-sided floppy disk

A **floppy disk** on which data can be recorded on only one side of the substrate. Though single-sided **5 1/4-inch floppy disks** were popular in the early days of PCs, they, like all 5 1/4-inch floppies, are obsolete. There is no such thing as a single-sided **3 1/2-inch floppy disk** for IBM-compatible computers.

slave

The second **Integrated Drive Electronics (IDE) hard disk drive** in a group of two attached to an IDE interface cable. "Slave" is a somewhat misleading term, since the **master** drive does not control the slave drive. Instead, the master drive interprets signals from the **host adapter**, eliminating the need for the slave drive to handle this function. *See* **master**.

slider

On **3 1/2-inch floppy disks,** the moveable piece of plastic in the **shell** that enables and disables **write-protection.** To write-protect a disk, move the slider away from the metal shutter so there is a hole through the shell. To write to a floppy disk, make sure the slider is down so the hole is closed.

Small Computer System Interface (SCSI)

As far as disk drives are concerned, SCSI is another **drive interface.** You may think of it as serving the same function as **Integrated Drive Electronics (IDE)** and **Enhanced IDE,** since it can be used to attach **hard disk drives** to the rest of your PC. But, taken on its own terms, SCSI is much more than a drive interface—it's a way of connecting all sorts of devices, such as **tape backup units,** CD-ROM drives (see Chapter 13), and other peripherals, to your PC.

Until recently, SCSI had a decided speed advantage: The **throughput** of SCSI hard disk drives is considerably higher than that of IDE drives. In addition, SCSI drives are not limited to 540 MB, as IDE drives are. But these advantages have evaporated in the face of **Enhanced IDE** drives, which rival or surpass SCSI in speed and capacity. A remaining SCSI advantage: SCSI also has the ability to connect as many as seven devices on a single host adapter in a "daisy chain," which makes it easy to install peripherals. The current SCSI standard is **SCSI-2.**

If you're thinking about adding SCSI peripherals, it makes good sense to get a system with a SCSI drive. You'll get the SCSI interface, which enables you to connect additional SCSI devices.

spindle

In a **floppy disk drive**, the drive shaft that clamps onto the disk's center and, powered by a **spindle motor**, makes it spin. Spindles may cause wear in **5 1/4-inch floppy disks**, so many of those disks have protective **hub rings**. In a **hard disk drive**, the spindle serves the same function, but it is permanently attached to the **platters**.

spindle motor

The electric motor in a **disk drive** that turns the **spindle**, causing a **floppy disk** or the **platters** of a **hard disk drive** to spin. In a floppy disk drive, the spindle motor turns only when a read or write operation is in progress. A hard disk drive's spindle motor turns constantly, as long as the PC is on.

sputtering

A means of applying **thin-film magnetic media** to the **substrate** of a **hard disk platter**. Sputtering relies on both heat and electrical attraction to coat the substrate smoothly and evenly. *Compare* **plating**.

ST506/412

The **hard disk drive** interface used in IBM XT, AT and early PS/2 models. The ST506/412 standard, developed by Shugart Technology, included a 34-conductor control cable and a 20-conductor data cable. These hard drives were often referred to as Modified Frequency Modulation (MFM) drives or RLL/RLE (Ren Length Limited and Run Length Encoded) drives. Because it transfers data very slowly, the ST506/412 standard is obsolete, replaced by the **Integrated Drive Electronics (IDE)**, **Enhanced Small Device Inter-**

face (ESDI) and **Small Computer System Interface (SCSI)**
standards.

stepper motor

See **stepping motor.**

stepping motor

An electric motor that, instead of spinning constantly, makes
a certain fraction of a turn each time it receives an electrical
pulse. Stepping motors, also called stepper motors, are used
to move the **read/write** head in most **hard** and **floppy disk
drive** designs.

substrate

The material, usually aluminum but sometimes glass in
hard disk drives and plastic in **floppy disks**, to which a
magnetic recording **medium** is affixed. Disk manufacturers
coat the substrate of floppy disks with a mixture of recording medium, **binder**, and sometimes a lubricant. Hard disk
drive manufacturers prefer thin-film magnetic media, which
is applied by **plating** or **sputtering.**

synchronous motor

The type of **spindle motor** used in early hard disk drives. Synchronous motors tie their speeds of rotation to the frequency of the electric current that powers them. Synchronous
motors are bulky and expensive, and require potentially
dangerous high-voltage electricity. They have been replaced
by **servo-controlled DC motors.**

Syquest drive

One of the most popular types of **cartridge drives.** Syquest Technology was the first to market such disks. Because these are SCSI devices, they can be used on other kinds of computers as well as the IBM-compatible PC.

tape backup unit

A tape drive, designed to work with **quarter-inch cartridges (QIC)**, that provides your system with crucial hard disk backup capability. If your hard disk fails, you can restore all your data from the backup tape. *See* quarter-inch cartridge (QIC), **QIC-wide.**

Try to get a unit that matches your hard disk's capacity. You won't have to switch cartridge's while backing up.

thin-film magnetic medium

A type of recording **medium** that replaces coatings of oxide with very thin layers of metals or metal alloys. Thin-film magnetic media have higher **areal densities** than oxide coatings and have higher **coercivities**. They are also more resistant than oxide coatings to scratches that result from contact with the **read/write head**. Thin-film magnetic media are applied by **plating** or **sputtering**.

throughput

A measure of how fast a **hard disk drive** transfers recorded information to the PC in which it is installed. Throughput takes into account operational overhead (the control signals and other administrative details that reduce efficiency) and gives a clear picture of how well a hard disk drive works with the rest of a PC. Measured in kilobytes per second (KB/sec), higher throughput is better. Typical modern hard disk drives have throughputs of several hundred kilobytes per second.

Throughput is a more accurate measure of hard disk drive performance than **data transfer rate** because it shows how fast a disk moves data under real-world conditions. Make sure you get throughput specifications when comparing hard disk drives — data transfer rates aren't enough.

track

One of several dozen concentric circles of recording **medium** that form the surface of a **hard** or **floppy disk**. When the read/write head stops somewhere between the **spindle** and the outer edge of a disk, and the disk spins beneath it, the circle of recording medium that passes underneath the head is one track. Tracks are divided into units called **sectors**.

track buffering

A process in which a **hard disk drive** reads the data recorded on an entire track into memory, regardless of how much of the information on the track the **host adapter** has asked for. Track buffering eliminates the need to optimize your disk's **interleave factor**, since an interleave factor of one is best for all track-buffered hard disk drives. All modern drives and most **Enhanced Small Device Interface (ESDI)** drives have track buffering and should not be interleaved.

track-to-track seek time

The time required for a **hard** or **floppy disk drive** to move its **read/write head** from one **track** to the next. In rating performance, track-to-track seek time is not as important as **average access time**.

transfer rate

See **data transfer rate**.

voice-coil actuator

See **servo-voice coil actuator**.

Winchester

A general term for any magnetic **hard disk drive**. The name "Winchester" derives from the first hard disk drive to use modern **read/write head** technology, the IBM 3030. Computer legend has it that someone nicknamed the drive after the famous Winchester 3030 repeating rifle, the long-range weapon of choice among lawmen and hunters on the American frontier.

write precompensation

The process by which a **hard disk drive** increases power to the **read/write head** as it nears the **spindle** to compensate for the need to pack data into the small **sectors** near the center of the **platters**. A hard disk drive begins write precompensation on a particular **cylinder** of a disk, the number of which is stored in read-only memory (Chapter 5).

write-protect notch

On a **5 1/4-inch floppy disk**, the little groove in the top-left corner that determines whether a disk is **write-protected** or not. To write-protect a disk, wrap one of the protective labels around both sides of the notch (masking tape will work just as well). To unprotect a disk, remove the protective label or tape.

write-proctection

Any means by which a **floppy disk drive** is prevented from writing data to a **floppy disk**. Write-protection prevents you from accidentally deleting your tax records or writing your database file of strudel recipes over your spreadsheet containing winning lottery numbers.

Several methods of write-protection exist. On **3 1/2-inch floppy disks**, you move the plastic **slider** up, so you see a hole, to protect the data. On **5 1/4-inch floppy disks**, you must apply tape over the write-protect notch.

zone-bit recording

Seagate Technologies' preferred term for **Multiple-Zone Recording (MZR)**.

Zoned Constant Angular Velocity (ZCAV)

See **Multiple-Zone Recording (MZR)**.

CD-ROM Drives

This chapter surveys the terms you're likely to encounter when you're contemplating adding a **CD-ROM drive** to your system, or buying a computer with one or more CD-ROM drives.

Although CD-Rom discs are a read-only medium (unless you can afford a pricey **CD-R** drive), they're increasingly indispensable as a distribution medium for voluminous amounts of data, such as multimedia presentations and application programs.

You'll be wise to get the fastest CD-ROM drive that you can afford. Much slower than hard disks, any CD-ROM drive will seem sluggish, but **quad-speed** drives are less sluggish than their **double-speed** counterparts (and not much more expensive).

2X.

See **double speed.**

4X.

See **quad speed.**

6X.

A **CD-ROM drive** capable of transferring data at a rate of 900 kilobytes per second, six times the rate of the earliest CD-ROM drives. Although a 6X drive transfers data 50% faster than a **quad speed** drive, the actual overall speed gain is not as great under normal conditions in which the optical head must first locate the desired data before transferring it to the computer (see **access time**).

access time

The time, measured in thousandths of a second (milliseconds, abbreviated ms), that a **CD-ROM drive** requires to locate the desired information, bring the disc to the correct speed, and initiate the transfer of data to the computer. Older CD-ROM drives required nearly a half-second to begin reading data; today's best drives cut the access time to 150 ms or less.

ATAPI

Acronym for Advanced Technology Attachment Packet Interface. A standard for connecting a **CD-ROM drive** to an Enhanced IDE (E-IDE) hard disk controller.

If your computer is equipped with an Enhanced IDE hard disk controller, installing an ATAPI-based CD-ROM drive can be as simple as hooking up the cables, attaching the drive with screws, and replacing the computer case's lid.

---

buffer

In a **CD-ROM drive**, a bank of random-access memory that serves as a temporary storage area for frequently-accessed data. A buffer substantially speeds a CD-ROM drive's performance frequently-accessed data can be retrieved from the buffer instead of the disk, which is many times slower. The larger the buffer, the better; most drives have at least a 128KB buffer, while the best drives offer buffers of one megabyte.

---

caddy

A plastic tray that holds a compact disc, allowing you to insert it into the drive without getting fingerprints or smudges on the disc's surface. Many **CD-ROM drives** require the use of caddies. The alternative to caddies is an automatic disk loading drawer, similar to those found on audio CD players.

Figure 13.1 A CD-ROM in a standard caddy

CD-DA

Acronym for Compact Disc-Digital Audio. A standard for audio compact discs jointly developed by Philips and Sony in the early 1980s, CD-DA makes possible the production of audio discs containing up to 72 minutes of stereophonic music. Virtually free from audible distortion or noise and relatively immune to damage, audio compact discs quickly replaced LP vinyl records.

CD-I

Acronym for Compact Disc Interactive. A standard developed by Philips for mass-marketed consumer multimedia devices. With CD-I, a single disk can hold up to 72 minutes of standard NTSC video. However, the mass market has not developed and little software is available for this format.

CD-R

An optical disk drive that can record data to a blank compact disk. At least ten times more expensive than read-only **CD-ROM drives**, CD-R drives may be cost-effective for businesses that must archive large amounts of information on a regular basis. In addition, CD-R technology makes it possible for individuals to begin their own CD-ROM publishing businesses with a low initial investment.

CD-ROM

Acronym for Compact Disc-Read Only Memory. A publishing medium that enables information producers to place up to 650 megabytes of information on a small, cheaply-produced optical disc, identical in appearance to a digital audio compact disc (**CD-DA**). Information is stored in the form of tiny pockmarks on the disc's surface, each corresponding to the 1s and 0s of binary data. You can read data from a CD-ROM disk, but you cannot write data to it (which is why it is called "Read-Only Memory"). Another disadvantage is that CD-ROM drives retrieve data about 10 to 20 times slower than a hard disk drive. Still, CD-ROM provides an ideal distribution medium for software, large collections of data (including video and graphics), and complex games. By providing high-density storage cheaply, CD-ROM technology has made the multimedia revolution possible. Increasingly, CD-ROM drives are standard equipment in new computer systems.

If you plan to use CD-ROMs extensively, consider buying a system with two CD-ROM drives. With one CD-ROM drive, you can only access applications or data on one CD-ROM drive at a time. With two drives, you can use two CD-ROM applications or data sets at the same time.

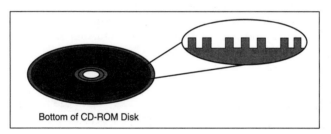

Bottom of CD-ROM Disk

Figure 13.2 *Pock marks on surface of CD-ROM disk*

| CD-ROM changer |

A **CD-ROM drive** that allows users to gain access as many as 100 CD-ROM disks simultaneously. With most units, at least five seconds is required to switch from one disc to the next. Synonymous with jukebox.

| CD-ROM drive |

A disk drive, similar in appearance to the disk drive in a compact audio disc player, that retrieves computer data from CD-ROM disks.

CD-ROM drive

Why are CD-ROM drives so much more expensive than audio compact disc players? It's because they must ensure that all the data is retrieved correctly and free of errors. Audio compact disc players are designed to gloss over read errors by substituting a predicted sound pattern; for computer programs, this technique is unacceptable. In addition, a CD-ROM drive's read mechanism must be able to move quickly across the surface of the disk, while an audio CD player simply plays the disc in sequence (except when you want to play a specific track).

CD-ROM drives retrieve data at rates substantially slower than hard disk drives. The reasons have to do with the large size of the laser reading device, which is several times the size of a hard disk's read-write head. It takes additional time to overcome the reading device's inertia when the device must be moved. In addition, the CD-ROM format calls for reading data at a constant linear velocity, which means that the disk must spin faster when the reading device is near the edge of the disk and slower when it's near the center. Because the reading device must often move laterally across the surface of the disc to access needed data, time is lost due to the necessity of speeding or slowing the rate of the disc's revolution.

CD-ROM drives differ their transfer rate (**double speed** or **quad speed**) and their interface to the computer (**SCSI** or **ATAPI**).

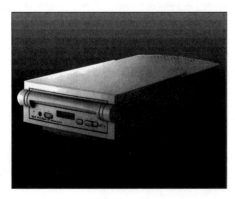

Figure 13.3 *A typical external CD-ROM drive*

CD-ROM/SD

Acronym for CD-ROM Super Density. A high-density compact disc storage format jointly developed by Toshiba and Matsushita. SD disks can store up to 9.6 gigabytes (GB) of data using both sides of the disk. The standard is not compatible with current **CD-ROM drives**. *Compare* **Multimedia Compact Disc (MMCD)**.

CD-ROM/XA

An extension to the original (Yellow Book) CD-ROM standard that adds some of the features of **CD-I (Compact Disk Interactive)** to the CD-ROM disks, including compressed audio and video. For full multimedia compatibility, make sure the drive you purchase is CD-ROM/XA-compatible.

double-speed drive

A **CD-ROM drive** that can transfer data to the computer at a rate of 300 kilobytes per second (Kbps), twice the minimum data transfer rate of 150 Kbps. However, a double-speed drive's overall performance is not twice that of a single-speed drive; most double-speed drives provide only marginal improvements in **access time**.

A double-speed drive should be considered the minimal, entry-level CD-ROM drive for your computer system—but note that many **quad-speed** drives are not very much more expensive!

Green Book

A standard developed by Philips for blending sound, audio, video, and text on a single compact disc. *Synonymous with* **CD-I (Compact Disc-Interactive)**.

High-Density Multimedia CD (HOMMCD)

See **MultiMedia Compact Disc (MMCD).**

High Sierra

An obsolete MS-DOS file storage format for CD-ROM disks. The standard has been published, with certain key modifications that render it incompatible with High Sierra, as the **ISO 9660** standard. Virtually all **CD-ROM drives** for PCs are ISO 9660-compatible.

ISO 9660

A standard published by International Standards Organization (ISO) that defines basic data storage and transfer characteristics of CD-ROM technology. Virtually all **CD-ROM drives** made for IBM PCs and compatibles are ISO 9660-compatible.

jukebox

See **CD-ROM changer.**

MPC-2

Acronym for Multimedia Personal Computer-2. A standard for multimedia personal computers developed by a consortium called the Multimedia PC Marketing Council. The MPC-2 standard, published in 1993, calls for a minimual multimedia system configuration of a 486SX-25 microprocessor, 8 MB of RAM, a color VGA display, and a **double-speed CD-ROM drive.**

MultiMedia Compact Disc (MMCD)

A standard proposed by Sony and Philips for storing 3.7 gigabytes (GB) of data, sound, and video on a single-sided compact disc, enabling smooth retrieval of full-screen, full-motion video (30 frames per second). The standard is not compatible with current CD-ROM drives. Sony's name for the format is High-Density Multimedia CD (HDMMCD). *Compare* **CD-ROM/SD**.

multisession PhotoCD

A Kodak **PhotoCD** standard that enables image processors to add more photographs to a partially-filled disk. The advantage to the consumer is that the disk can be returned for additional processing until it is filled, thus taking full advantage of the PhotoCD format's efficient storage capabilities.

Ordinary CD-ROM disks have a single index located at the beginning of the disk. This index contains a table of the information stored on the disk. When you return your PhotoCD disk to Kodak to add new pictures, the existing index cannot be modified. Instead, the new data begins with a new index. A multisession-compatible drive knows how to look for the additional indexes.

Not all CD-ROM drives are multisession PhotoCD-compatible. A single-session drive can only handle PhotoCD disks that are pressed in one session (probably leaving some of the disc empty). If you're planning to take advantage of PhotoCD, make sure your CD-ROM drive can handle Kodak's multisession disks.

PhotoCD has not become the consumer success that Kodak hoped for. Instead, PhotoCD technology has found a niche in professional and semi-professional publishing.

PhotoCD

A technology developed jointly by Kodak and Philips that allows consumers to place pictures taken using ordinary 35mm cameras and film on a digital compact disk that can hold up to four 24-exposure rolls of digitized images. The images on the disk can be displayed on a TV equipped with a PhotoCD player or, for higher resolution, on a computer display.

If you think you'd like to try PhotoCD, make sure the **CD-ROM drive** you're buying is **multisession PhotoCD**-compatible.

proprietary interface

An interface between a **CD-ROM drive** and a computer, developed by a single company, that works only with that firm's products. The use of proprietary interfaces is giving way to **ATAPI** interfaces, which allow CD-ROM drives to connect to Enhanced IDE hard disk controllers.

quad speed

A **CD-ROM drive** that transfers data at four times the standard data transfer rate of 150 kilobytes per second (Kbps). Rated at 600 Kbps, quad speed drives are actually not four times faster than single-speed drives; any CD-ROM drive's overall performance is limited by technical constraints on **access time**, the time it takes for the laser reading mechanism to locate the desired data and to begin the actual transfer. In practice, quad-speed drives are roughly 40 percent faster than **double-speed** drives.

Red Book

A standard (ISO 10149) published by the International Standards Organization with a distinctive red cover. The Red Book defines the original **CD-DA** (digital audio) compact disc standard.

| SCSI |

Acronym for Small Computer Systems Interface. An independent, system-level input/output bus for a variety of computer peripherals, including hard disks, **CD-ROM drives**, and scanners. The current specification, SCSI-2, was published in 1994, and provides for high-speed data pathways up to 32 bits in length. Up to seven additional devices can be "daisychained" to a SCSI port with a simple installation procedure.

To connect a SCSI-based CD-ROM drive to your computer, the computer must be equipped with a SCSI port. Sometimes found on the motherboard, this is more often provided by an expansion board that fits into the computer's expansion bus. With most computers, this is an optional accessory.

In CD-ROM drives, SCSI interfaces provided an attractive alternative to **proprietary interfaces** until the advent of **ATAPI**-based interfaces (using a direct connection to an Enhanced IDE hard disk controller).

| Yellow Book |

A standard published by the International Standards Organization that defines CD-ROM data storage and retrieval, including the **CD-ROM/XA** standard that adds interleaved sound and video to CD-ROM text.

Sound Cards and Speakers

This chapter surveys the terms you'll encounter when you're considering an essential system addition: **a sound card**. The PC's tinny speaker just won't cut it for today's multimedia applications. To equip your system with stereo sound, you'll need a sound card, which is an expansion card designed to fit into one of your computer's expansion slots, and **self-powered speakers**.

8-bit sound card

A sound card that can represent and process sounds expressed in units of 8 bits, which is barely adequate for voice and system sounds (beeps) but not for music. 8-bit sound cards are no longer marketed and should be avoided. *See* **resolution**.

12-bit sound card

A sound card that can representing and processing sounds expressed in units of 12 bits. A 12-bit sound card can reproduce voice, system sounds, and simple music; however, the sound quality is poor and suffers from audible noise and distortion. This level of quality is judged sufficient for **business audio**. *See* **resolution**.

16-bit sound card

 A sound card that can represent and process sounds expressed in units of 16 bits, the minimum necessary to produce sound comparable in quality to that produced by audio compact discs. Most 16-bit sound cards can automatically detect and process sounds recorded with 12- or 8-bit resolution. *See* **resolution**.

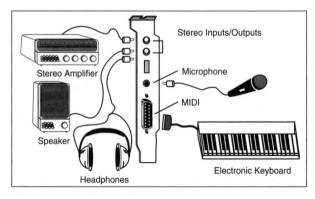

Figure 14.1 Typical connections on a sound card

business audio

In a sound card, a level of quality in sound reproduction that is considered to be sufficient for business uses of the computer, such as recording and playing back voice annotations and playing various beeps and other system sounds. **12-bit sound cards** or 12-bit **onboard audio** circuits are judged to be sufficient for business audio; however, there is little justification for purchasing 12-bit sound cards since full **16-bit sound cards**, which are capable of producing music with quality approaching that of audio CDs, are available for less than $100.

CD-ROM interface

In a sound card, a connector and supporting circuitry that lets you directly connect the sound card to a CD-ROM drive. The advantage of a CD-ROM interface is that the audio output of the CD-ROM drive can be routed directly to the sound card, bypassing the computer's circuitry and reducing load on your computer's microprocessor.

Watch out for proprietary CD-ROM interfaces which force you to buy a CD-ROM drive made by the same manufacturer. Creative Labs makes a sound card with a SCSI interface, enabling you to connect it to any SCSI-compatible CD-ROM drive.

digital signal processor (DSP)

A programmable sound processing circuit. In a DSP, signal-processing characteristics that formerly required separate hard-wired circuits, such as advanced filtering and sound effects like reverberation, can be initiated and controlled by programming the DSP circuitry. In effect, a DSP is a "virtual" sound processor, the DSP can be programmed to emulate one of many physically distinct kinds of signal processors. In modems, DSPs are used to switch between different modulation protocols. In sound cards, DSPs are used to switch between differing sound reproduction standards. In the popular Sound Blaster 16 sound card, for example, a DSP is used to switch among a number of **waveform sound** formats, ranging from 8-bit monaural sound all the way up to full 44.1 KHz, 16-bit stereo with audio CD quality.

FM synthesis

 In **MIDI** play back devices, including sound cards, a method of simulating the sound of musical instruments by electronically varying the timbre of a generated sound. FM synthesis is inexpensive to implement but it produces tones that sound like those produced by a cheap electronic organ. *Compare* **wave table synthesis**.

General MIDI (GM)

In **MIDI**, a industry-wide standard for identifying 128 distinct musical voices, such as Acoustic Grand Piano, Church Organ, String Ensemble, and Alto Sax. Included are sound effects, ethnic instruments, and percussion sounds. A sound card that is GM-compatible can correctly play sounds corresponding to these 128 instruments, using **FM synthesis** or **wave table synthesis**.

MIDI

See **Musical Instrument Digital Interface (MIDI)**.

MIDI interface

See **MIDI port**.

MIDI port

Also called MIDI interface. A port that is designed to exchange **MIDI** control signals with another MIDI-compatible device, such as a synthesizer.

A MIDI port includes a Universal Asynchronous Receiver-Transmitter (UART) similar in function to the one you'll find in every standard serial port, except that MIDI UARTs exchange data at a fixed rate of 31,250 bps through specially-designed MIDI cables. MIDI cables have matching male 5-pin connectors on each end, and can be 15 meters (about 50 feet) in length. Most MIDI ports include an In and Out jack for these cables; some also include a Thru jack for special-purpose applications.

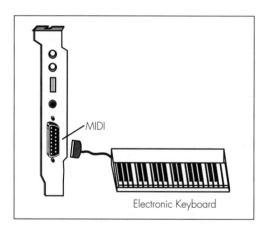

Figure 14.2 Most PC sound boards provide MIDI port

MPU 401

An industry-standard **MIDI port**, created by Roland, for connecting **MIDI**-capable musical instruments to the computer. The interface contains its own processing circuitry, which minimizes demand on the computer's microprocessor.

MPU 401   polyphony

If you're looking for a sound card that includes a **MIDI port**, make sure it is MPU 401-compatible.

Muscial Instrument Digital Inerface (MIDI)

 An industry-wide standard for the representation of music in digital form. Unlike audio CDs, MIDI files do not contain a digitized version of actual sounds. Instead, they contain tables that tell a MIDI-compatible synthesizer when to start and stop playing a given note. MIDI files are thus much more compact than files that contain digitized music. Moreover, the MIDI file format lets users connect musical devices made by more than one manufacturer. When a MIDI-compatible device plays a MIDI file, it does so without audible noise or distortion. If the intention is to simulate real musical instruments, the best results are obtained with a playback unit that uses **wave table synthesis** rather than **FM synthesis**.

onboard audio

A **business audio** sound circuit that is contained on a computer's motherboard. Suitable for use with Windows applications, onboard audio generally does not reproduce the sounds generated by DOS games and employs **FM synthesis**. For the highest-quality sound, you can add a **16-bit sound card** with **wave table synthesis** to a system with onboard audio, but you may have to disable the onboard audio first.

polyphony

The reproduction of more than one tone simultaneously. High-end **wave table synthesis** sound cards such as the Sound Blaster AWE32 can reproduce up to 20 tones simultaneously.

resolution

The number of bits that are available for the encoding of recorded sound. This number determines the maximum number of discrete sound levels that can be assigned to represent the sounds being recorded. With 8-bit resolution, a digital recording device can represent only 256 sounds levels, a number that is adequate for voice, if one is willing to live with audible distortion and noise, but it is not sufficient to capture the range of sounds found in music.

sampling rate

The number of times per second that the digital recording or playback device samples the sound during recording. The standard sampling rate for audio compact discs is 44.1 KHz per second. In general, the higher the sampling rate, the fuller and richer and sound, and the wider the frequency response, which (for musical purposes) should at least equal the frequency range of FM radio, 20-15,000 Hz. Sampling rates of 11 KHz or 22 KHz may be acceptable for voice recordings, but not for music. *Compare* **resolution**.

Look for a sound card that uses a sampling rate of at least 44.1 KHz, conforming to the audio compact disc standard. This capability is assumed by many of today's multimedia compact disks, which contain CD-quality audio sound.

self-powered speaker

A speaker, designed for use with a computer sound card or a personal tape or CD player, that contains its own integrated amplifer. The amplifer is needed because the line output from sound cards and personal players is insufficient to generate the desired volume level. Power may be supplied by means of batteries or an AC line adapter.

self-powered speaker   sound card

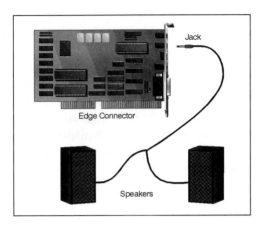

Figure 14.3 *Connecting a pair of powered speakers to your sound card*

---

shielded speaker

A speaker that contains insulation ot isolate the speaker's magnetic field so that it does not interfere with your computer. Speakers produce sounds using powerful magnets, which can distort the image on your monitor or, at the extreme, disturb data recorded on hard and floppy disks. A shielded speaker prevents the problems.

Sound Blaster compatible

Compatible with the popular Sound Blaster sound card. Sound Blaster compatibility is very important if you want to hear the sound generated by DOS games. It isn't necessary if you just want to hear sounds generated by Windows applications.

---

sound card

An expansion card (Chapter 6) that adds digital stereo sound to your computer system. Most sound cards can reproduce two kinds of sounds: **MIDI** sounds (text files that tell the sound card how and when to reproduce sounds) and **wave form sounds** (sound files that contain digitized recordings of music or sounds). Early **8-bit sound cards** reproduced sound with audible noise and distortion, but today's **16-bit sound cards** approach—but do not equal—the quality of audio compact discs. When reproducing MIDI sounds, cards that employ **wave table synthesis** do a much better job than those that use the less expensive **FM synthesis**. If you want to hear the sounds generated by DOS games, look for **Sound Blaster compatibility**. A desirable feature is a **CD-ROM interface** that allows you to connect the sound output of your CD-ROM drive directly to the sound card, thus reducing the processing load on your computer..

| wave table synthesis |

In **MIDI** playback devices, including sound cards, a method of simulating the sound of orchestral instruments by retrieving and modifying a stored sample of the sound these instruments produce. Although wave table synthesis-based sound cards cannot reproduce the dynamics of real musical instruments (including sustain, attack, and the decay of notes), they reproduce digitized music much more realistically than **FM synthesis** sound cards.

Many computer games and CD-ROM multimedia disks make extensive use of MIDI files to provide music. To reproduce these sounds realistically, look for a sound card that includes wave table synthesis capabilities, and avoid FM synthesis. Be prepared to pay a premium for wavetable synthesis capabilities.

If you already have an FM synthesis sound card, you may be able to purchase an adapter that upgrades the card to wave table synthesis. Contact the sound card's manufacturer for details.

waveform sound

One of two basic types of digitized sounds (the other is a **MIDI** sound). In a waveform sound, the sound file contains a digitized version of an actual, recorded sound. On a **16-bit sound card** these sounds play back with impressive realism. However, waveform sound files consume massive amounts of disk space at its highest levels of fidelity (the Windows WAV format requires 27MB of disk storage for each minute of recorded sound). *Compare* **MIDI**.

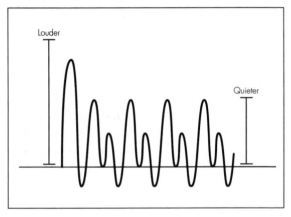

Figure 14.4 Graphic representation of a wave form sound

Modems and Fax Modems

This chapter surveys the terminology related to computer **modems** and **fax modems**. Look here to find definitions, tips, and hints for any term that concerns modems or the **communications programs** required to run them. You'll find these definitions invaluable when you're shopping for a new modem or upgrading an existing one.

A modem enables your computer to connect with distant computers by means of the world telephone system. Sitting in a cabin along the Russian River in California, you can link your computer with another PC in a friend's house down the road—or a gigantic mainframe computer, half a continent away. And once you're connected, you can take advantage of the rapidly-expanding world of computer online services, including **bulletin board systems (BBS), online information services**, and the **Internet**. You can exchange electronic mail with computer users world-wide, **download** computer files and programs, search for information, and join computer discussion groups. Fax modems include the circuitry required to send and receive faxes.

16450

An integrated circuit that provided the **Universal Asynchronous Receiver/Transmitter (UART)** for the IBM Personal Computer AT, introduced in 1984. The 16450 is too slow to work with today's fast microprocessors and high-speed modems. If your computer has a 16450-based UART, you may need to replace it with a 16550A. For more information, see Chapter 7.

16550A

An integrated circuit that provides the **Universal Asynchronous Receiver/Transmitter (UART)** for today's fast computer systems. If you're buying a used computer, make sure it has a 16550A UART so that you can use the system with a high-speed modem. For more information, see Chapter 7.

acoustic coupler

A **modem** that is shaped to accommodate the handset of a desk telephone. Once in common use, an acoustic coupler is needed only if the telephone with which you're trying to connect doesn't have a **modular jack** (a plug designed for use with telephones), also known as RJ-11 Jack. Today's modems plug directly into the modular jack.

active configuration

The set of **modem** operating options that you've chosen during an operating session by using your communications program and the AT commands that tell your modem what to do. This is accomplished by means of the **initialization string** which the program sends to the modem. The active configuration applies for the rest of the current operating session; when you turn off your modem or reboot your system, the active configuration choices are lost and the modem returns to its **factory configuration**.

American Standard Code for Information Interchange (ASCII)

A code consisting of seven binary digits (bits) that is used for representing text, graphics, and control characters for use in the computer. There are a total of 128 character codes in the standard ASCII set. The first 32 are used to symbolize keyboard and printer operations, such as backspace, carriage return, and line break. The remainder represent the characters you find on any standard computer keyboard, including lowercase and uppercase letters, numbers, and punctuation marks. ASCII lacks accented characters (such as e´)and ligatures (conjoined characters such as æ, common in Danish and Norwegian), which are widely used in European languages.

Personal computers use an eight bit **extended character set** that employs an additional 128 codes, for a total of 256. To represent the additional characters, computers encode characters using an 8-bit code. These codes are used to provide foreign language characters, mathematical and technical symbols, and graphics characters. However, extended character sets are not standardized. For example, the IBM PC's extended character set differs from that of the Macintosh.

---

analog

The representation of information by means of continuously-varied electrical properties, such as voltage, in such a way that the variations capture the patterns of the original information. For example, an analog telephone converts the intensities and frequencies of the human voice into electrical signals; the signal varies in proportion to the strength and frequency of the voice. *Compare* **digital**.

analog modem

A **modem** designed to work with analog telephone lines; the type of modem in most common use today. *Compare* **digital modem**.

ANSI graphics

ANSI is an acronym for American National Standards Institute, a non-profit consortium of computer and technical industry organizations. Among the ANSI standards are a set of cursor control codes, commonly referred to as "ANSI graphics," that allows a **bulletin board system (BBS)** to display graphics characters and colors on your screen.

Set your **communications program** to emulate an ANSI terminal when you call a BBS; with this **terminal emulation** enabled, the BBS software can display graphics and colors on your screen.

archive

A file that contains one or more files that have been compressed using a **data compression program**, such as PKZIP. Most of the files available on **bulletin board systems** are archive files. After you **download** an archive file, you use a data compression program to decompress the files so that you may use them.

The archive's file extension—the three-letter part of the file name that follows the period—tells you which program was used to compress the file. The de facto standard data compression program in the BBS world, PKZIP, creates archives with the extension .ZIP. An older data compression program, PKARC, uses the extension .ARC.

ASCII transfer

A **file transfer protocol** that transfers **ASCII** text between two computers linked by modems and a telephone connection. This simple transfer method has no **error correction protocol** or **flow control**, so you should use it only for non-critical files. For error-free transfer of programs or text files, use a protocol such as **Zmodem** that provides error correction.

Many communications programs can be customized to strip unwanted characters, such as unwanted control characters or extraneous foreign language characters, from incoming ASCII text. If the files you receive have unwanted characters (for example, a Greek character at the beginning or end of each line), check your program's documentation to find out whether you can strip this character from the incoming text.

---

asynchronous communication

A method for solving the chief problem in **serial communication**: How to demarcate the beginning and the end of a unit of transmitted data. In asynchronous communication, the method used is simpler than that of **synchronous communication**, which involves the use of a timing signals to synchronize the arrival of units of data. Instead, the beginning of each unit is marked with a **start bit**—which says, in effect, "Here comes a unit of data." And the end of the unit is marked with a **stop bit**, which says, "That's the end of the data." In PC data communications, the start and stop bits are added to each eight-bit unit (**byte**) of transmitted data. This means that each character, normally one byte (eight bits) in length, requires the the transmission of 10 bits of data.

If your new **modem** doesn't seem to be performing up to its full potential, remember that the modem must transfer ten bits of information for every character, not just the eight bits that define the character itself. For this reason, a 14,400 **bps** modem probably won't manage to transfer 1800 characters per second; you'll be lucky to get 1,400. (Most **communications programs** show you how many bits or characters per second your modem is transferring while a file transfer is in progress.) To get the maximum performance out of your modem, consult your modem's and communication program's documentation to learn how to establish a synchronous connection using an **error correction protocol** such as **V.42** or **MNP4**.

AT command set

A command language that lets you (or your **communications program**) tell a **modem** what to do. Originated by Hayes Microcomputer Products, Inc., the AT command set has become a de facto industry standard. A modem that responds to the AT command set is said to be **Hayes-compatible**. *Synonymous with* **Hayes command set**.

When your **communications program** is in its **terminal mode**, in which everything you type is sent out the **serial port** to the modem, you can use the AT command set to give direct commands to your modem. To shut up the speaker, for example, type +++ to enter the **command mode**, then type ATM. Press Enter to send the command to the modem.

at sign

The character @, which is frequently used in electronic mail addresses.

audio monitor

A tiny audio speaker mounted on the **modem's** circuit board that lets you hear what's happening when you attempt to make a connection. For example, if the line's busy, you hear a busy signal. If you make the connection, you hear tones and a hissing noise, indicating that the receiving modem is ready to engage in communication with your modem. And if you hear a voice that says "Hello? Hello? Is this some kind of prank?" you'll know that you dialed the wrong number!

If you don't like hearing the obnoxious wails and hissing that signals the onset of a successful modem link-up, you may be able to choose an option in your **communications program** to shut the modem up—check your program's manual. If there's no command to silence the modem, you can add a command to the modem **initialization string** that your communication program automatically sends to the modem every time you begin a communications session: Just add the letter M after the letters AT that begin the string. (It's OK to type all the letters in lower case.)

auto-answer mode

A **modem** operating mode in which the modem automatically answers incoming calls. The modem detects the incoming ringing signal and answers the line, just as if you had picked up the handset. The answering modem then sends a signal to the calling modem and begins the process of **handshaking** that occurs at the beginning of the link. This capability is convenient if you're running a **bulletin board system (BBS)** or making your computer available to someone else in **host mode**. With most modems, this mode isn't turned on by default; you must use an **AT com-**

mand (or choose an appropriate option in your **communications program**) to turn the mode on. *Compare* **originate mode**.

Don't engage the auto-answer mode if you use the same phone line for voice calls—your callers will hear a piercing shriek and hissing noise when they ring you up! User your communications program to disengage the modem's auto answer mode.

auto-dial modem

A **modem** that can generate pulse or tone dialing signals, without requiring the use of a telephone. You can plug an auto-dial modem directly into the modular telephone jack. (If the modem did not have this capability, you would have to dial the number manually using a telephone, and then hang up so that the modem could take over.) All of the modems on the market today are auto-dial modems.

auto-logon

A feature of most **communications programs** that lets you write or record a **script** to automatically dial and **log on** to a remote computer system.

Don't buy a communications program that can't record your log on procedure and "play it back" automatically. Otherwise, you'll find yourself typing the same commands over and over again.

automatic speed sensing

A capability of today's popular **modems** that permits them to exchange control information with another modem at the beginning of a call. A modem with this capability can automatically adjust its speed to match the capabilities of the modem on the other end of the line. If the other modem cannot operate at the calling modem's maximum speed, the calling modem **falls back** to the next lower speed, and continues doing so until a connection is established. This is part of the process of **handshaking** that occurs at the beginning of a link.

bandwidth

A measurement of the amount of information that a given communication line can transmit. A line's bandwidth is defined by the range of frequencies that the line can carry, ranging from the lowest to the highest. Bandwidth is measured in Hertz, abbreviated Hz, which is the number of cycles per second of the frequency.

The bandwidth of a standard telephone line spans 3000 Hz, ranging from 300 Hz to 3300 Hz. These limits were originally determined by the amount of bandwidth needed to carry the human voice, but they impose severe limitations on computer communications that must use telephone lines. Coupled with limitations imposed by the presence of noise in the lines, telephone lines can carry a theoretical maximum of less than 60,000 **bits per second (bps)**.

batch file transfer

In **file transfer protocols**, the ability to **upload** or **download** more than one file at a time. Among the protocols widely used to access files in **bulletin board systems (BBS)**, **YModem** and **Zmodem** are two that support batch file transfers.

baud

A measurement of a **modem's** performance that indicates how many times per second the modem can change the electronic

signal it sends into the telephone line. A 300 baud modem
can change the signal 300 times per second.

Don't refer to a modem's **data transfer rate** using the
term baud. Today's modems employ clever techniques that
allow them to convey more than one bit of data for each
change in the signal; a modem capable of transferring 2400
bits per second, for example, operates at 600 baud. Inse-
tad, use the term **bits per second (bps)** to describe a
modem's data transfer rate. This measurement is more
closely related to a modem's actual performance and
enables you to compare the performance of two modems
meaningfully.

Bell 103

An early **modulation protocol** developed by American
Telephone & Telegraph (AT&T) that governs transmission at
speeds of 300 **bits per second (bps)**. The Bell 103 protocol
employs **frequency shift keying** to signify information. Only
used in North America, the protocol conflicts with the **V.21**
standard used in the rest of the world to govern transmission
at 300 bps.

Bell 212A

A **modulation protocol** developed by American Telephone
& Telegraph that governs transmission at speeds of **1200 bits
per second** (bps). This protocol adds **quadrature modulation**
to a 600-**baud** signal. Only used in North America, the protocol conflicts with the **V.22** standard used in the rest of the
world to govern transmission at 1200 bps.

bit

Contraction of binary digit; a basic unit of digital data, consisting of a 1 or a 0.

bits per second (bps)

The number of binary digits (bits)—1s and 0s—that a communication device can transfer from one point to another within one second. The bps rate is the fundamental measure of a modem's **data transfer rate**. Since today's modems can transfer thousands of bits per second, the abbreviation Kbps (kilobits per second, or thousands of bits per second) has come into common use. In high-speed networking, the abbreviations Mbps (megabits per second, or millions of bits per second) and Gbps (gigabits per second, or billions of bits per second) are in common use.

block size

In a **file transfer protocol** or **error correction protocol**, the size (in **bytes**) of the chunk of data that is transmitted in a unit. The **Xmodem** protocol, for instance, transmits data using a block size of 128 bytes.

bulletin board system (BBS)

A do-it-yourself on-line computer information system that is created with a personal computer, a **modem**, and BBS software.

Usually operated on a volunteer basis by computer hobbyists, BBS systems typically offer hundreds or even thousands of programs and graphics files to **download**, local electronic mail, games, and—increasingly—access to the **Internet**. Most levy a modest fee, such as $35 for one year of unlimited access. There are an estimated 45,000 BBSs in the U.S. alone.

> Looking for a bulletin board in your area? Check out Computer Shopper or Boardwatch, monthly magazines you'll find in many bookstores and newsstands.

byte

A basic data unit consisting of eight binary digits (**bits**), which are sufficient to represent the entire **extended character set** that is in common use in personal computing. For this reason, the term is often used synonymously with "character."

call waiting

 An option made available to most home telephone customers that allows you to detect and answer an incoming voice call while you're talking to somebody else. Call waiting is great for voice communication, but it's murder on your **modem**: If someone tries to call you while your modem is using your phone line, you may lose data, or even lose the connection.

 Disable call waiting when you use your modem. To do so, press *70 (star-70), wait for the dial tone, and dial the number. In your **communications program**, you can add this code to the phone number for a **bulletin board system (BBS)** or some other online resource. Before you can enter the telephone number, type *70 followed by a comma (the comma tells the modem to wait a second before resuming dialing). If this doesn't work, check with your local phone company to find out how to disable call waiting.

capture

 To record incoming data from your screen to a disk file. Most **communication programs** include a capture command that enables you to name the file and store incoming data.

| capture | Class 1 |

If your communications program has a capture command, find out if you can pause capturing data without closing the capture file. This capability is convenient because it lets you omit any information that you don't need from the file, such as the menus that **BBS** systems display to guide you to files and other resources.

| carrier |

A continuous tone that, when sent by one **modem** and received by another, constitutes a valid connection. The sending modem conveys data by changing this tone.

| carrier detect signal |

A signal conveyed by the **modem** to the computer indicating that a valid connection has been established with another modem. If you have an **external modem**, the carrier detect (CD) light comes on when a connection is established.

| checksum |

A simple **error correction** technique that determines whether a block of data was transmitted accurately. The checksum involves performing an arithmetic operation on the bit values contained in the block, resulting in a value. This value is calculated before transmission and afterward. If the two values don't agree, the error-checking software assumes that an error occurred during transmission, discards the block, and requests a re-transmission.

| Class 1 |

A standard for **fax modems** that specifies the extensions to the **AT command set** to handle the sending and receiving of faxes. The job of processing the fax data—for example, of digitizing the image—is left to fax software. The Class 1 standard was jointly developed by the Electronics Industry Association and the Telecommunications Industry Association. Compare **Class 2**.

If you're shopping for a modem, Class 1 isn't a liability compared to Class 2. Today's high-powered personal computers can handle fax processing easily. Just be sure to equip your computer with a Class 1-capable fax program.

Class 2

A standard for **fax modems** that, like **Class 1**, specifies extensions to the **AT command** set to handle the sending and receiving of faxes. The difference lies in the fact that Class 2 transfers most of the processing operations, such as digitizing and compression, to the modem. The Class 2 standard was jointly developed by the Electronics Industry Association and the Telecommunicatoins Industry Association. *Compare* **Class 1**.

The theory underlying the Class 2 standard is that underpowered personal computers need assistance handling the complex processing operations needed to send and receive faxes, such as digitization and compression. With a Class 2 modem, fax operations could run in the background without making demands on your computer's microprocessor.

Like many nice theories, the one underlying Class 2 hasn't worked out in practice. First, it's not really necessary. Today's "underpowered" personal computers aren't so underpowered anymore. Even a 386SX-25 can handle

Modems and Fax Modems

Class 2   Comité Consultif...

Class 1 fax operations. There's no compelling need to transfer the processing to Class 2 fax modems, which are much more expensive than Class 1 modems because they must include additional processing circuitry.

The second reason Class 2 hasn't worked out well lies in the development of conflicting Class 2 standards. The Class 2 specification was published in 1992, but only after several fax modems appeared that followed a provisional Class 2 specification, which differed in some respects. To distinguish the two, the published (official) version of the protocol is called Class 2.0, while the interim version is simply called Class 2. Most of the "Class 2" modems observe the interim (Class 2) protocol. As if this isn't confusing enough, modem manufacturers introduced their own proprietary discrepancies between their implementation of the interim protocol and the final, published version (2.0). As a result, Class 2 is not a uniform standard.

Don't spend money on Class 2 fax compatibility— arguably, you'll be throwing money away needlessly. Although a modem with Class 1 compability requires your computer's processor to handle digitization, compression, and other fax-processing operations, most of today's standard systems (486 and higher) can handle these tasks quite well, even while you're running other applications.

Comité Consultif International de Télégraphique et Téléphonique (CCITT)

See **International Telecommunications Union—Telecommunications Standards Sector (ITT-TSS).**

command mode

One of the **modem**'s two operating modes in which the modem interprets the text you type as a command. With a **Hayes-compatible** modem, you enter the command mode by typing the **escape sequence**, three plus signs (+++). To return to the terminal mode, you type ATO and press Enter. But don't worry that you'll have to become a programmer to use your modem: a good **communications program** will handle the mechanics of switching modes and issuing commands. *Compare* **communications mode**.

communications mode

One of the **modem**'s two operating modes in which the text you type is sent through the telephone line to the modem on the other end of the line.

communications parameters

See **communications settings**. *Compare* **command mode**.

communications program

A program that transforms your PC into a **remote terminal** (a keyboard and screen that are linked to another computer located elsewhere) that can be linked to another computer by means of a **modem**. In addition, a communications program gives you the ability to control the modem, save and recall phone numbers easily, **upload** and **download** files, and **capture** incoming data to a file.

If you have a **high-speed modem** that supports **V.42** error correction and **V.42bis** compression, select a communications program that supports these features for the brand and model of modem you're using. Otherwise, you might not be able to take full advantage of your modem's capabilities.

communications settings

The choices you must make to configure your **modem** before you attempt to log on to another computer, such as a **bulletin board system (BBS)** or **online information service**. These choices concern the use of **parity checking** (no parity checking, **odd parity**, or **even parity**), the number of **data bits** that the receiving computer expects to receive (6, 7, or 8), and the number off **stop bits** that it expects (1, 1.5, or 2). You use your **communications program** to choose the correct communications settings.

Almost all BBSs and online information systems expect no parity, 8 data bits, and 1 stop bits. In their advertisements, these settings are often abbreviated as N81. If you're not sure which communications settings to use, try N81 to start.

compression

The reduction of the number of bits in a unit of data. There are two kinds of compression that are important to understand—on the fly compression, handled by the modem, and regular file compression, in which you use a separate utility program to reduce the size of specific files. Most of today's **high-speed modems** can compress data "on the fly" (that is, while transmission is taking place) and decompress incoming data without loss. The result is a gain in the modem's **effective transmission rate**: one technique, for example, allows a 14,400 Kbps modem to transfer data at an apparent rate of 38,400 Kbps. The modem isn't actually transferring the data any faster—the gain is produced by compressing the data so that fewer bits need to be transmitted.

Mathematical techniques called "compression algorithms" make it possible to compress data without loss. In one technique, commonly-occurring characters (such as the vowels e and a) are given a short code, while infrequently-occurring characters (such as the consonants w and q) are given long codes. The result is a reduction of 50% or more in the size of the transmitted data. Nevertheless, this data can be fully restored on the receiving end by simply retranslating the codes to their original values.

For **on-the-fly compression** to work, both the transmitting and the receiving modem must conform to the same **data compression protocol**. The earliest high-speed modems used **proprietary protocols** (standards used only by the manufacturer who invented them). Most modems now conform to the **MNP5** or **V.42bis** data compression protocols.

Many computer users compress their files using a data compression utility such as PKZIP prior to uploading them, thus eliminating the need for on-the-fly compression. And many of the files you'll retrieve from **bulletin board systems (BBS)** and **online information services** such as CompuServe are precompressed. Because these files are already compressed, a modem capable of data compression cannot transfer them any faster than an ordinary modem.

Don't enable **on-the-fly data compression** if you're uploading or downloading a file that has already been compressed. Although doing so won't damage the file, the on-the-fly compression can actually increase the size of the precompressed file.

---

connect speed

The speed at which your **modem** actually achieves a connection with the modem on the other end of the line. This speed may not be the same as your modem's top speed because your modem will **fall back** to a lower speed if necessary to achieve the connection. For example, a 14,400 bps modem will fall back to 9600 **bps** if the receiving modem's top speed is only 9600 Kbps.

control character

In the **ASCII** character set, one of 32 non-printing codes for computer operations such as line feeds and carriage returns.

copper pair

The standard, unshielded wire, consisting of two pairs of wires in a plastic sheath, that makes up the bulk of residential telephone wiring. These wires are not suitable for digital data communication and will have to replaced before services such as **ISDN** can be implemented. Recently, the use of **twisted pair** wiring (four pairs of cables in a single sheath) has become more common in residential installations. Twisted pair wiring, in common use in low-bandwidth local area networks (LANs), can be used for the lowest-speed ISDN service.

core set of modulation protocols

A set of **modulation protocols** (standards for encoding data for serial transmission) that, when built into a **modem,** enables the modem to communicate with virtually any other modem. A modem that offers the core set includes the two older U.S. standards (Bell 103 at 300 bps and **Bell 212** at 1,200 bps), as well as the most popular international standards (**V.22** at 1,200 bps, **V.22bis** at 2,400 bps, **V.32** at 9,600 bps, and **V.32bi**s at 14.4 Kbps).

CTS/RTS

A type of hardware **handshaking** that employs the RTS (Request to Send) and CTS (Clear to Send) signals on a standard **serial port** connection. CTS/RTS handshaking, which is a form of **flow control**, is used to ensure that your computer does not send more data to the modem than it can handle.

cyclic redundancy check (CRC)

A commonly-used method of checking for errors in a data transmission. Before a data **frame** is transmitted, a utility program performs a complex computation on the data contained in the frame and produces a **checksum**. If even a single **bit** of the frame has been altered or lost in the transmission, the receiving station will be able to detect the loss and discard the corrupted frame. *See* **error correction protocol**.

data bits

One of the three fundamental **communications settings** (also see **parity** and **stop bits**). This setting specifies the number of bits (usually seven or eight) that the system you're contacting uses to represent one character of data. Before contacting an online resource such as a **bulletin board system (BBS)**, you use your **communications program** to specify the number of data bits.

 With the exception of a few dinosaur mainframe systems, most of the computers you can contact with your modem use eight data bits. Try this setting first.

Data Communications Equipment (DCE)

In the standard **serial port** specification (RS-232; see Chapter 7), the equipment that connects the computer to a **modem**, **fax modem**, or fax machine.

data compression program

A program that is designed to compress a program or data file, so that it takes up considerably less storage room (and transfers more quickly in telecommunications). A compresed file created by a data compression program is called an **archive**. *See* **compression**.

data compression protocol

A standard that specifies how two **modems** can communicate so that the sending modem compresses the data and the receiving modem decompresses it. For compression to work, both the sending and the receiving modems must conform to the same protocol, such as **MNP5** or **V.42bis**.

data modem

A **modem** that lacks fax capabilities (*compare* **fax modem**).

Don't buy a data modem—for just a few dollars more, or even for the same price, you should be able to get a fax modem, which will enable your computer to send and receive faxes as well as exchange data with other computers.

Data Terminal Equipment (DTE)

In the standard **serial port** specification (RS-232; see Chapter 7), a device that is capable of originating or receiving data communications (such as a personal computer or a terminal).

data transfer rate

The speed at which a **modem** can convey data via the phone line, measured in **bits per second (bps)**. *Compare* **connect speed**.

A modem can achieve its maximum data transfer rate only when it is connected with another modem that has the same (or higher) maximum rate. Most modems can automatically **fall back** to a lower rate if the modem on the other end cannot communicate at a higher one.

DCE

See **Data Communications Equipment**

DCE speed

The speed at which two **Data Communications Equipment (DCE)** devices, such as **modems** or fax machines, can reliably communicate with each other via a telephone line.

demodulation

 The process of transforming an incoming audio signal, inwhich varying tones signify information, into **digital** information that a computer can process. *See* **Modem, Modulation.**

dialup access

 A method of connecting to a computer by means of apersonal computer equipped with a **modem** and a **communications program**. "Dialup access" most commonly refers to accessing the Internet, but can also describe the way you connect to a **BBS**. For Internet access, you use your computer and modem to connect to a system that has high-speed dedicated access (a permanent connection) to the Internet. By far the simplest and cheapest method of using the Internet, this is also the least capable (for example, you will not be able to run graphical applications such as Eudora or Mosaic). Using your computer and communications program, you dial a connection to an Internet computer, and once this connection is established after the **logon** procedure, your computer becomes a remote terminal of the system you've contacted.

To contact the Internet by means of dial up access, you must have an account on an Internet-connected host system, such as a university's central computing system. If your organization does not offer dial up access to an Internet host, you may be able to obtain dial-up access by means of a freenet, an Internet-linked **bulletin board system (BBS)**, or a commercial dial-up access provider such as Performance Systems International (PSI), located in Herndon, Virginia. Commercial **online information services** that are accessible by means of dial up access, such as CompuServe, also offer limited Internet access.

With dialup access, your personal computer isn't really connected to the Internet, although the host system is. Depending on the host's resources, you can use standard Internet applications such as electronic mail, FTP, Usenet, and Gopher.

Ask your organization's computer center whether Internet dialup access is available. You may be able to get Internet access for free.

Don't subscribe to a commercial access provider or online service without first finding out just which Internet services are available. Many systems that advertise "Internet access" provide only electronic mail.

| dialup IP |

A method of **Internet** access that allows computer users to establish a temporary but direct Internet connection by means of a **high-speed modem** and **POTS** (plain old telephone system). Requiring special software both on your computer and on the Internet host you contact, dialup IP works by presenting your computer to the Internet as if it were a node with a unique IP address. As a result, Internet data can go directly to your computer (this is not possible with ordinary **dialup access**). The programs required to implement dialup IP are governed by two protocols called **SLIP** and **PPP**.

Dialup IP has a number of advantages over dialup access. Because the data packets can travel directly to your computer, you can obtain files without the intermediary step of downloading them from the host system (which is required when you use dialup access). Unlike dialup access, dialup IP allows you to run graphical browsers such as Mosaic on your computer system, and has other advantages such as convenient file transfer (files obtained through FTP, for example, go directly to your computer's hard disk instead of being stored temporarily on a minicomputer or mainframe computer host system).

Dialup IP is still something of an art; much of the required software is in the public domain and as a result is poorly documented. With the growing availability of high-speed modems, dialup IP is certain to become more widely used and more user-friendly products are sure to emerge.

| dialup modem |

A **modem** that is designed to work with a standard telephone line, as opposed to a leased line modem that is designed to work with a **leased line** (a cable that is permanently dedicated to connecting two computers). As the name implies, a dialup modem can dial a telephone number, make a connection, and terminate the connection when the data transfer is complete. The modems used with most PCs are dialup modems.

digital

The representation of information by means of discrete digits (units), which can be absolutely and unambiguously distinguished from each other. In computers, information is represented by low and high currents, which represent the basic units of binary encoding (0 and 1). Although, information stored within the computer is digital, the information must be transformed (through a process called **modulation**) before it can be sent via the telephone system. *Compare* **analog**; *see* **modem**.

digital modem

A device, usually available as an internal expansion card, that enables a personal computer to connect with a high-speed digital cable system, such as the conditioned **twisted pair** wiring used with **Integrated Services Digital Network (ISDN)** telephone service. Digital modems usually include the **terminal adapter (TA)** that is needed to connect your computer to a digital telephone line.

The term "digital modem" is a contradiction in terms, since digital cabling systems such as ISDN do not require the **modulation** and **demodulation** that enables computer signals to traverse the **analog** telephone system. Still, some kind of interface is needed between the computer and digital lines, provided by so-called "digital modems."

In a world where analog lines predominate, a digital modem wouldn't prove of much value if it didn't include all the core set of **modulation protocols** that lets a modem communicate with virtually all analog modems. Ideally, a digital modem would also work transparently with existing **communications programs**. An example of a digital modem designed to meet these criteria is IBM's WaveRunner modem for Microsoft Windows systems.

download

To transfer a file from another computer to your computer by means of a modem and a telephone line. *Compare* **upload**.

To download a file to your computer, you must use a **file transfer protocol** which assures that the transmission is free from errors. The file transfer protocol of choice for computer **bulletin board systems (BBS)** is **Zmodem**. If you're accessing a UNIX computer system (such as a university's mainframe computer), you may use another protocol, such as **Kermit**. Most popular **communications programs** can transfer files with either of these protocols.

DTE

See **Data Terminal Equipment**

DTE speed

The speed at which a **Data Terminal Equipment (DTE)** device such as a personal computer or terminal can communicate with a **Data Communications Equipment (DCE)** device, such as a modem.

If you're using a modem that implements hardware **compression**, you should set the DTE speed as high as possible (with most systems, that's 57.7 Kbps). Otherwise, you will create a bottleneck between your computer and the modem that will slow down the effective rate of transmission. To set the DTE speed, use your operating system's control panel to adjust the speed of the serial port to which your modem is connected.

dual-tone multi-frequency (DTMF) tones

The tones generated by a touch-tone telephone and emulated by most **auto-dial modems.**

duplex

The simultaneous transmission of data in two directions. A duplex modem can send and receive information at the same time. All of the popular modems for PCs are duplex modems. *Compare* **half duplex.**

effective transmission rate

The rate at which a **modem** equipped with **on-the-fly** **data compression** capabilities appears to transfer data. The modem does not actually transfer data through the telephone line any faster than a modem that lacks on-the-fly compression, but because the data is compressed, less time is required to send the same data. The result is an apparent increase in the modem's speed. For example, a 9600 **bps** modem equipped with **MNP5** compression capabilities can transfer data at an effective rate of 19,200 bps. Modems equipped with **error correction protocols** can also generate gains in the effective transmission rate. *See* **compression.**

> Note that the effective transmission rate may be lower if you're transferring data that has already been compressed using a compression program such as PKZIP. Further compression of compressed files can actually slow down the transmission rate.

| error correction protocol |

 A standard that governs a **modem**'s capacity to correct errors in the transmitted data before they reach your PC. To enable error correction, both the sending and receiving modem must conform to the same error correction protocol. The two most common error correction protocols for PC modems are **V.42** and **MNP4**.

An error correction protocol differs from a **file transfer protocol** in two ways. The first difference is that the error correction protocol is built into the modem's hardware, unlike a file transfer protocol, which is enabled by the **communications program** you are using. (See **hardware error control**.) Because the error correction processing is handled by the modem, there's less demand on your computer's processing circuitry.

The second difference between an error correction and a file transfer protocol is that error correction is "on" at all times. File transfer protocols correct errors only when you're **uploading** or **downloading** a file. Line noise may generate **garbage characters** when you're sending or receiving text, such as electronic mail. Error correction protocols eliminate such errors during the entire transmission.

When two modems have established a connection by means of **V.42** or **MNP4**, they have achieved a **reliable connection**. You can assume that all the data you send and receive will be free from errors. In addition, you can expect gains in the modem's **effective transmission rate**. The use of the error correction protocol makes it unnecessary to use the **start bits** and **stop bits** that add two **bits** to each **byte** of transmitted data. With 20% less data to transmit, a modem rated at 9600 **bps** can transmit data at speeds up to 11,500 bps. (The gain does not equal 20% because of processing overhead introduced by the error correction method.)

Don't use an error-correcting file transfer protocol such as **Xmodem** if you have established a reliable link. The use of a file transfer protocol isn't necessary and can slow down the transmission.

escape sequence

A series of characters that you type to engage the **modem's command mode**. The escape sequence for **Hayes-compatible** modems is +++(three plus signs).

even parity

A type of **parity checking** in which the parity bit a bit in each transmitted **byte** of data that is set aside for error-correction purposes is set so that the number of 1 bits in the transmitted byte always adds up to an even number. If the number turns out to be odd when the byte is received, the receiving modem concludes that an error has occurred, discards the byte, and requests a retransmission. *Compare* **odd parity**.

extended character set

An IBM-defined set of 256 characters and control codes that includes the 128 standard characters of the **American Standard Code for Information Interchange (ASCII)**, as well as 128 additional characters that include technical, foreign language, graphics, and mathematical characters.

external modem

A modem that has its own case and power supply. To connect an external modem, you use a standard cable that runs from the modem to one of your computer's **serial ports**.

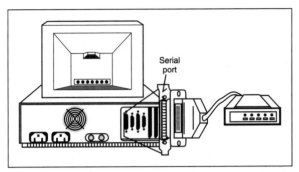

Figure 15.1 A standard external modem configuration

An external modems may have an advantage over an **internal modem** in some situations. Because you can easily disconnect an external modem, you can use it with more than one computer. In addition, the light-emitting diode (LED) indicators on the case's control panel can let you know what's happening with your connection (however, some communications programs, such as WinComm Pro, simulate these indicators on-screen even if you're using an internal modem). If your computer has a free serial port, an external modem may be easier to install. Since you are connecting the modem to a known serial port, you don't have to worry about port conflicts or IRQ conflicts, which can cause headaches when you're installing an internal modem. For more information on port conflicts and IRQ conflicts, see Chapter 7, Ports.

| factory configuration |

The set of **modem** operating options that were set by the modem's manufacturer. For example, most modems are configured so that they automatically wait for a dial tone before dialing a number. You can change the factory configuration by using **AT commands**. The resulting **active configura-**

tion applies for the rest of the current operating session; when you turn off your modem or reboot your system, the active configuration choices are lost and the modem returns to its factory configuration. *See* **initialization string**.

fall back

To revert automatically to a slower **data transfer rate** if the receiving **modem** cannot handle the faster rate. A modem capable of transmitting data at 14,400 **bps**, for instance, can fall back to 9600, 4800, 2400, and 1200 bps. This ensures compatibility with systems that have not upgraded their modems to the fastest available speed. Almost all modems can fall back to the speeds of earlier communications standards.

fall forward

To move to the next higher speed if changing line conditions make faster data transmission possible. A **modem** with fall-forward capabilities can restore faster communication after being forced to fall back due to **line noise**.

fax

An abbreviation of *facsimile*. The transmission of a digitized image of a page by means of a telephone line. Fax-capable devices (fax machines or **fax modems**) are required on both ends of the transmission. A fax machine optically scans the original piece of paper, digitizes the image, and transmits the digitized image via the telephone line. At the other end, the receiving fax machine receives the digitized image and prints it. If your modem has fax capabilities, you can send and receive faxes from your computer (*see* **fax modem**).

fax	fax modem

Like data communications, faxing is governed by international standards maintained by the ITU-TSS. *See* **Class 1**, **Group 3**.

---

fax modem

A modem that can send and receive faxes as well as computer data. You need a fax program, such as WinFax Pro (Delrina Corporation), to make use of your modem's fax capabilities.

Like other data communications, faxing benefits from the widespread adoption of international standards (called **protocols**) that govern the transmission of fax data. The standards relevant to fax modems are **Class 1**, **Group 3**, **V.17**, **V.27ter**, **V.29**, and **V.34**. Your fax modem should be able to communicate with most fax machines if it is compatible with the Class 1 and Group 3 standards.

Faxing from your computer, instead of a fax machine, has both advantages and disadvantages. When faxes arrive directly at your computer, they're more secure than they would be if they arrived at a fax machine used by many people. You can store copies of all your faxes (the ones you've received as well as the ones you've sent) on your computer's hard disk, and retrieve them when you please. Software for fax modems includes many more features than fax machines, such as a phone book that lets you select a destination number just by choosing an item from a list. On the negative side, with a fax modem you can only send faxes that you've created with your computer, such as word processing documents or graphics files. If you want to fax something that's already printed on paper, you'll need a scanner—an expensive peripheral—which might cost more than a good fax machine.

---

fax switch

An accessory that can distinguish between incoming voice, fax, and data calls, and route them accordingly.

> Buying a fax switch is a good idea if you're using the same line for a telephone and a **fax modem**. With the fax switch, you can leave your fax modem set to the **auto-answer mode** without fear that callers will hear the fax tone.

---

file transfer protocol

A standard for the error-free transfer of program and data files between two computers linked by modems. File transfer protocols in common use include **Xmodem, Xmodem-1k, Xmodem/CRC, Ymodem**, and **Zmodem**. The generic term "file transfer protocol" should not be confused with File Transfer Protocol (FTP), the **Internet** standard for file exchange.

---

flow control

A method of controlling the amount of information that is sent so that the transmitted data does not overwhelm the receiving system. This is accomplished by messages that say in effect, Wait, I'm busy." or "OK, I'm ready." In **modem**-to-modem communication, **software handshaking** (called **XON/XOFF** handshaking) handles the flow control between the two linked modems, while **hardware handshaking** (called **CTS/RTS**) handles flow control between your computer and your modem.

> If your **communications program** supports it, turn on hardware flow control between your computer and your modem.

frame

A unit of data of a specified size, such as 128 bytes, that has been set aside for error-checking purposes. *See* **cyclic redundancy check (CRC)**.

frequency shift keying (FSK)

A simple **modulation** technique that involves shifting the frequency of the **carrier** signal as a means of conveying information. Frequency shift keying is a simple modulation technique employed in the early **Bell 103** protocol (300 bits per second). In frequency shift keying, every change in the carrier signal conveys 1 bit of data; thus the **baud** rate and the **bits per second (bps)** rate of FSK **modems** are identical. *Compare* **group coding**, **trellis-code modulation**.

full duplex

See duplex.

garbage characters

 Extraneous, meaningless characters that are introduced by **line noise** during data communications.

 If you see many garbage characters, you may have a "dirty line"—a connection that's especially noisy. Try hanging up and redialing.

Gbps

See **bits per second (bps)**.

Group 1

An obsolete international standard for **fax** machines that requires six minutes to transfer a single page of information.

Group 2

An obsolete international standard for **fax** machines that requires about three minutes to transfer a single page of information.

Group 3

The reigning international standard for **fax** machines and **fax modems** that can transfer a single page of information in a minute or less. A fax modem that is compatible with the Group 3 standard should be able to communicate with most of the fax machines in common use today. The Group 3 standard is maintained by the **ITU-TSS**.

The Group 3 fax standard does not specify the speed at which fax transmission occurs; this is handled by additional standards. The **V.27ter** standard specifies fax transmissions at rates of 4800 **bits per second (bps)**. The **V.29** standard regulates fax transmissions at rates of 9600 bps, while the **V.17** standard regulates speeds of 14,400 bps.

Group 4

An advanced standard for **fax** transmission adopted by the **ITU-TSS** in 1987. The Group 4 standard calls for near-typeset quality reproduction of fax images, but it requires high-speed, digital transmission lines and expensive, specialized equipment. **Group 3** is expected to remain the most widely-used standard for faxing until telephone companies succeed in their aim of extending **digital** services to homes and offices. This aim won't be achieved anytime soon—certainly not in the twentieth century.

group coding

A method of improving the **data transfer rate** of a modem by signifying two or more **bits** of data with each change in the **modem**'s signal. For example, a modem that can produce four completely different signals can signify four two-bit patterns (00, 01, 10, and 11). A modem that can produce 16 different signals can represent all the possible combinations of 4 bits. A modem that can produce 256 different signals can represent all the possible combinations of 8 bits. To produce the necessary number of distinct signals, group coding techniques employ more than one **modulation** technique. For example, **quadrature modulation** varies the phase (by shifting the wave forms of the outgoing signal) as well as the amplitude (by varying the volume). *Compare* **frequency shift keying**.

half duplex

The transmission of data in one direction at a time (*compare* **duplex**). A half duplex modem can send information or receive information, but it cannot do both at the same time. All of the popular **modems** for PCs today are duplex modems, but can shift to half duplex if you're trying to connect to a really ancient mainframe computer.

handshaking

 An automatic process in which a **modem** determines the best **modulation protocol**, **error correction protocol**, and **data compression protocol** to use when a connection is established. *Synonymous with* negotiation.

When your modem establishes a link with another modem, a complex series of exchanges takes place. First, the remote modem sends its answer tone, which gives human callers a chance to recognize that they've reached a machine instead of a person, and hang up. Next, the remote modem sends out what sounds to human ears like a piercing hiss or a burst of static. This signal is part of the process by which the modems negotiate the fastest possible data transfer rate they can achieve between them. Subsequent negotiations settle on error correction and data compression protocols, if the modems are capable of these advanced communications functions. **High-speed modems** exchange test data so that they can equalize their response to the unique properties of the specific connection they've established; for example, a particular connection may not provide flat frequency response across the entire frequency spectrum. The modems compensate by boosting their output in the frequencies suppressed by the connection.

> You know that the modem on the other end of the line is capable of 14,400 **bits per second (bps)** and **V.42** error correction—but the modems establish a 9600 bps connection. What gives? The likely culprit is extraordinary **line noise**. Hang up and try again.

---

hardware error control

The provision of an **error correction protocol**, such as **MNP4** or **V.42**, within the **modem** rather than in the **communications program**. Locating the error control in the modem reduces the demand on your computer's internal processing circuitry. *Compare* **software error control**.

> If you're shopping for a modem, insist on hardware error control. Software error control results in a cheaper modem, but only by transferring the processing to your computer. Worse, the error correction will be available only

if you're using a communication program that enables it, and there are very few that do.

hardware handshaking

A type of **flow control**, designed to moderate the amount of information that is sent so that the transmitted data does not overwhelm the receiving system, that governs the transfer of data between your computer and your modem. In hardware handshaking, the two linked devices send messages concerning information flow by means of signals sent on wires set aside for that purpose. *Synonymous with* **CTS/RTS**.

Hayes command set

See **AT command set**.

Hayes-compatible

Able to respond to the **AT command set**. Hayes Microcomputer Products, Inc., originated the AT control language that is widely used to control **modems**. **Communications programs** translate your on-screen choices, such as selections from menus, into the AT commands that Hayes compatible modems recognize.

You'll be wise to choose a Hayes-compatible modem, as they are supported by all communications programs.

high speed modem

Conventionally, a **modem** capable of **data transfer rates** of at least 9600 **bits per second (bps)**—but this is considered slow at this writing. In practical terms, 14,400 bps is the minimal definition of high-speed, and that's particularly true now that 28,800 bps modems are becoming widely available at low prices.

Should you upgrade to a high-speed modem? With most commercial **online information services**, you'll pay more for high-speed access. But it's well worth it to pay the higher costs of high-speed access—you'll save when it comes to connect-time charges—and even more if you must pay for long-distance telephone access to the remote system).

High Speed Technology (HST)

A **proprietary protocol** developed by U.S. Robotics, a **modem** manufacturer, to govern data transmission at rates of 14,400 **bits per second (bps)** in one direction and 450 bps in the other direction. The modem can switch directions depending on which modem is originating the heaviest flow of data.

Because HST is a proprietary protocol, an HST modem can't communicate with another modem unless it is also HST-compatible. HST was an early high-speed protocol but has been supplanted by modems conforming to the **V.32bis** protocol.

Don't buy a modem that offers only a proprietary **modulation protocol** like HST unless you're doing so for a very specific reason—for example, you must establish a connection with a host system that's using a modem with the same proprietary protocol.

host mode

A modem operating mode in which the modem is set up to answer calls automatically. *See* **auto-answer mode**.

initialization

The configuration of a **modem** at the beginning of an operating session. Every modem comes with a **factory configuration**, but it is usually desirable to add some **AT commands** to your **active configuration**, which applies during the current operating session. The easiest way to do this is by using your **communications program** to choose an **initialization string** that's appropriate for your modem (*see* **initialization string**).

If your communications program won't hang up at the end of a session with a **bulletin board system (BBS)** or online information service, add the string &D2 to your modem's initialization string.

initialization string

A series of **AT commands** that your **communications program** automatically enters at the beginning of every session with your **modem**. The initialization string amends the **factory configuration** with your **active configuration** choices.

Most communication programs come with a prepared list of initialization strings for popular modems. You probably won't have to alter the string your program enters for the brand and model of modem you're using.

Integrated Services Digital Network (ISDN)

A set of standards for high-speed **digital** communications that can make use of existing telephone lines. Widely implemented in Europe, ISDN is capable of delivering graphics, sound, low-resolution video, and text data as well as noise-free voice transmission to home users without requiring a massive capital investment. In North America, ISDN implementation has been so slow that wags have renamed it "It Still Does Nothing."

Still, it's certain that digital telephone lines will one day reach homes, schools, and offices, and for a very simple reason: The present system is obsolete.

The existing telephone system was designed to handle the human voice. by using **analog** technology. A microphone converts the human voice into an undulating current, whose variations match the changing frequencies of human vocal output. At the other end, a speaker reproduces the voice— but, as generations of phone users can attest, with sometimes less fidelity than the original and with the addition of a substantial amount of **line noise**. During a conversation, line noise can be irritating, but during computer data transmission it's often more so: error-free data transmission via the telephone system requires **modems** and **file transfer protocols** (such as **Zmodem** or **Kermit**) that retransmit units of data if line noise disturbs the transmission. This substantially lowers the speed of data transmission.

As millions of audio compact disc enthusiasts have discovered, **digital** techniques provide accurate reproduction of the original sound while virtually eliminating extraneous noise. This is done by converting the audio signal into **bits** (1s and 0s), the basic units of digital information. A digital telephone system could bring the same benefits to telephone and computer users: accurate rendition of the human voice against a silent, noise-free background, and it would bring benefits to computer users, as well. By eliminating line noise (and consequently the need for retransmission), digital telephone lines bring significant gains in data transmission speeds. Existing ISDN systems can handle 64,000 **bits per second (bps)** of data, a figure that can be increased to 200,000 bits per second with data compression. Compared to the 14,400 bits per second achieved with today's standard modems and analog phone lines, the benefits in the increased **effective transfer rate** are obvious. A high-resolution graphic that today takes ten minutes to **download** could be received in a minute or less. But ISDN lacks sufficient **bandwidth** to realize the lofty goal of distributed computing, in which—from the user's perspective—all network resources are accessible at speeds at least approaching those of directly-connected peripherals such as disk drives.

ISDN is a proven digital telephone technology that is already widely implemented in Europe and Japan. The standard was originally proposed by the **ITU-TSS**, a United Nations organization that coordinates international telecommunications, in 1984. In the United States, the regional Bell companies have been slow to offer ISDN. The delay is partly attributable to incompatible standards. This problem has been resolved by the 1991 publication of the ISDN-1 standard, which makes the regional Bell offerings compatible not only with each other but also with foreign ISDN systems. More than 50% of regional Bell system lines were expected to have ISDN capability by the end of 1994.

For telephone subscribers, the immediate advantage of ISDN lies in the quality of the incoming signal and the ability to use two devices with one line. When an ISDN device "rings," the receiver—whether a **digital modem**, a fax machine, or a digital phone—receives a complex message including the originating phone number, the data transfer rate that has been established, and additional information that helps to assure the fastest possible connection. And because even the least-expensive ISDN services provide two digital data pathways, it is possible to operate a modem and place a telephone call over the same line.

If your telephone company extends an ISDN line to your home, you can kiss your old, **analog modem** good-bye. An ISDN line removes the last vestige of analog transmission—and with it, the rationale for modems, which transform the computer's digital impulses into the warbling, analog sounds required by standard analog telephone lines. But you'll still need some equipment, such as a **terminal adapter (TA)** that links your computer directly to the ISDN lines, a **network termination-1 unit (NT-1)** that terminates the digital telephone line, and a digital modem. This equipment could cost as much as $750 at current price levels (which are expected to decline).

In the United States, ISDN services fall into to three categories: Basic Rate ISDN (BRI), Primary Rate ISDN (PRI), and Broadband ISDN (B-ISDN). Designed as the basic option for consumers, Basic Rate ISDN offers two 64,000 bit per second channels for voice, graphics, and data, plus one 16,000 bit per second channel for signalling purposes. Primary Rate ISDN provides 23 channels with 64,000 bits per second capacity. Broadband ISDN, still under development, would supply up to 150 million bits per second of data transmission capacity, which is sufficient for high-definition television (HDTV); however, this would require the replacement of twisted-pair telephone lines with optical fiber.

If you're like many home computer users these days, you're probably thinking about getting an extra POTS ("plain old telephone service") line for your home so that you and others can place and receive voice calls while your modem's in action. But before doing so, call your local telephone company to find out if ISDN service is available for your residence. A single ISDN line can carry two "B" (64,000 bps) channels, and might be cheaper—or the same price—as two POTS lines. But bear in mind that you'll run into additional costs for the equipment needed to connect your computer system to the ISDN line. Also, expect to pay a stiff fee ($200 is the going rate) for ISDN installation, which requires extensive line testing to make sure that the circuits can handle the increased data flow.

| internal modem |

A **modem** designed to fit within one of your computers expansion slots (see System Units) or PCMCIA slots (see Ports). Internal modems for notebooks (see Notebooks and Personal Digital Assistants) use a special, proprietary design to link with the computer. Compared with **external modems**, internal modems are cheaper because no power supply or case is required.

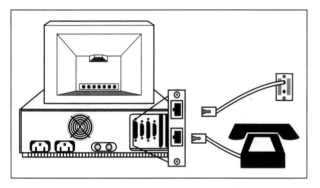

Figure 15.2 A standard internal modem configuration

If you're adding a modem to an older PC, you may have an additional reason for preferring an internal modem besides lower cost. Older PCs are equipped with slow **Universal Asynchronous Receiver/Transmitter (UART)** circuits that may not be able to accommodate today's **high-speed modems**. To connect an external modem to your PC, you must do so through the computer's serial port (see Ports), and you're stuck with your PC's UART. You could find that you're unable to use the modem's highest speed unless you replace the UART, adding additional cost. But internal modems come with their own, high-speed UART (called a 16550 UART), which is designed to work with **high-speed modems**.

International Telecommunications Union-Telecommunications Standards Section (ITU-TSS)

An international organization, headquartered in Switzerland, responsible for developing the standards for the international exchange of telephone, telegraph, and data communications. ITU-TSS's parent organization is the International Telecommunication Union (ITU), a United Nations agency that also deals with international radio broadcasting. More than 160 nations belong to ITU-TSS and send representatives to its conferences. ITU-TSS standards are published every four years in volumes called fascicles, with the color of the covers varying by year.

ITU-TSS is responsible for the key **protocols** used in **modem** telecommunications. These include **modulation protocols** (such as **V.21, V.22, V.22bis, V.32,** and **V.32bis**), an **error correction protocol (V.42)**, and a **data compression protocol (V.42bis)**.

Internet

The Internet (uppercase I), as opposed to *an* internet (lowercase i). The emerging world network of thousands of physical networks that can exchange data by means of the **TCP/IP** protocols. The result is a cyberspace of prodigious dimensions, an enormously valuable global resource of information and collaboration. Personal computer users can access the Internet by means of a **modem** and **dialup access**, but the preferred means of modem-based access is to use a **high-speed modem** and a connection based on the **Serial Line Internet Protocol (SLIP)** or **Point-to-Point Protocol (PPP)**.

The Internet is the computer space created by the Internet's technical means of connecting dissimilar networks so that they can exchange mail and data quickly and transparently. In fact, the TCP/IP protocols can and are used on very different kinds of networks, spanning the gamut from local area networks (LANs) such as Ethernet, metropolitan area networks (MANs) and regional networks that link the LANs in a city or region, to one of several high-speed transmission lines that carry Internet data over transcontinental and transoceanic hauls. Along the way, Internet data may traverse a variety of physical media, telephone wires, fiber optic cable, communications satellites, and microwave relay systems. In the future, Internet data will traverse the experimental gigabit networks of the coming National Information Infrastructure (NII). In short, the Internet isn't a physical network. It's a way of getting dissimilar physical networks to work together so that users of these networks can exchange data.

Networks come and go, but the Internet remains—and grows. The Internet is growing an estimated 10 to 15% per month so any mention of specific numbers of networks and hosts quickly becomes inaccurate. At this writing, well over 2 million computers were directly addressable through the Internet, including an estimated 20 million people in 69 countries, with strong penetration in the U.S., Canada, Mexico, most of Europe, Russia, China, Singapore, Australia, and New Zealand. According to National Science Foundation (NSF) statistics, the rate at which new networks are added to the Internet in foreign countries (183%) exceeds domestic U.S. network growth (160%). It's estimated that by 1998, the Internet may have 100 million users worldwide.

The Internet is growing so rapidly for many reasons.

- The Internet's ability to link physically dissimilar networks frees users to choose the equipment they need. A graphics artist in Cupertino uses a high-end Macintosh, while an engineer in Gothenberg, Sweden uses a Sun workstation. Yet the Internet can link them, and provide them the means to exchange files and data.

- The Internet is fast becoming the world's de facto electronic mail system. By means of gateways, Internet users can exchange electronic mail with users of many additional networks that don't use TCP/IP, widening the Internet's impressive reach even further. An estimated 25 million people are now thought to have the ability to exchange electronic mail by means of the Internet and Internet gateways.

- The Internet's protocols (standards) are in the public domain and are supported by virtually every manufacturer of network equipment. These manufacturers are also experiencing phenomenal growth—manufacturers of Internet routers (devices that route **TCP/IP** data packets) have recently experienced some of the fastest business growth rates ever observed in the U.S. With this growth comes the economies of scale that send prices of Internet equipment are plummeting. The Internet is a textbook example of the economic and technological benefits of effective standardization.

- Once confined to universities, research centers, and government agencies, the Internet is quickly moving out into the mainstream of society. Freenets and online information services make Internet access available to individuals, while commercially-oriented network service providers are hooking up corporations and small businesses at rapidly accelerating rates. In 1993, the amount of commercial traffic on the Internet exceeded other uses for the first time. Firms everywhere are concluding that the Internet is an indispensable resource for business. The commercialization of the Internet, as well as the concomitant process of privatization, will change the network's character—but no one is certain just how.

- Viewed as a public communication medium, the Internet is a revolution. As opposed to broadcast media that sends you only what the broadcaster wants you to see, read, or hear, the Internet is a two-way communication that lets every participant become an originator as well as a consumer of information and resources. The quality of the resources contributed by individuals varies, of course, but it's quite possible to discover some material on the Internet that will prove of tremendous value to you—a bibliography, a utility program, a graphic, or just a few wise words from a very knowledgeable person. These resources don't have much (if any) commercial value and wouldn't be available in a broadcast medium. And suffusing the Internet is what Mitch Kapor, president of the Electronic Frontier Foundation (EFF), calls a "gift economy": an ethic that stresses the common good that arises from everyone contributing to the network in an unselfish spirit.

interoperability

The capacity of a computer device to work with and control another computer device, even though the other device was made by a different manufacturer. With respect to modems, interoperability is ensured by conformity to published international standards, such as those developed by the **ITU-TSS**. For example, a Supra modem that conforms to the v.32bis protocol can interact with a Hayes modem that conforms to the same protocol.

ITU-TSS

See **International Telecommunications Union-Telecommunications Standards Section**

Kbps

See **bits per second (bps)**.

Kermit

 A **file transfer protocol** for use with **modems** that allows a mainframe and a PC to reliably exchange data by means of **dialup access**. Unlike the file transfer protocols commonly used in personal computing (**Xmodem**, **Ymodem**, and **Zmodem**), Kermit is designed to deal with the problems that arise when one of the linked computers uses the **7-bit ASCII** code, commonly used on mainframe computers, while the other one uses the 8-bit **extended character set** used with PCs. The protocol transmits data in variable-length blocks with error checking by means of a **checksum**. Enhancements to the original protocol include data **compression** and the ability to send data in long-length packets of 1,024 **bytes**.

leased line

A permanently-connected telephone line allows constant transmission between two computers. A leased line is conditioned to eliminate noise and allow the transmission of data at high rates. Typically, leased lines can handle between 56,000 and 64,000 **bits per second** of data.

line noise

In a telephone line, any extraneous or random signal introduced by interference of many possible kinds, such as telephone company switching operations, lightning storms, crosstalk between adjacent lines, and current fluctuations.

Link Access Protocol for Modems (LAPM)

An **error correction protocol** that is included in the **ITU-TSS V.42** standard. V.42 attempts to establish a connection with LAPM; if the other **modem** does not recognize LAPM, the protocol attempts to use **MNP4**. If the other modem does not recognize MNP4, error correction is abandoned and a non-error-correcting connection is established. Like other **error correction protocols**, LAPM can eliminate **garbage characters** attributable to **line noise**. It also increases the effective **data transfer rate** by eliminating the use of start and stop bits for each byte of transmitted data.

local echo

In a **communications program,** when the characters you type are displayed on-screen at the same time the **modem** sends them to the computer with which you're communicating.

Local echo isn't often required. Most **bulletin board systems (BBS)** and **online information services** send the characters you type back to your screen so that you can see whether they were correctly received.

local loop

The **copper pair** wire that runs from the local telephone company's central office to your house. Employing **analog** transmission technology that was designed to accommodate the human voice but not computer data, these wires have limited **bandwidth** for computer data communications (56 Kbps is a frequently-cited theoretical maximum with analog technology). A **modem** is required to transmit computer signals via the local loop.

log

A record of your transactions. A **communications program,** for example, can keep a log of your online activity.

log off

To end your online connection by choosing the command that ends the session. In a **bulletin board system (BBS),** for example, you usually log off by typing bye or g (short for "goodbye").

Don't log off by just hanging up (without issuing the log off command). Although most systems can handle this, some computers leave processes running when you exit this way, and that ties up computer resources so that others can't use them.

---

log on

To make an online connection with computer by typing your **login name** and password.

---

login name

The name you type as part of the procedure you use to **log on** to a **remote system**.

---

lossless compression

A method of data **compression**, used with program and data files, that seeks to preserve all of the original data without alteration. Lossless compression techniques are used in compression programs such PKZIP.

---

lossy compression

A method of data **compression**, used with graphics and video files, that sacrifices some loss of the data in ways that are not apparent to a person who is viewing or listening to the file after it has been transmitted. An example of a lossy compression standard is the Joint Photographic Expert's Group (JPEG) technique.

Mbps

See **bits per second (bps)**

Microcom Networking Protocol (MNP)

A series of **error correction** and **compression protocols** originally developed by Microcom, Inc., a **modem** manufacturer. There are a total of 10 MNP protocols, of which the first (MNP1) is obsolete. MNP2, MNP3, and MNP4 are error correction protocols that have been incorporated into the international ITU-TSS **V.42** error correction protocol (*see* **MNP4**). **MNP5** is a compression protocol. Most of today's popular modems support MNP2 through MNP5. MNP6 through MNP10 are **proprietary protocols** for advanced error correction, compression, and handshaking and are not widely used.

MNP 4

An **error correction protocol** that is incorporated into the **ITU-TSS V.42** standard as an alternate. (The default error correction protocol is called **Link Access Procedure for Modems (LAPM)**. MNP4 can actually improve the **effective transmission rate** because it strips the **start bits** and **stop bits** from the transmitted data, reducing the amount of information that must be conveyed by 20 percent. Also, MNP4 varies the length of the packets depending on the quality of the line; the better the quality, the larger the packet, and the more efficient the transmission.

MNP5

A **compression protocol** that is widely supported by popular **modems** as an alternative to **V.42bis**. MNP5 is an **on-the-fly data compression** protocol that compresses outgoing data and sends it to an MNP5-compatible modem, where it is decompressed. By reducing the amount of data that has to be transmitted, MNP5 can double the **effective transmission rate** of a modem.

Don't let the promise of a doubled transmission rate get you excited. Much of the information you're **downloading** from **bulletin board systems (BBS)** has already been compressed. Data that has already been compressed cannot be compressed further—and in fact, doing so may actually increase rather than decrease the size of a file.

modem

A peripheral that permits your computer to communicate with other computers via the telephone system, which can't handle computer signals without modification (called **modulation**). To send signals, a modem modulates (changes) them so that they can be sent over the telephone line; it also demodulates incoming signals. The term "modem" is an abbreviation of MOdulator/DEModulator.

You can't connect your computer directly to the telephone line because the telephone system wasn't designed for computer communications. The telephone system is an **analog** communication system that was designed for the human voice. When you speak into your telephone's handset, a microphone transforms your voice into a continuously fluctuating electrical current, which modifies a **carrier**—a continuous tone that you can't hear. The fluctuations in the current mimic those of your voice. On the receiving end, the receiving phone transforms these fluctuations back into sounds.

Computers don't communicate using continuously-varying tones. In contrast, they use on-off pulses, which correspond to the basic units of digital information (bits). Since the phone system can't handle a computer's on-off pulses, the modem transforms these pulses into tones that fall within the normal frequency range of the human voice (from about 100 to 3000 cycles per second). This process is called modulation. The modem also transforms incoming sound signals, sent from the computer at the other end of the line, back into the **digital** form your computer can recognize (called demodulation).

To communicate with each other, the modems at the sending and receiving ends of the line must obey the same **modulation protocol**, a standard that specifies the modulation method. The modulation protocol in turn determines the maximum **data transfer rate** that the modem can achieve, provided it is linked with a modem that conforms to the same protocol.

Modems will be rendered obsolete by innovations such as **ISDN** (a high-speed digital telephone system that can use existing telephone lines), cable TV systems carrying Internet as well as all those junky TV channels, and the National Information Infrastructure (NII), which will extend high-speed digital communications links to homes, offices, and schools. But you'll still need devices such as a **terminal adapter (TA)** to connect your computer to these high-speed lines.

Going with the herd is always a good idea when you're considering computer communciation choices—you want to be able to communicate with as many computers as possible. By this reasoning, you won't go wrong with a modem confirming to the **V.32bis** protocol, which enables communication at speeds up to 14,400 **bits per second (bps)**. On the horizon are modems conforming to the new **V.34** protocol, which will enable communication at speeds up to 28,800 bps.

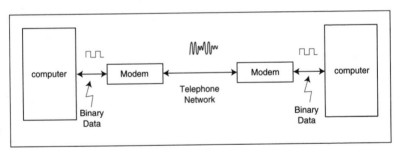

Figure 15.3 Modems linked by telephone connection

modular jack

In a telephone system, a standard, wall-mounted receptacle that is designed to accept the modular telephone cable packaged with most modems. If your home was constructed prior to 1970, it may have an obsolete, four-prong connector; you can purchase an adapter (code-numbered RJA1X) that provides the needed receptacle. *Synonymous with* **RJ-11**.

| modulation |

The process of transforming digital information into a varying audio tone that contains the same information. This is done by making changes to a continuous tone, called a **carrier**. The technique by which this is achieved is called a **modulation protocol**. Computer **modems** modulate outgoing computer signals so that they travel through the telephone system, which is designed for voice communications rather than digital computer signals. *Compare* **demodulation**.

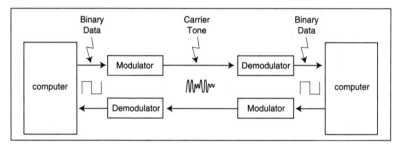

Figure 15.4 Modulation and demodulation

| modulation protocol |

The standard that describes the precise technique by which a **modem** changes **digital** signals into varying tones that convey information over telephone lines. The modulation protocol determines the maximum **data transfer rate** that the modem can achieve. Early modulation protocols were developed by AT&T's Bell Laboratories (*see* **Bell 103**, **Bell 212A**), but these found use only in North America. World-wide standards, preceded by a V as in **V.32bis**, are set by the **ITU-TSS** (formerly called CCITT). Most modems now observe the ITU-TSS standards, although some include **proprietary protocols**.

Make sure that you buy a modem that conforms to a recent ITU-TSS protocol, such as **V.32bis** (14,400 **bps**) or **V.34** (28,800 bps). The use of international standards has led to the explosive growth of computer networking. If you use a modem conforming to a proprietary standard, you probably won'e be able to use many services.

negotiation

See **handshaking**

network termination 1 unit (NT-1)

In an **Integrated Services Digital Network (ISDN)** telephone system, a device that terminates the digital connection at the subscriber's end of the circuit, and provides inputs for up to eight of the subscriber's digital devices (such as digital telephones, **digital modems**, and digital fax machines). The NT-1 is usually mounted on the wall, like a **modular jack**, and requires its own power supply (typically, a small transformer that plugs directly into a wall outlet). In the U.S., ISDN subscribers must typically buy their own NT-1s, adding significantly (from $125-$300) to the cost of ISDN installation.

null modem cable

A cable designed to connect to the **serial ports** of two computers. The cable's wiring hoodwinks the computers into thinking they're linked via **modems**. If both computers are running **communications programs**, they can exchange data.

odd parity

A type of **parity checking** in which the **parity bit,** a **bit** in each transmitted byte of data that is set aside for error-correction purposes, is set so that the number of 1 bits in the transmitted **byte** always adds up to an odd number. If the number turns out to be even when the byte is received, the receiving modem concludes that an error has occurred, discards the byte, and requests a retransmission. *Compare* **even parity, no parity.**

offline

Not connected to another computer via a telephone connection or a network. While offline, you can perform tasks such as editing and updating the list of numbers you can dial, and choosing settings for the **modem.** *Compare* **online.**

on-the-fly data compression

A method of compressing transmitted data during the transmission rather than before the transmission takes place. On-the-fly compression requires **modems** that conform to a **compression protocol,** such as **V.42bis** or **MNP5.** The sending modem compresses the data, while the receiving modem decompresses it. *See* **compression.**

online

Directly connected to another computer via a telephone connection or a network. *Compare* **offline.**

online information service

A for-profit, subscription-based computer service that makes computer resources available to dialup users. These resources typically include up-to-the-minute news, weather, sports results, discussion groups, thousands of files to **download**, technical information on computer products, and games. The most popular online information services are CompuServe, Prodigy and America Online.

Online information services are professional versions of **bulletin board systems (BBS)**, the do-it-yourself computer services set up by computer hobbyists. Many BBSs are free. If you're interested in trying an online service you can learn the basics, such as establishing the communication and downloading files by practicing on a local BBS.

originate

To place a call to another computer via a **modem** and a telephone line.

originate mode

A mode of computer modems, usually the default mode, in which the modem is set to originate calls but not to answer them. *Compare* **auto-answer mode**.

parity

In computer **error correction protocols**, whether or not a transmitted value is the same at the receiving end as it was when it was transmitted. If the value is not the same, the receiving computer concludes that an error has occurred and requests a retransmission. *See* **parity checking**.

parity checking

A common **error correction protocol** in which the sum of the **bits** in a **byte** of data is taken at the sending and receiving points in the transmission. Parity checking works by adding an eighth bit, called the **parity bit**, to the 7-bit code used to represent characters. In **even parity**, the eighth bit is set so that the sum is always an even number. In **odd parity**, the eighth bit is set so that the sum is always an odd number. With even parity checking, the receiving station rejects the data if the sum is odd; with odd parity, the receiving station rejects the data if the sum is even.

Don't rely on **file transfer protocols**, such as Xmodem, that use nothing but parity checking. Parity checking techniques can't guarantee that the data has been received free from errors. Multiple errors may result in the sum looking as if it is correct to the receiving station. *Compare* **cyclic redundancy check (CRC)**.

PCMCIA modem

A **modem** designed to fit within one of your notebook computer's PCMCIA slots (see Chapter 7, Ports).

Plain Old Telephone Service (POTS)

The standard telephone service provided to residences, consisting of a **copper pair** wire that's set up for **analog** transmission. POTS is not suited for **digital** communication; to communicate via POTS, computers need a the assistence of **modems**. *Compare* **Integrated Services Digital Network (ISDN)**.

pocket modem

A miniature, battery-powered **external modem** designed for use with notebook computers.

Point-to-Point Protocol (PPP)

One of the two most prominent protocols for **dialup IP access** to the Internet (the other is **SLIP**). PPP establishes a method of Internet access in which a personal computer, linked to an Internet computer via a telephone connection and a high-speed modem, appears to the rest of the world as if its directly connected to the Internet. PPP temporarily establishes a direct Internet connection in which Internet data can travel directly from and to your computer system, eliminating the mediation of the mini- or mainframe host computer (compare **dialup access**). Because a direct Internet connection is established, you can run graphical programs such as Mosaic on your computer system. Also the successor to SLIP, PPP offers superior data compression, handshaking, and error correction.

proprietary protocol

A **modulation protocol** or **error correction protocol** that a given manufacturer has developed but refused to share with other manufacturers or submit to the standardization process. If you are using a **modem** with a proprietary protocol, you may not be able to get the best performance unless your modem is linked to another modem made by the same manufacturer.

Whatever else you do when you buy a modem, avoid proprietary protocols like the plague. Choose a modem that conforms to established **ITU-TSS** standards and includes the **core set of modulation protocols**.

| protocol |

A technical standard that specifies how two computers can communicate and exchange data with each other. Protocols relevant to **modems** include **modulation protocols** (such as **V.32bis**), **error correction protocols** (such as **V.42** or **MNP4**), and **compression protocols** (such as **MNP5** and **V.42bis**).

| quadrature modulation |

A **group coding** technique for **modulating** the modem's **carrier** signal so that it can convey 2400 **bits per second** of data across a telephone line. In this technique, two methods of modulation are combined so that the **modem** can send a total of 16 separate signals, which can represent all the possible combinations of four bits of information. Quadrature modulation combines amplitude modulation (varying the loudness of the signal) as well as phase modulation (varying the arrival times of the peaks and troughs of the signal's wave form). *Compare* **trellis-code modulation.**

| reliable connection |

A connection established between two **modems** that share the same **error correction protocol** such as **V.42** or **MNP4**.

| remote system |

The computer system to which you establish a connection by means of your **modem**. Your **communications program** transforms your computer into a **remote terminal** of this system.

remote terminal

 A terminal (video display and keyboard) that is connected via telephone lines or network cables to a distant computer. With a **modem** and a **communications program**, you can transform your personal computer into a remote terminal of another computer. You operate the computer remotely by means of the remote terminal. This term derive from the heyday of mainframe computing, when remote terminals provided the only means of communication with computers.

RJ-11

See **modular jack**.

RJ-11 jack

 A modular telephone wall plug that is designed to work with modular telephone cables. Using a standard modular cable, you can plug most **modems** directly into RJ-11 jacks.

S register

A special memory storage area inside a **modem** that allows for the expansion of the basic **AT command set**. The options that are stored within the S registers include the ability to answer on a specific ring number and the time to wait for the **carrier** to appear.

serial port

An asynchronous port, conforming to the RS-232C standard of the Electronics Industry Association (EIA), that transforms the parallel bit stream within your computer into a single-file, one-after-the-other series that can be transferred by a two-wire connection. For more information, see Chapter 7.

setup switches

In older **modems**, a bank of DIP switches that permits the user to choose modem operation settings, such as whether the unit will answer an incoming call. In newer modems, these settings are selectable through your **communications program**. *See* **initialization**.

script language

In a **communications program**, a programming language that permits you to write (or record) a series of commands that can automatically perform repeated actions, such as **logging on** to a **bulletin board system (BBS)**.

serial communication

The transmission of data between computers by means of a single circuit, which requires the **bits** of data to be sent in a stream, one after the other, like cars on a one-lane road. Within the computer, data is transmitted in parallel, like cars on a multi-lane freeway. As the road analogy suggests, serial communication is slower than the parallel communications that take place inside your computer— and with **modems**, speed is further limited by the inherently low **bandwidth** of **plain old telephone service (POTS)**. Serial communications can employ **asynchronous communication** techniques (in which each **byte** of data is demarcated by **start** and **stop bits**) or **synchronous communication** techniques (in which a block or **frame** of data is transmitted along with control information that synchronizes the arrival of each frame).

Serial Line Internet Protocol (SLIP)

One of the two most prominent **protocols** for **dialup IP access** (the other is **PPP**). The SLIP protocol establishes a method of **Internet** access in which a personal computer, linked to an Internet computer via the telephone system and a **high-speed modem**, appears to the rest of the world as if it were directly connected to the Internet. SLIP establishes a temporary direct Internet connection in which Internet data can travel directly from and to your computer system, eliminating the mediation of the mini- or mainframe host computer (compare **dialup access**). Because a direct Internet connection is established, you can run graphical programs such as Mosaic on your computer system.

SLIP dialer

A program, running on a personal computer or UNIX workstation, that dials the number of an **Internet**-connected computer, and establishes a **Serial Line Internet Protocol (SLIP)** connection.

When you're using SLIP (or **PPP**, for that matter), no other **communications program** is necessary, and for a very simple reason: With SLIP and PPP, your computer is no longer acting as the remote **terminal** of a distant computer that has direct network connections. SLIP and PPP appear to actually give your computer a direct network connection. With SLIP and PPP, your computer is part of the Internet, and you can access and download all of the Internet's resources directly from your own computer.

software error control

 The provision of an **error correction protocol**, such as MNP4 or **V.42**, within the the **communications program** rather than the **modem**. Requiring error control in the software reduces the cost of designing and manufacturing a modem. *Compare* **hardware error control**.

If you're shopping for a modem, insist on hardware error control. Software error control results in a cheaper modem, but only by transferring the processing to your computer. Worse, the error correction will be available only if you're using a communication program that enables it, and there are very few that do.

software handshaking

A type of flow control, designed to moderate the amount of information that is sent so that the transmitted data does not overwhelm the receiving system, that governs the transfer of data between two modems. In software handshaking, the two linked devices send ASCII control characters to each other along the same channel that carries the transferred data (*compare* hardware **handshaking**). *Synonymous with* **XON/XOFF handshaking**.

start bit

In **asynchronous communication**, the **bit** that signals the beginning of a character.

stop bit

In **asynchronous communication**, a **bit** that signals the end of a **byte** of data. The number of stop bits employed by a given system is one of the fundamental **communications settings** (the other ones are **data bits** and **parity**) that you must specify before calling a remote computer. Most systems use one stop bit.

synchronous communication

One of two methods of solving the chief problem of **serial** communication: How to denote the beginning and the end of a unit of transmitted data (the other method is **asynchronous communication**). In synchronous communication, the two linked computers exchange timing and control messages so that they can exchange blocks of data, called **frames**. **Modems** that conform to the **V.42** error correction protocol can set up a synchronous link with another V.42-capable modem; this has the benefit of improving the **effective transfer rate** because it is not necessary to include a start and stop bit with each **byte** of transmitted data.

TCP/IP

Acronym for Transport Control Protocol/Internet Protocol. A set of related protocols that allow computers made by varying manufacturers to exchange messages and share resources across a computer network. The TCP/IP protocol suite, as well as specific programs based on these protocols, form the technical basis for the **Internet**. This network of networks is a packet switching network, in which a given message is broken up into packets of data—blocks of information that contain the addresses necessary to deliver them. The packets travel through the network independently, taking whatever route is freely available as they seek their destination. The packets are reassembled at their destination.

Personal computer users can connect to the Internet, and join in the give and take of TCP/IP data packets by using high-speed modems and computers equipped with the **Serial Line Interface Protocol (SLIP)** or **Point-to-Point Protocol (PPP)**. Such a connection is superior to **dialup access**, in which your computer becomes a remote terminal to a distant computer that has direct TCP/IP access. With SLIP or PPP, downloaded data comes directly to your computer, and you can use graphical Internet resource discovery tools such as Mosaic.

TCP/IP is the current world standard for internetworking compatibility; even Microsoft Corporation announced it is planning to include TCP/IP support in the next version of its phenomonally successful Windows software (Windows 95). TCP/IP's widespread acceptance is attributable to its openness (the protocols are in the public domain and are freely available), its hardware independence (the protocols are not tied to any specific brand or model of computer or networking hardware), and its transparency (from the user's perspective, the entire Internet is a single logical network, such that the differences among the many different computers and physical networks is hidden from the user's view).

terminal

A computer monitor and keyboard that can be connected via data communications links to a distant computer system. A "dumb" terminal has no processing circuitry of its own; its only function is to serve as a remote communication station for a computer that's installed somewhere else. A "smart" terminal has its own processing circuitry and disk drives for the storage of information. A **communications program** enables your computer to emulate a terminal so that you can access a **remote system**. To do this successfully, you must choose the correct kind of terminal to emulate. *See* **terminal emulation**.

terminal adapter (TA)

A device that connects computers and fax machines to an **Integrated Services Digital Network (ISDN)** telephone line. Like a **modem,** a TA can be installed internally in a computer's expansion slot or you can get an external TA with its own power supply.

Before shelling out money for a TA, check out the latest crop of **digital modems**. Increasingly, they come with a built-in terminal adapter, saving you the expense and hassle of installing a separate TA.

terminal emulation

The use of a **communications program** to transform your computer into a device that electronically simulates the functions of a **terminal**. Most communications programs permit you to choose from many terminals to emulate.

For dialup access to the **bulletin board systems (BBS)**, the most commonly-used terminal emulation is called **ANSI**.

terminal mode

In a **communications program**, the operating mode in which your computer becomes a **remote terminal** of a distant computer.

throughput

Synonymous with **effective transfer rate;** the effective rate at which two **modems** can transfer data, taking into account the effect of the **data compression protocol** and **error correction protocols**. The maximum throughput of a **V.32 bis** modem (nominally rated at 14.4 Kbps) is 57,600 **bits per second (bps)**, while the maximum throughput of a **V.34** modem 28.8 Kbps is 115,200 bps. However, these figures border on the imaginary because most of the data you'll exchange with other computers has been precompressed, and further compression cannot reduce its bulk.

trellis-code modulation (TCM)

A **group coding** technique for **modulating** the modem's **carrier signal** so that it can convey 9600 **bits per second** of data or more via a telephone line. Unlike slower group coding techniques, TCM works by assigning one modulation method to one axis of signal variation and a second modulation method to another, producing a matrix (a "trellis," if you like) in which each point on the matrix can be assigned a distinct value. This technique allows the modem to represent 16, 24 or more **bits** of data with each change in the modem's signal (**baud**). **High-speed modems** (more than 9600 bits per second) employ trellis-coded modulation techniques.

twisted pair

A high-quality telephone line, consisting of pairs of insulated copper cables that are twisted together in a helical form like a braid. This reduces interference from other wires, because two parallel wires form an antenna (consider the dipole antenna supplied with most stereo receivers). Twisted-pair wiring is now the standard for high-quality residential and office telephone installations, and is used in low-bandwidth local area networks (LANs). Twisted-pair wiring can handle low-speed **digital** transmission, such as the lowest level of **Integrated Services Digital Network (ISDN)**.Still, the provision of high-bandwidth data communications to homes, schools, and offices will probably require the rewiring of the **local loop** (the "last mile" of twisted pair wiring that extends from telephone company switching centers to residences and offices). The price tag? An estimated capital investment of $300 billion.

Universal Asynchronous Receiver/Transmitter (UART)

An integrated circuit that provides the key processing functionality of a serial port, namely, transforming the parallel bit stream of the computer into a single-file, one-after-the-other series of data bits. Once transformed by the UART, the serial data stream is ready for **modulation**, a task performed by the **modem**, so that it can be sent out via the telephone line. For more information on UARTs, see Chapter 7.

---

upload

To transfer a file from your computer to another computer by means a **modem** and a telephone line. *Compare* **download**.

Uploading is one of the several inconveniences of **dialup access**: If you want to send a file to a user elsewhere on the Internet, you must first upload the file to the **host** you're using. If the file is large, this can be a very time-consuming process in comparison with the speed of host-to-host links on today's Internet. A file that takes 12 minutes to upload with a 9600 bps modem can be transferred by FTP between two computers connected by something faster than a telephone connection in a matter of seconds.

To upload a file to your host, you must use a **file transfer protocol** which assures that the transmission is free from errors. The file transfer protocol of choice for computer **bulletin board systems (BBS)** is **Zmodem**. If you're accessing a UNIX host, you're more likely to use **Kermit**. Most popular **communications programs** can transfer files with either of these protocols.

V.17

A **modulation protocol** for **fax modems** and fax machines that governs fax transmissions at 14,400 **bits per second (bps)**, with the ability to fall back to 12,000 bps, 9600 bps, or 7200 bps if line conditions deteriorate. The protocol is regulated by the **ITU-TSS**.

V.21

A **modulation protocol** that governs transmissions at 300 **bits per second (bps)**. The protocol is regulated by the **ITU-**

TSS. This standard conflicts with the **Bell 103** standard widely used in North America.

V.22

A **modulation protocol** that governs transmissions at 1200 **bits per second (bps)**. The protocol is regulated by the **ITU-TSS**. This standard conflicts with the **Bell 212A** standard widely used in North America.

---

v.22 bis

A **modulation protocol** for **modems** that governs transmissions at 2400 **bps**, with the ability to **fall back** to 1200 and 600 bps. The protocol is regulated by the **ITU-TSS**. The first modulation protocol to gain world-wide acceptance, V.22bis employs **trellis-code modulation** techniques. V.22bis modems are in widespread use.

> Don't buy a v.22bis modem! For just a few dollars more, you can get a V.32bis modem that's capable of transmitting data at 14,400 bps.

V.27ter

A **modulation protocol** for **fax modems** and fax machines that governs fax transmissions at 4800 **bits per second (bps)**, with the ability to **fall back** to 2400 bps if line conditions deteriorate. The protocol is regulated by the **ITU-TSS**.

V.29

A **modulation protocol** for **fax modems** and fax machines that governs fax transmissions at 9600 **bits per second (bps)**, with the ability to **fall back** to 7200 bps if line conditions deteriorate. This standard is also used for 9600 bps transmission on **leased lines**. The protocol is regulated by the **ITU-TSS**.

v.32

A **modulation protocol** that governs transmissions at **9600 bps**, with the ability to **fall back** to 4800 bps. The protocol is regulated by the **ITU-TSS**. The v.32 protocol employs **trellis-code modulation** at the 9600 bps speed.

v.32 bis

A **modulation protocol** that governs transmissions at speeds of 14,400 **bps**, with the ability to **fall back** to 12,000 bps, 9600 bps, 7200 bps, and 4800 bps. The protocol is regulated by the **ITU-TSS**. Employing **trellis-code modulation**, V.32bis **modems** are inexpensive and in widespread use.

v.32terbo

A **modulation protocol** that governs transmissions at speeds of 19.2 K **bps**, with the ability to **fall back** to all the rates supported by the **V.32bis** standard. Despite the official-sounding name, V.32terbo is not an **ITU-TSS** standard; it is a proprietary standard developed in 1993 by AT&T.

The word "terbo" is a rather ugly neologism that plays on the similarities between the ITU-TSS's official term, ter ("the third"), and turbo.

Don't bother with a V.32terbo modem; now that the **V.34** has been published, V.32terbo will quickly fade into oblivion.

V.34

A **modulation protocol** that governs transmissions at speeds of 28,800 **bits per second (bps)**. Only recently made available, the protocol is regulated by the **ITU-TSS**. To achieve the high transmission rate, V.34 **modems**

adapt to changing line conditions in an effort to eke out all the possible **bandwidth** in a telephone line.

Because the ITU-TSS publishes standards only once every four years, the technology to produce 28,800 bps modems preceded the dissemination of the V.34 standard. As a result, several manufacturers have released what they call **V.fast** modems, which anticipate the V.34 protocols. Most of these modems can be upgraded to the V.34 protocol now that it has been published. To avoid the hassle of upgrading, avoid V.fast modems in favor of the newest ones that implement V.34.

V.42

An **error correction protocol**, regulated by the **ITU-TSS**, for the correction of errors that occur as a result of **line noise**. V.42 is a **hardware error control** protocol that is implemented within the **modem**, rather than in the communications software. When both the sending and receiving modems conform to the v.42 standard, errors are automatically detected and the sending modem is instructed to repeat the transmission until the information is received intact. V.42 incorporates **MNP4** as an alternative protocol, which will be employed automatically if the other modem cannot use the preferred method, **Link Access Protocol for Modems (LAPM)**.

V.42bis

A **compression protocol**, regulated by **ITU-TSS**, that produces the effect of speeding transmission because there is less data to transmit. The protocol specifies how data should be compressed on the sending end and decompressed on the other. If the data is not already compressed, gains in **effective transmission rates** of up to 400% can be realized. A competing standard is **MNP 10**.

V.Fast Class (V.FC)

A **proprietary standard** that was developed by a consortium of modem manufacturers in anticipation of the long-delayed **V.34 modulation protocol** (28,800 bps). Most V.FC modems can be upgraded to the V.34 standard.

voice-capable modem

A **modem** that can distinguish between incoming voice, fax, and data calls, and routing them accordingly. With a voice-capable modem and **voice mail** software, you can use your computer to set up a computerized answering machine and voice mail system. Future voice-capable modems linked with high-speed digital transmission lines will allow multi-party computer conferencing.

voice mail

A telephone answering system that permits the caller to make choices, leave messages, and route calls by pressing touch-tone keys on the telephone. With a **voice-capable modem** and the appropriate software, you can use your computer to set up an impressive voice mail system.

Xmodem

An early **file transfer protocol** for use with **modems** that allows two computers to exchange data reliably by means of **dialup access**. Xmodem employs a simple (but far from perfect) **error correction protocol** that performs a **checksum** operation on each transmitted 128-**byte frame** of data. If the checksum at the transmitting and receiving ends do not agree, the receiving modem abandons the frame and requests retransmission.

Xmodem	Ymodem

Created in 1978 by Ward Christiansen, this protocol is considered obsolete and may even degrade the performance of today's fast (14.4 **Kbps**) modems. Worse, Xmodem cannot assure valid data transfers: Certain kinds of errors in a transmitted frame can produce a valid checksum. A more advanced version is called **Xmodem/CRC**. *Compare* **Xmodem, Xmodem-1k,Zmodem**.

Don't use Xmodem unless the remote computer you're contacting supports no other protocol. The best file transfer protocol for most purposes is **Zmodem**.

Xmodem/CRC

An improved version of **Xmodem**, this **file transfer protocol** allows two computers to exchange data reliably by means of **dialup access**. Xmodem/CRC employes **Cyclic Redundancy Check (CRC)** on every two **bytes** transmitted. CRC error checking is more reliable than the **checksum** techniques employed in **Xmodem**, but it introduces **overhead** that slows down the **effective transfer rate**. *Compare* **Ymodem-1K, Zmodem**.

Xmodem-1K

An improved version of **Xmodem/CRC**, this **file transfer protocol** reduces the **overhead** of the Xmodem/CRC protocol by performing a **Cyclic Redundancy Check (CRC)** check only on large blocks of data (1,024 bytes). *Compare* **Ymodem, Zmodem**.

Ymodem

An improved version of **Xmodem-1K**, this **file transfer protocol** transfers files in 1,024-**byte** blocks and perfoms **Cyclic Redundancy Check (CRC)** error checking on each transmitted **frame**. It also allows multiple files to be sent in a single session called a batch transfer. *Compare* **Zmodem**.

Ymodem-g

A variant of **Ymodem**, this **file transfer protocol** does not perform any error checking. It's designed for use with **high-speed modems** capable of **V.42** or **MNP4** error-checking, which looks for errors in all the transmitted data (not just the data transmitted during file transfer operations).

The theory underlying Ymodem-g is that a file transfer protocol doesn't require error-checking if the modems themselves can provide this service. This eliminates the processing **overhead** that slows down the **effective transfer rate**. As a result, Ymodem-g is more than twice as fast as Ymodem, but only under good line conditions—and if an error is detected during the transfer, the entire file transfer is abandoned. **Zmodem** is even faster, and provides error checking and retransmits blocks of data that were not received correctly.

XON/XOFF

A type of **software handshaking** that employs standard ASCII control characters (called XON and XOFF). These control characters enable two linked modems to tell one another when they are ready to receive more data. *See* **flow control**.

Zmodem

 A **file transfer protocol** that, in the judgment of many **modem** users, is the best choice for file transfer operations, even if you're using modems equipped with an **error control correction protocol**. Zmodem transmits data in 512K blocks on which it uses **Cyclic Redundancy Checks** (CRC). However, the protocol reduces processing **overhead** by sending confirmation messages only when the receiving modem detects an error in the file. As a result, the sending modem dumps out the data in a continuous stream, as fast as it can, unless it receives a message that one of the blocks was incorrect. It then retransmits the damaged block and resumes sending the data. Zmodem incorporates many convenient features, such as the ability to restart a transmission that's interrupted for any reason. *Compare* **Kermit**, **Xmodem**, **Ymodem**.

If you're **downloading** files from a **BBS**, set your **communications program** so that it uses the Zmodem protocol. This is the most advanced and convenient file transfer protocol for this purpose.

Printers

This chapter surveys the terms you're likely to encounter while you're shopping for a printer, whether for use in a home office or a busy network setting. You'll find full coverage of the various printer technologies, including the latest color printers, as well as printer accessories (such as **fonts**, **network interface cards**, and **consumables**).

A-sized paper

As defined by the American National Standards Institute (ANSI), a page sized 8.5 by 11 inches (210 x 297 mm).

aliasing

In low **resolution** printers, a printing defect in which curves and diagonal lines appear with an unattractive, step-wise distortion. This effect is commonly known as "jaggies." *See* **resolution enhancement technology**.

automatic emulation switching

A feature common in today's printers that allows the printer automatically to identify the incoming printer signal's **printer control language**, and to adjust accordingly so that the document can be printed. Many printers can respond to the printer control languages developed by Epson and Hewlett-Packard.

automatic network switching

An advanced feature of **departmental laser printers** and workgroup printers that allows them to automatically detect the protocol (communications standard) of an incoming print signal (such as EtherTalk, TCP/IP, and LAN Manager) and to receive the signal for printing. With automatic network switching, a single printer can serve a network that connects Macintoshes, Windows systems, and UNIX workstations. Hewlett-Packard's LaserJets can switch among twelve network protocols. Synonymous with protocol switching. *Compare* **automatic emulation switching.**

B-size printer

A printer capable of printing on B-size paper (11 by 17 inches).

B-size paper

As defined by the American National Standards Institute (ANSI), a page sized 11 by 17 inches (297 x 420 mm).

bidirectional communication

An advanced feature of high-end printers that lets the printer return messages to the user's computer, alerting the user to problems such as low toner, paper jams, or lack of paper.

Bidirectional communication is a necessity for workgroup laser printers and **departmental laser printers**, which are networked and located in a departmental office. Without bidirectional communication, you won't know whether your document has printed unless you take that long walk down the hall.

The extent of bidirectional communication is sharply limited by the standard Centronics parallel port, however (see Chapter 4). This port sets up a one-way information transfer, permitting only five status signals to travel from the printer to the computer: paper empty, fault, busy (printer not ready), acknowledge (data received), and select (printer is available).

bidirectional parallel port

An advanced, two-way parallel port for printers and other peripherals that conforms to the Institute of Electrical and Electronics Engineers (IEEE) standard 1284. In contrast to the slow, one-way communication allowed by the standard **Centronics parallel interface**, a bidirectional parallel port transfers data to the printer at up to ten times the speed, and lets the printer send detailed messages to the computer. Several printer manufacturers have announced printers confirming to the IEEE 1284 standard, and it is expected to replace the standard Centronics parallel port in coming years.

bit-mapped font

 A **font** that is stored as a complete set of characters in a particular font size; each character is made up of a matrix of dots. Bit-mapped fonts print quickly but they cannot be scaled without introducing the unattractive distortions of **aliasing**. Additional disadvantages of bit-mapped fonts is that they consume memory, both on disk and in a printer's on-board memory. *Compare* **scalable font**.

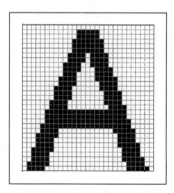

Figure 16.1 A bit-mapped letter

bit-mapped graphics

A method of producing a graphic image through the use of thousands of tiny dots. Although bit-mapped images can produce semi-**photorealistic** effects, they consume large amounts of disk space and print slowly. In addition, they cannot be resized without introducing unattractive distortions.

black-write technique

In a **laser printer**, a printing technique in which the toner adheres to the negatively-charged areas that were illuminated by the laser beam. This is the most common technique used in today's laser printers. *Compare* **white-write technique**.

bleed capability

The capability of a printer to print all the way to the edges of the paper (*see* **full bleed**). With most laser printers, there is a nonprintable area (typically about one-fourth of an inch wide) around the edges of the paper.

bubble-jet printer

A type of **ink jet printer** that uses a heating element instead of a piezoelectric crystal to expel droplets of ink from the print head's nozzles.

buckyball toner

An advanced toner made from buckminsterfullerene, a new, synthetic form of carbon. Discovered in the mid-1980s, buckminsterfullerene forms spherical molecules whose polyhedral shape reminded researchers of the inventor Buckminster Fuller's domed structures. These molecules are larger and easier to control than the carbon molecules normally used in printer toner.

built-in font

See **resident font**.

cartridge font

A **font** that is made available to the printer by means of a read-only memory (ROM) cartridge, which is inserted into a font receptable in the printer's case. For printers that use **bit-mapped fonts**, an advantage of cartridge fonts is that they do not consume any of the printer's limited on-board memory.

Centronics parallel interface

The standard IBM parallel port, with a 25-pin connector, that conforms to the standards established by Centronics, a once-prominent manufacturer of computer printers. Because the Centronics parallel interface permits only limited bidirectional communication, it is considered obsolete in view of users' needs for more information about the status of their printers. *Compare* **bidirectional parallel port**.

characters per inch (cpi)

In a **monospaced font** such as Courier, the number of characters that occur within an inch, measured horizontally across the page.

CMYK

A **color model** in which all colors are produced by combining cyan, magenta, yellow, and black in varying percentages. Unlike the RGB and HSB color models, commonly

CMYK	color laser printer

used for computer displays, the CMYK model can support **device-independent color**, in which a designer can select a specific color from a matching chart and be reasonably sure that the printout will match the chosen color.

| | coated paper |

A paper that has been specially prepared to increase the **resolution** of color printer output. Coated paper is expensive but required by high-end color printers such as **thermal wax transfer printers**.

| | color ink jet printer |

An **ink jet printer** that can produce color output. The cheaper models print just three colors (cyan, magenta, and yellow); slightly more expensive, but significantly better in quality, are true CMYK printers that can also print black, producing richer colors and deeper blacks.

| | color laser printer |

A **laser printer** that can print in color, using plain paper at low overall printing costs (approximately $.20 to .30 per page).

Color laser printers work the same way monochrome laser printers do. A laser beam traces a detailed image on an electrostatically-charged surface. The printer applies dry toner to this charged surface, which adheres only to the laser-exposed areas. Then, the printer draws the paper over this surface, using heat to fuse the toner to the paper. In a color laser printer, this process is repeated for each of the four primary colors.

Color laser printers offer many advantages over competing technologies. The dry toner won't bleed or smudge, as do water-based inks. Laser printers produce output much faster than ink jet printers, and they cost far less than **thermal wax transfer print-**

| color laser printer | consumables |

ers and **dye sublimation** printers. Plain paper costs much less than the coated papers required by most color printers.

On the down side, they do cost more than monochrome laser printers, so they're a good choice only for applications that demand color. Moreover, color laser printers cannot produce the deep color saturation generated by high-end color printers, such as **thermal dye transfer printers**. The time is soon to come, though, when color laser printers will be considered an essential component of a minimal PC system. *See* **direct-to-drum imaging**.

| color model |

The schema by which the differences among colors are represented and manipulated. The RGB model, appropriate for monitors, uses percentages of red, green, and blue to generate colors. The HSB model specifies colors according to the three fundamental color parameters of hue, saturation, and brightness. The **CMYK** model employs percentages of cyan, magenta, yellow, and black to produce a full range of colors, with deep, rich blacks. Of the three models, the CMYK model is the only one suited for **device-independent color** systems, such as the **Pantone color matching system**, which lets designers specify colors and be reasonably sure that the printout will match their expectations.

| consumables |

The supplies required to keep a printer running, such as paper and toner.

Don't underestimate the cost of consumables when you're shopping for a printer. Check out reviews in computer magazines for the printer's cost per page; for color printers, this figure can be as high as $3.50!

continuous-tone image

A picture formed from shades of gray or colors that imperceptibly blend into each other, producing a **photorealistic** effect.

continuous-tone output

In a color printer, a method of creating **photorealistic output** that varies the color intensity at each pixel. *Compare* **dithering**.

control codes

The first 32 characters in the ASCII character set, which includes several characters that have been set aside to send control messages to the printer. For example, ASCII character 12 will eject a page if this character is sent to the printer. You can enter some control characters manually, but normally this is done by a **printer driver**. *See* **escape sequences**; *compare* **printer control language**.

convenience copier

A fax machine that can also be used to produce photocopies under light-duty conditions.

corona wire

In a **laser printer**, a wire that applies a positive electrostatic charge to the paper.

cost per page

For a given printer, an estimate of the approximate cost of the **consumables** the printer uses, such as ink and paper. For color printers that require special **coated paper** and expensive ribbons, the cost per page may be a significant cost item, as high as $3 per page for **thermal dye sublimation printers**. For ink jet printers, costs per page may be difficult to estimate, since graphics-intensive pages consume more ink than text-only pages.

daisywheel printer

A **fully-formed character printer** that employs a wheel-like printing element in which the characters are arranged around the edge, like daisy petals. An **impact printer**, a daisywheel printer works by rotating the wheel until the desired character is in the printing position, and hammering the character against the ribbon to form an impression on the paper.

Daisywheel printers were once considered the *sine qua non* of business computer printing, and still have a following in law firms, where their output appears as if it had been typed by a top-notch legal secretary. Even the cheapest **laser printer** is capable of outperforming a daisywheel printer, both in terms of speed of output and quality of the printed image.

departmental laser printer

A laser printer that incorporates the network connectivity, printing speed (12 **pages per minute** or more), remote management capabilities, and the durability required to survive **monthly duty cycles** of up to 12,000 pages per month. Among the advanced features generally found in such printers are **automatic network switching**, **auto-**

matic emulation switching, **bidirectional communication**, **duplex printing**, and **remote management**.

Desktop Management Interface (DMI)

A standard, proposed by the **Desktop Management Task
Force (DMTF)**, for the management of networked laser
printers. The DMI standard is widely expected to replace the
dated **Simple Network Management Protocol (SNMP)**.
Taking advantage of the two-way communication afforded
by computer networking, DMI-compatible printers notify users
when conditions such as paper jams, low toner, or open
covers arise.

Desktop Management Task Force (DMTF)

A consortium of computer industry vendors that collabo-
rate on industry standards, such as the **Desktop Management
Interface (DMI)** and the **Plug and Print** standard. DMTF's
Printer Working Group includes Compaq, Hewlett-Packard,
IBM-Pennant Systems, Intel, Lexmark International, Okidata,
QMS, Tektronix, Texas Instruments, Unisys, and Xerox.

---

device-independence

Freedom from the peculiarities of a particular brand and
model of computer hardware. With respect to printers,
device independence is a property of the **PostScript** page
description language, which can control PostScript-com-
patible printers made by a wide variety of manufacturers.

---

device-dependent color

A color printing technology that produces colors whose
characteristics (brightness, hue, and saturation) are entirely governed by the idiosyncrasies of the hardware involved,

and cannot be easily compared or matched with the colors produced by other printers. The color red printed by one color printer may not match the red printed by another printer. All but high-end printers print device-dependent color. *Compare* **device-independent color.**

device-independent color

A method of standardizing colors so that imaging devices are forced to modify their output to conform to the color standard, rather than modifying the color to conform to their hardware peculiarities. *Compare* **device-dependent color.**

direct-to-drum imaging

A **color laser printing** process developed by Hewlett-Packard that uses multiple drum rotations to produce the color image. The drum rotates four times, picking up one of the four primary colors with each rotation. On the fifth rotation, the drum fuses the image to the page. Using this technology, the HP Color LaserJet can print four to five color pages per minute.

dithering

The process of simulating colors or grays by mixing dots of available colors or grays to simulate the ones that are missing.

dot matrix printer

An **impact printer** that forms an image by hammering a pattern of extruded wires against a ribbon. The end of each individual wire forms a dot, and the pattern of dots forms a character. The earliest dot-matrix printers used a nine-wire design, but more recent models, capable of **near-letter-quality printing,** use 18 to 24 wires. All but displaced from the market by **ink jet printers**, dot matrix printers still play a role where their impact technology enables printing multi-part carbon copies.

All but the best dot matrix printers produce output that is easily recognized by the unattractive spaces between the dots, which make the document hard to read. At more than a few colleges and universities, bleary-eyed professors refuse to accept dot matrix–printed papers. An even greater draw-back is that dot matrix printers generate high levels of unpleasant noise, which has been compared to the sound produced by an approaching storm of five-foot-long mosquitos or a concerto of dentist's drills.

Dot matrix **print heads** can become very hot while working. If you're trying to clear a paper or ribbon jam after a lengthy job, don't touch the print head.

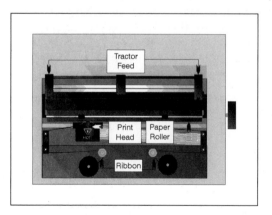

Figure 16.2 *Inside a dot matrix printer*

| dots per inch (dpi) |

A commonly-used measurement of a printer's **resolution** that specifies the hightest number of discrete dots the print-er can place within a horizontallly drawn line on the printed page, exactly one inch in length. Low-end printers can print 300 linear dots; better laser printers can print 600, and the best print 1200 (but see **effective resolution**). Printer resolutions specifications frequently state the number of vertical scan lines as well as the number of horizonal dots; a 300 x 600 printer, for example, can print 300 dpi horizontally and 600 dpi vertically.

download

To transfer from the computer to the printer's memory. **Downloadable fonts** are handled in this way.

downloadable font

 A **font** that is stored on the computer's disk drive, ready to be downloaded to the printer if required. The disadvantage of downloadable fonts is that you must wait while the computer transfers the font to the printer. *Synonymous with* **soft font**. *Compare* **resident font**.

driver

For a printer, a file stored on the computer's hard disk that contains the specifications a program needs to work with a particular brand and model of printer. *See* **printer driver**.

drop-out

A printing flaw commonly encountered with **laser printers** in which some of the printout appears to be light while other areas are dark. The usual cause of this problem is excess moisture content in the paper. Try using a fresh, dry ream of paper. If this does not solve the problem, clean the **corona wire**.

duplex printing

An advanced printer capability that lets the printer print on both sides of the paper, without requiring the user to re-insert the paper so that the second side can be printed.

duplication station

A scanner that is designed to work with a specific brand and model of printer, allowing it to work as a photocopying machine as well.

economy mode

In **ink jet printers**, an ink-saving mode that produces draft-quality output, suitable for review and editing but not for final presentation.

effective resolution

In contrast to true **resolution**, a measurement of a printer's resolution that takes into account the effect of **resolution enhancement** techniques. For example, some 600 **dpi** printers claim an effective resolution of 1,200 dpi, but their output may not match the quality of true 1,200 dpi printers. Some of the enhancement techniques these printers use have a detrimental effect on **grayscale** images, such as scanned photographs.

electrostatic printer

A printing technology that forms an image by creating an electrostatic charge on a rotating drum, applying toner to the charged areas, and fusing the toner to paper using a heat process. **Laser printers** and **LED printers** are electrostatic printers.

emulation

The ability of a printer to respond to, and work with, the **printer control language** of another brand and model of printer.

emulation sensing

See **automatic network switching.**

emulation switching

See **automatic emulation sensing.**

Energy-Star-compliant printer

A printer that complies with the U.S. Environmental Protection Agency (EPA) standards for Energy Star certification. Such a printer can power down to use 45 watts or less during periods of inactivity.

escape sequence

A series of ASCII characters preceded by the Esc value (27). Many printers use escape sequences to control the operation of the printer. Although standard escape sequences exist, most printer manufacturers have elected to define their own escape sequences, reflecting the special characteristics and capabilities of their printers. Among these proprietary mappings of escape sequences are those created by Diablo and Qume for **daisywheel printers**, Epson and IBM for early **dot matrix printers**, and Hewlett-Packard for **laser printers** (*see* **PCL**). Because these escape sequences vary, many printers use **emulation** so that they can respond to another manufacturer's escape sequence mappings. Together with control characters, escape sequences comprise the

print control language of many simple printers. *Compare* **page description language.**

| FinePrint |

In the **laser printers** made by Apple Computer, a **resolution enhancement technology** that generates 600 x 600 dpi resolution. *Compare* **PhotoGrade.**

| firmware |

Software that is encoded on a **read-only memory** circuit within the printer.

| font |

In typography, a complete set of characters, all of one size, in a single, distinctive **typeface.** In computing, this term is often used synonymously (albeit incorrectly) with typeface, the distinctive, named design of all the characters in a font (such as Garamond or Times Roman).

A font has the following attributes:

- Spacing. In **proportional spacing,** a thin character such as "1" receives less horizontal space than a thick character such as "m." In **monospacing** (fixed spacing), each character receives exactly the same space.

- Pitch. In a **monospaced font,** this figure (expressed in **characters per inch,** or **cpi,** corresponds to the old typewriter standards Pica (10 cpi) or Elite (12 cpi).

- Point Size. The height of characters, measured in printer's **points** (72 per inch).

- Style. Options include upright (normal) characters, and enhancements such as italics, underline, or bold, as well as width (expanded or condensed) and special effects such as outlining and shadowing.

- Stroke Weight. Thickness (light, medium, or bold) of the strokes used to construct the characters.

- Typeface. The distinctive, named design of all the characters in a font (such as Garamond or Times Roman).

- Orientation. The direction in which the font is printed on the paper. **Landscape fonts** print horizontally across the long dimension of the page (11 inches for standard 8.5 x 11 inch paper), while **portrait fonts** print across the narrow (8.5") dimension.

font cartridge

A **read-only memory** (ROM) cartridge, designed to fit into a corresponding receptacle of a given brand and model of printer, that contains one or more **fonts**. The fonts available in font cartridges operate much more quickly than fonts that most be downloaded from the computer (*see* **downloadable font**), but both font cartridges and downloadable fonts are inferior, in terms of cost and convenience, to Microsoft's **TrueType** font technology.

footprint

The amount of space that a printer takes on up the printer stand or desk.

form feed

An instruction that tells the printer to eject a page from the printer mechanism.

full bleed

Printing from one edge of the page to the other.

fully-formed character printer

A printer that, like a typewriter, is capable of printing a single, fully-formed character at a time, such as a **daisy-wheel printer**.

fuser wand

In a **laser printer**, a heating element that fuses the toner to the page.

If your printouts are marred by a vertical line, chances are some dried toner has accumulated on the fuser wand. See your printer's manual to find out how to clean the fuser wand.

garage

In an **ink jet printer** that combines color and monochrome printing capabilities, a receptacle that lets the user temporarily park a cartridge that isn't being used so that it does not dry out.

Graphical Device Interface (GDI) printer

A printer that is designed to work exclusively with Microsoft Windows applications (synonymous with **Windows printer**). In a GDI-compatible printer, the printer itself lacks the **raster image processor** (**RIP**) circuitry needed to decode the incoming print signal; this processing occurs in the computer, where the Windows print output is converted into a bitmap and sent to the printer. GDI printers can print anything that Windows can display and they are cheaper than printers requiring rasterizing circuitry, but they cannot work with PostScript fonts (unless they are displayed with Adobe Type Manager). In addition, GDI printers cannot print from DOS and cannot work with computer networks.

 Is GDI is good bet? GDI places heavy burdens on your computer's processing circuitry, and may not be fully supported in future versions of Microsoft Windows. Microsoft Corporation is reportedly trying to convince printer manufacturers to employ its At Work printer technology instead of GDI; the At Work technology handles some of the processing at Windows' end, but the printer is expected to perform the rest of it.

grayscale

In a printer, a method of simulating the tonal range of a color graphic through the use of a series of gray tones, ranging from very dark to very light.

grayscale support

The extent to which the printer can produce fine gradations in shades of gray, which enables the printer to produce realistic-looking printouts of photographic images. The more the shades of gray that the printer can handle, the better the results.

halftone

A copy of a photograph, which has continously-graded shades of gray, that has been prepared for printing by breaking the continuous gradations down into patterns of tiny dots. A halftone is superior to a digitized photograph in that the dots are superimposed, producing more realistic tone gradations.

I/O buffering

An advanced and desirable feature of **network laser printers** that allows the printer to accept the input for a new print job while it is still producing the output from a previous job.

impact printer

A printer that forms an image on the paper by physically striking a ribbon that is pressed against a sheet of paper; the impact forces ink out of the ribbon and on to the paper. *See* **daisywheel printer** and **dot matrix printer**.

Non-impact printers, such as **laser printers** and **ink jet printers**, have all but forced impact printers off the market, as impact printers are very noisy and, for this reason, unpleasant to use. Still, impact printers are necessary for producing multi-part carbon copies.

ink jet printer

A **non-impact printer** that forms an image on the page by spraying droplets of ink. Like a **dot matrix printer**, an ink jet printer uses a matrix of printing elements—in this case, tiny nozzles, which fling droplets of ink when directed to do so by the printer's computerized controls. Ink jet printers are quiet and fast, and they produce results that may be almost indistinguishable from the output produced by **laser printers**.

In most of today's ink jet printers, the flinging device is a piezo-electric crystal. The crystal oscillates at a constant rate when voltage is applied. When placed in a tiny ink channel, the oscillating crystal functions as a pump, squeezing ink out of the ink jet as it expands, and sucking new ink into the channel as it contracts.

In **bubble-jet printers**, a small heating element is used instead of a piezoelectric crystal. When voltage is applied to the element, it heats the ink, causing an air buble to form and expand. When it bursts, a droplet of ink escapes from the nozzle.

Ink jet printers cost less than laser printers, but be aware that their operating costs are currently about twice that of laser printers ($.06 per page, vs. $.03 per page for laser printers).

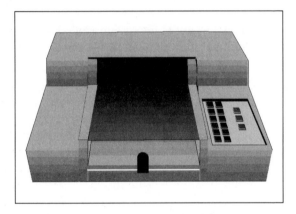

Figure 16.3 *An HP ink-jet printer*

| internal hard drive |

In a **laser printer**, a hard disk drive that is devoted to storing fonts for the printer's use.

| jaggies |

Synonymous with **aliasing**.

| landscape font |

A **font** that is designed to print vertically on the page.

| landscape printing |

A printing orientation in which the output appears across the long dimension of the page's surface. Using standard 8.5 by 11-inch paper, the 11-inch sides are the top and bottom of the page. *Compare* **portrait painting**.

| laser printer |

A **non-impact printer** that uses a laser **print engine**, similar to the print engines used in photocopiers, to produce output.

Most laser printers work in the following way. First, the printer decodes the print output and constructs a bit-map image of the page. Then the printer uses a laser beam to record the image on a rotating, photosensitive drum. A key element in this process is a complex optical system, consisting of movable mirrors and lenses, which focuses the laser beam on the drum and produces precisely-focused dots of light. The Illuminated areas take on a static charge, which attracts the toner. This technique is called the **black-write technique** because the toner is attracted only to the areas struck by the laser beam (*compare* **white-write technique**). Then, the paper-feed mechanism feeds the paper past the **corona wire**, which charges the paper with a strong static charge, which draws the toner off the drum. Finally, the toner is fused to the paper using a heated roller.

Laser printers have some disadvantages. A non-impact technology, laser printers cannot create carbon or carbonless copies. The processing circuitry needed to decode the incoming print signal is complicated (*see* **raster image pro-**

cessing) and expensive, and the printer must have enough **on-board memory** to retain a full page of text and graphics (2 MB of on-board memory may be required for some applications). If the delicate optical assembly goes out of alignment, you're in for an expensive repair. Toner cartridges aren't cheap. Finally, laser printers require periodic **printer maintenance**, which is more extensive and costly than the maintainence costs of other printers.

Almost all the laser printers on the market today are designed to print in black and white, although **color laser printers** are available.

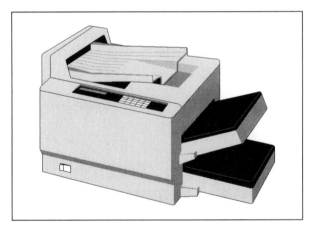

Figure 16.4 *A laser printer*

light-emitting diode (LED) printer

A printer that works like a **laser printer**, except that an array of as many as 2,400 light-emitting diodes is used to produce the light that illuminates the print drum. Like **liquid crystal shutter (LCS) printers**, LED printers have fewer moving parts than laser printers and may yield a longer service life.

| line feed |

An instruction that tells the printer to move the print head down one line.

| liquid crystal shutter (LCS) printer |

A printer that works like a **laser printer**, except that the printer does not use a laser to generate an electrostatic charge on the print drum. Instead, the printer uses a halogen lamp or some other light source and an array of lenses and shutters to focus the light on the drum. LCS printers have fewer moving parts than laser printers and may yield a longer service life.

| matte finish |

Print output that does not reflect light, as does a glossy finish. In color laser printing, users tend to prefer matte finishes to glossy ones because the matte finish matches the finish of monochrome text in the rest of the document.

| MIB/MIF |

See **Plug and Print**.

| microfine toner |

A specially-manufactured toner composed of extremely fine particles, which enable the printer to form sharper text and more precise images.

| Microsoft At Work |

A set of standards for the computer control of a series of office devices, including telephones as well as printers, fax machines, and copiers. A scaled-back version of Microsoft At Work, restricted to the control of printers and fax machines, is included in Windows 95.

monochrome printer

A printer that can produce black and white, but not color.

monospaced font

A font that always prints with **monospacing**, even if the printer is capable of **proportional spacing**. Courier is a monospaced font.

monospacing

In a **font**, a method of spacing in which each character receives exactly the same amount of horizontal space. *Compare* **proportional spacing**.

monthly duty cycle

The number of pages that a printer is designed to print in an average month. High-end, heavy-duty **departmental laser printers** (such as the QMS 3225) are rated to print as many as 200,000 pages per month.

near-letter-quality printing (NLQ)

In **dot-matrix printers**, a method of simulating the output of office-quality typewriters by repeatedly printing a letter with a slight offset on each pass. The offset serves to fill in the spaces between the dots. A disadvantage of near-letter-quality printing is lower printing speed.

network interface card (NIC)

An adapter card, designed to work with a particular brand and model of printer, that allows the printer to be connected to a local area network (LAN). Printers equipped with network interface card can be used by two or more network workstations at the same time.

network laser printer

A **laser printer** that is designed to connect to a local area network (LAN), enabling more than one user to access the printer simultaneously. Network laser printers are designed to withstand heavy use.

non-impact printer

A printer that does not form an image by physically striking a ribbon. Examples of non-impact printers include **laser printers** and **ink-jet printers**. A major advantage of non-impact printers is quiet operation.

page description language (PDL)

A true programming language that is capable of describing the precise placement of text and graphics on the printed page. In contrast to a **printer control language**, which is merely a catalog of commands to which a given brand and model of printer can respond, a PDL is independent of the peculiarities of printer hardware (see device independence); properly written, a file composed in PDL can be printed on any PDL-capable printing device, ranging from an inexpensive laser printer to a high-end typesetting machine. One disadvantage of PDLs is that PDL-capable printers require their own microprocessor, which is required to decode the programming instructions. PDL-capable printers are therefore more expensive than printers designed to work with printer control languages. A popular PDL is PostScript.

page printer

A printer, such as a **laser printer**, that constructs an image of an entire page in its on-board memory, and then prints the complete page in one operation. The three most common page printer technologies are **laser printers**, **liquid crystal shutter (LCS) printers**, and **light-emitting diode (LED) printers**.

If you plan to use a page printer, make sure the printer has enough memory to contain the most complex page you plan to create. Graphics require much more memory than text. If you plan to do desktop publishing involving heavy use of graphics, you will need at least 2 MB of on-board memory.

pages per minute (ppm)

A measurement, often inaccurate and always misleading, of the number of pages that a given brand and model of printer can crank out in the space of 60 seconds. Printer manufacturers are prone to exaggerate this statistic, and in any case it applies only to plain text output, not to output containing fonts other than the printer's **resident fonts** or to output containing graphics.

Pantone color matching system

A **device-independent color** system in which designers may choose a specific **spot color** (solid color) from a handbook, specify the color in the software they are using, and then print the color on a printer that has been professionally calibrated to match Pantone output. The advantage of using the Pantone system is that you can be reasonably sure that the color on the printout will match your expectations. *Compare* **device-dependent color**.

PCL3

The version of Hewlett-Packard's **Printer Control Language** (PCL) that was used on the firm's original LaserJet. PCL3 restricts LaserJet users to **cartridge fonts** and is considered obsolete.

PCL4

The most widely-used version of Hewlett-Packard's **Printer Control Language** (PCL). PCL4 drives HP's LaserJet Series II printers and others that use **emulation** to recognize the Series II printer commands. Unlike **PCL3**, this version of PCL lets users place multiple fonts on the same page and use **downloadable fonts**.

PCL5

A version of Hewlett-Packard's **Printer Control Language** (PCL) introduced in 1990 with the firm's LaserJet III series. Created in response to the needs of today's offices for basic desktop publishing capabilities, PCL5 allows the use of **vector graphics** and **scalable fonts**.

PCL5e

An updated version of the PCL5 printer control language, released with the LaserJet IV printer series, that incorporates numerous advanced features. These include **bidirectional communication** and data compression that speeds the transfer of information from the computer to the printer.

permanent font

In Hewlett-Packard laser printers, a **font** that, after being downloaded (*see* **downloadable font**), resides in the printer's memory until the power is switched off.

personal laser printer

A **laser printer** designed to be connected directly to a personal computer, and designed to accommodate one user's printing needs. *Compare* **network laser printer**.

PhotoGrade

A **resolution enhancement technology** created by Apple Computer that is designed to enhance the printing of **grayscale** images.

photorealistic

Like a photograph; detailed, with rich, thoroughly-saturated colors.

photorealistic output

Continuous-tone printer output that closely resembles the resolution, saturation, finish, and overall quality of a photograhic image.

At this writing, only **thermal dye sublimation printers** are capable of producing true photorealistic output. To achieve this effect, be prepared to pay up to $3.00 per sheet for the special, **coated paper** these printers require. **Thermal wax transfer printers** come in second; the colors are brilliant and saturate the page, but it's obvious that you're not looking at a photograph.

| **Plug and Play** |

A management standard jointly developed by Microsoft, Compaq, and Intel that will allow users to configure new printers and other peripherals with ease and to control printer functions (and cope with printer problems) from Microsoft Windows.

| **Plug and Print** |

A standard created by the **Desktop Management Task Force** (DMTF), an industry consortium, that allows improved communication between printers and desktop computers. The Plug and Print standard calls for printers to include a Management Imformation Base (MIB), a database containing information about the printer's characteristics, configuration, and status. For printers connected directly to PCs, a similar file, called the Management Information File (MIF), runs on PCs. Unlike Microsoft's **Microsoft at Work** (MAW) standards, Plug and Print is designed to be an open standard, accessible and usable by any vendor. *Synonymous with* MIB/MIF.

| **point** |

A unit of measurement equal to 1/72 inch. The height of a **font** is measured in points.

| **portrait font** |

A **font** that is designed to print so that the text runs across the short (8.5") dimension of the page.

portrait printing

A printing orientation in which the print appears across the narrow dimension of the page's surface. Using standard 8.5 by 11-inch paper, the 8.5-inch sides are the top and bottom of the page.

PostScript

A **page description language** (PDL), developed by Adobe Systems, that precisely defines the text and graphics elements of the printed page. Each element is defined in terms of its relationship to the others, positionally or mathematically, instead of as a **bit-mapped image**. PostScript fonts, for example, are defined in terms of mathematical equations which, when decoded, can be scaled up or down with the same, beautiful results (*see* **scalable fonts**). Printing involves the computer sending a PostScript page description to a **PostScript printer**, which is equipped with an on-board computer. The printer's computer then decodes this description, transforms it into a bit-mapped image, and generates the print output. In 1990, a new version of PostScript, called **PostScript Level 2**, was introduced.

A major advantage of PostScript is its **device independence**; a PostScript page description is not tied to the printing capabilities of a particular printer. This means that you can print a PostScript-formatted file on a 300 dpi laser printer, and then take the same file to a graphics service bureau for printing on a high-resolution typesetting machine. PostScript printing devices always print PostScript files at the device's maximum possible resolution.

Disadvantages of PostScript include the high cost of PostScript printers, which must contain a fast and capable microprocessor and sufficient on-board memory to decode the incoming PostScript page description.

An updated version of **PostScript**, a **page description language**, that improves PostScript's overall performance through the use of optimized code and support for file compression, and allows color printing.

| PostScript printer |

A printer that contains the microprocessor, memory, and programming needed to print **PostScript** files. Because they contain the special-purpose computing circuitry needed to decode PostScript, PostScript printers are more expensive than printers that respond to proprietary **printer control languages**. However, serious desktop publishing requires the PostScript printer's versatility and print quality.

| print engine |

In a **laser printer** or **LED printer**, the mechanism that generates the image and fuses the toner to the page. Although there are many brands of laser printers, print engines are manufacturered by a relatively few firms. Printers sharing the same print engine are likely to have similar durability, performance, and print quality.

| print head |

In a computer printer, the mechanism that delivers images to the page's surface. The four basic print head technologies are impact, thermal, ink jet, and electrostatic (*see* **impact printer**, **thermal printer**, **ink jet printer**, and **electrostatic printer**).

printer control language

A set of commands that, under the direction of a **printer driver**, tell a printer how to print a document. No single, standard printer control language exists; instead, there are a number of proprietary standards, each associated with a particular manufacturer. However, many printers are designed to emulate commonly-used printer control languages. Commonly-used and emulated printer control languages include Epson's (for dot-matrix printers) and Hewlett-Packard's Printer Control Language (PCL) for laser and ink-jet printers. Printer control languages, which are merely a set of printer control commands, should be differentiated from true **page description languages (PDL)** such as **PostScript**. A printer control language is merely a set of commands that a given brand and model of printer can recognize; a PDL is a programming language that is independent of particular hardware devices.

Printer Control Language (PCL)

A **printer control language** developed by Hewlett-Packard in 1981, and currently in its fifth version (see **PCL5**). Not a true **page description language**, PCL is a proprietary set of **control characters** and **escape sequences** that are designed to control all the capabilities of HP's LaserJet printers, including font selection. *See* **PCL3**, **PCL4**, and **PCL5**.

printer driver

 A file containing the information that an application needs to control a given brand and model of computer.

Printer drivers are needed because each brand and model of computer has its own specific capabilities. They are also

| printer driver | raster image processor |

needed because different manufacturers use different **print-er control languages** to send command and control signals to the printer.

printer maintenance

The procedures that must be followed periodically to keep a printer running. In particular, **laser printers** require periodic cleaning of the **corona wire**, optical lens, and rollers.

process color

In professional color printing, one of the four primary colors that are used to produce color images: cyan, magenta, yellow, and black. By combining percentages of these four colors, printers can produce virtually any color. *Compare* **color model**, **spot color**.

proportional spacing

In a **font**, a method of spacing in which a thin character such as "l" receives less horizontal space than a thick character such as "m." *Compare* **monospacing**.

protocol switching

See **automatic network switching**.

raster image processor (RIP)

A special-purpose circuit or program that transforms a screen image into a bitmap that can be printed on a graphics printer.

read-only memory (ROM)

In a printer, a memory circuit that contains a permanently-encoded program. For example, ROM is used to provide fonts in **font cartridges**.

remote management

A feature of advanced **departmental laser printers** that allows the printer's administrator to obtain on-screen reports regarding the printer's status (such as toner level, paper availability, and usage levels) and the status of print jobs.

resident font

 A **font** that is automatically loaded into the printer's on-board memory every time the printer is switched on. Resident fonts can be printed quickly because they are readily available for the printer's use.

resolution

 In printers, a measurement—expressed in horizontal and vertical **dots per inch** (dpi)—of the print output's sharpness. Low-end laser printers produce a resolution of 300 x 300 dpi, while the better laser printers produce 600 x 600. Professional typesetting equipment and high-end laser printers produces resolutions of 1200 x 1200 or more.

resolution enhancement technology

A means of improving the apparent **resolution** of a printed image by smoothing the **aliased**, or jagged, edges of **fonts** and graphics. The smoothing effect is accomplished by varying the size of the printed dots and placing smaller dots between larger ones.

satellite

In **ink jet printer** output, a flaw resulting from extra flecks of ink adhering to the white area surrounding characters.

scalable font

A **font** that is stored as a mathematical equation, which describes precisely how the printer should construct the printed output for each character.

serial printer

A printer that is designed to be connected to a personal computer by means of an RS-232C serial port. Best avoided, these printers are substantially more difficult to install and configure than printers designed to connect with the standard parallel interface.

Simple Network Management Protocol (SNMP)

A standard that defines how to create, maintain, and access a database of information regarding the status of hardware devices connected to a computer network. With SNMP, a network administrator can keep track of these devices, and respond to problems as they arise. SNMP-capable printers are capable of generating status messages, describing problems such as jams and paper outages.

soft font

See **downloadable font**.

spot color

In professional offset printing, a solid color that is specified using the **Pantone color matching system**, producing **device-independent colors**.

stroke weight

The width of the basic strokes of a **font**, typically indicated by the terms "light," "medium," or "bold" in the font's name.

style

In a **font**, the formatting attributes that have been given to a character or set of characters, such as italic, underline, bold, outline, or shadow.

tabloid printer

A printer capable of printing on **B-sized paper** (11 by 17 inches). *Synonymous with* **B-size printer**.

temporary font

In Hewlett-Packard **laser printers**, a **font** that, after being downloaded (*see* **downloadable font**), resides in the printer's memory only while it is being used. It is deleted when the printer is reset, freeing the printer's on-board memory for other fonts.

thermal dye sublimation printer

A high-end color printer that works by focusing a heat source, which is capable of precise temperature variations, on a page-sized panel of dyes. As the dyes heat, they evaporate from the ribbon and diffuse on to specially coated paper, forming areas of color whose hues differ according to the intensity of the heat. The result is a **resolution** of 300 **dots per inch** (dpi), but the effect is of much greater resolution, and of **photorealism**, because the colors are intense and fully saturate the page. *Compare* **thermal wax transfer printer**.

This technology is beyond the reach of the average PC user as thermal dye transfer printers can cost as much as $15,000. A major drawback of such printers is their slow speed; as many as fifteen minutes may be required to print a single page. And these printers require coated papers that can cost as much as $4 per page, and for each page printed, the printer uses an entire section of the very expensive, dye-saturated ribbon. Recently available are several **B-size printers** that can produce **full-bleed** images of up to 11 inches by 25 inches in size.

thermal fusion printer

A printer that uses a heat-sensitive ribbon to transfer ink from the ribbon to the page, producing high-quality output on plain paper. Thermal fusion technology is common in battery-powered portable printers because it consumes very little power.

> Are you working in a high-security field? Be aware that thermal fusion printers have a significant security drawback—the ribbon contains a record of what you've printed, and could be read by somebody other than your intended audience.

thermal printer

A printer that uses heat to produce an image on special, heat-sensitive paper (called thermal paper). The thermal print head moves across the surface of the paper, and

| thermal printer | transparency |

tiny resistive elements, called dot heaters, respond to the printer's electronic signals by heating and cooling rapidly, producing printed characters on the page. Thermal printers are quiet and reasonably fast, and they require very little electricity to operate, making them a good choice for battery-powered portable printing. On the down side, they require thermal paper, which is prone to discoloration (*see* **thermal fusion printer**).

thermal wax transfer printer

A high-end color printer that works by focusing a heat source on a page-sized panel of wax-based dyes. As the tightly-focused heat source heats the dyes, they melt and transfer to the paper or transparency. Unlike **thermal dye sublimation printers**, thermal wax transfer printers cannot vary the color intensity of the dots they print. On close inspection, the brilliantly-colored images turn out to be made up of tiny, discrete dots, which nevertheless saturate the page and give an effect that is nearly **photorealistic**. Thermal wax transfer printers are much less expensive than thermal dye sublimation printers; several cost less than $1,000. These printers require printers have acceptable **costs per page** ($.50 is a common figure).

transparency

A transparent sheet of acetate, which can be placed on the display surface of an overhead projector. A major advantage of **page printers** and **ink-jet printers** is that you can load these printers with transparencies; the printers can print directly to the transparency's surface, giving you high-quality presentations for a very low price.

 Be sure to get the right kind of transparencies for your printer; there are different types for laser printers and ink-jet printers.

TrueType

A **scalable font** technology jointly developed by Microsoft Corporation and Apple Computer Inc. as an alternative to the costly **PostScript** technology developed by Adobe. True-Type fonts can be displayed on-screen, and their print output exactly matches the display. TrueType fonts are an excellent choice for most users.

typeface

The distinctive, named design of all the characters in a font (such as Garamond or Times Roman). *Compare* **font**.

vector graphics

A method of producing a graphic image in which the shapes are composed of mathematically-generated lines and shapes. In comparison to **bit-mapped graphics**, vector graphics consume less disk space and print faster. In addition, illustrations created with vector graphics techniques can be resized without apparent distortion.

white-write technique

In a **laser printer**, a printing technique in which toner adheres to the unexposed areas of the drum. This technique can produce darker and denser print images. *Compare* **black-write technique**.

Windows printer

See **Graphical Device Interface** (GDI) printer.

D

daisy chaining
  of monitors, 177
  of peripherals, 241
data bits, 290
Data Communications Equipment (DCE),
    290, 292
data dependency, 58
Data Terminal Equipment (DTE), 291,
    speed of, 296
data transfer rate, 210-11, 224, 245
  of modems, 280, 281, 291, 301, 306, 323
data-striping, 210, 237
demodulation, 292, 295
Desktop Management Interface (DMI), 359
Desktop Management Task Force (DMTF),
    359, 379
device-independence, 359, 380
dialup access, 292-3, 330
dialup IP, 293-4
dialup modem, 294, 295
digital, 295, 311, 323
digital signal processor (DSP), 263-4
DIP, 27, 39, 58
Direct Access Storage Device (DASD), 211
direct memory access controller, *see* DMA
direct-to-drum imaging, 360
disk drive, 211
  size of, 15, 199
diskette, 211
display, 178
display adapter, 4, 8, 160-1, 163, 169
  bit-size of, 158, 159
  color depth of, 159
Display Power Management Signaling
    (DPMS), 178-9, 182, 192
dithering, 360
DMA, 26, 27
  Multiword Mode 1, 34
dongle, 125
dot matrix printer, 360-1
dot pitch, 171, 173, 179
download, 296
  fonts to printer, 362
downloadable font, 362
dpi (dots per inch), 361-2
DRAM, 28, 107-8, 113, 161

drive activity indicator, 212
drive arrays, 212
drive bay, 14-15
  full-height, 15
  half-height, 15
drop-out, 362
DSP, *see* digital signal processor
DTMF, *see* dual-tone multi-frequency tones
dual in-line packages, *see* DIP
dual-issue processor, 56, 59, 101
dual-scanned passive matrix, 171, 179
dual-stripe magneto-resistive (DSMR)
    head, 213
dual-tone multi-frequency (DTMF)
    tones, 297
duplex, 297
duplex printing, 363
duplication station, 363
dynamic beam forming, 180
dynamic random access memory, *see* DRAM

E

E-IDE, 28, 214
economy mode, 363
ECP, *see* port
effective resolution, 363
electromagnetic radiation, 181
  standards, 187-8
electron gun, 180-1
elevator seeking, 213
emulation, 59, 338, 364
Energy Star, 181-2, 364
Enhanced IDE, *see* E-IDE
enhanced small device interface (ESDI), 214
EPP, *see* port
escape sequence, 364
expansion board, 4, 29
expansion bus, 4, 115-22, 157
  bottleneck, 117, 119
  Enhanced ISA (EISA) expansion bus, 116
  Industry Standard Architecture (ISA)
      expansion bus, 117
  local, 118
  Micro Channel Architecture (MCA)
      expansion bus, 119
  PCMCIA, 120, 313